With illustrations by
P Endsleigh Castle ARAeS
J Goulding
R Ward

Aircraft in Profile

Volume 1/Part One

General Editor   **Charles W Cain**

Profile Publications Ltd Windsor Berkshire England
Doubleday & Company Inc Garden City New York

© Profile Publications Limited 1965

Doubleday & Company Inc. edition 1965

First published in England in 1965
by Profile Publications Limited
Coburg House Sheet Windsor
Berkshire England

Revised (4th) edition 1975

ISBN 0 85383 410 5

ISBN (USA) 0 385 09982 7

Acknowledgements
Credit where credit is due. The authors, artists, the general editor and the publishers, Profile Publications Ltd., take this opportunity of acknowledging with sincere and grateful thanks the immense amount of invaluable assistance rendered unstintingly by government departments, military bureaux, the aerospace industry, learned bodies, historical associations and museums—not least, people as people who have opened up their own private archives simply because of their real affection for aviation in one form or another. In the case of the more recent parts of *Aircraft in Profile*, authors have been invited to make 'Acknowledgements' an integral facet of their overall work. To everyone who has helped in the past and will feel free to do so in the future. . . . Thank you! from the team that makes up *Aircraft in Profile*.—CWC.

Note to readers
Authenticated additional or corrected information, together with appropriate photographic or other material evidence, will be welcomed by the Editor, the specific author will be notified accordingly.—CWC.

Uniform with this volume

Aircraft in Profile Series *3rd Edition*
AFVs of the World Series *1st Edition*
Locomotives in Profile Series
Warships in Profile Series
Small Arms in Profile Series
Cars in Profile Series

Printed in England by Mears Caldwell Hacker Limited, London

Foreword

This is a unique experience. Never before has anyone attempted to produce such a great aviation library series. The original objective was to create a wide variety of aircraft monographs aimed to satisfy the most discerning of aviation buffs, fans and enthusiasts in every part of the world.

What has resulted from the original concept of reaching out for the highest standards is a product unique in the annals of aviation publishing. Today, the collected works total well in excess of 1,000,000 words and more than 250 individual Aircraft Profiles.

Undeniably, there is an insistent demand for warplane subjects and essentially civil aircraft are in the minority. But *Aircraft in Profile* as a series is prepared by historians who are more concerned with the accuracy of their researching than presenting the reader with less exacting popular histories.

This first volume sets the style for subsequent volumes by ranging over aviation's horizons from World War One through the years to the Second World War and on into the 1950s. In fact, some more recent Profiles are concerned with aircraft of the 1970s. To help the newcomer find his way around, this volume contains a quick-reference section called 'Aircraft Profile Finder'.

Finally, for those who like to know what is between these hard covers statistically-speaking, there are no fewer than 296 black and white photographs, 24 pages of full-colour artwork views (140 separate drawings) and about 50,000 words.

January 1975   **Charles W Cain**

Contents

Index to Volume One Part One

Key : (c) colour drawings ; (p) photographs

Aircraft Profile Finder Parts 1–258 inclusive.
Country of Origin and Period of Use.

(1) ■□□□ World War 1 : 1914-18
(2) □■□□ Post-W.W.1 : 1920s-1930s
(3) □□■□ World War 2 : 1939-45
(4) □□□■ Post-W.W.2 : 1950s-1970s

Austria-Hungary (1914-18)

Ö. AVIATIK (BERG)
- 151 ■□□□ Berg D I

PHÖNIX
- 175 ■□□□ Scouts (D I-IV)

Australia

COMMONWEALTH
- 178 □□■□ Boomerang
- 154 □□■□ Wirraway

Canada

CANADAIR
- 186 □□□■ Sabres (Mks. 1-6 ; see also U.S.A./North American F-86 Sabre)

Czechoslovakia

AVIA
- 152 □■□□ B-534

France

AEROSPATIALE/BAC
- 250 □□□■ Concorde

BLOCH (see M. BLOCH)

BREGUET
- 157 ■□□□ †Breguet 14 (Type XIV)

DASSAULT (M. DASSAULT)
- 230 □□□■ †Mirage III-5 (& Milan)
- 143 □□□■ M.D. 450 Ouragan

DEWOITINE
- **135** □□■□ D.520

HANRIOT
- 109 ■□□□ †HD-1

LIORE ET OLIVIER
- 173 □□■□ LeO 45 Series

MARCEL BLOCH
- 201 □□■□ (M.B.) 151 & 152

MORANE SAULNIER
- 147 □□■□ M.S.406

NIEUPORT
- **49** ■□□□ †N.17C-1
- 79 ■□□□ †N.28C-1

POTEZ
- 195 □□■□ Potez 63 Series

SPAD
- **17** ■□□□ †S.P.A.D. XIIIC.1

SUD-AVIATION
- 180 □□□■ Caravelle 3 & 6

Germany

ALBATROS
- 127 ■□□□ †D I-D III
- 9 ■□□□ †D V

ARADO
- 215 □□■□ Ar 234 Blitz

AVIATIK (see Ö. Aviatik: Berg D I, Austria-Hungary)

BÜCKER
- 222 □□■□ Bü 131 Jungmann

DORNIER
- **164** □□■□ **Do 17 & 215**

FIESELER
- 228 □□■□ †Fi 156 Storch

FOCKE-WULF
- **3** □□■□ **FW 190 A**
- **94** □□■□ **FW 190 D/Ta 152 Series**
- **99** □□■□ **FW 200 (Condor)**

FOKKER
- **25** ■□□□ †D VII
- 67 ■□□□ †D VIII
- 55 ■□□□ †Dr I (Triplane)
- 38 ■□□□ †Monoplanes (Eindeckers)

GOTHA
- 115 ■□□□ G I-G V

HEINKEL
- **15** □□■□ **He 111 H**
- **203** □□■□ †He 162 (Salamander)
- 234 □□■□ He 177 (Greif)
- 219 □□■□ He 219 Uhu

HENSCHEL
- **69** □□■□ Hs 129

JUNKERS
- **177** □□■□ **Ju 52 Series (Ju 52/3m)**
- **76** □□■□ **Ju 87 A & B ('Stuka') ('A'—'Anton'; 'B'—'Berta')**
- 211 □□■□ †Ju 87 D Variants ('Stuka') ('D'—'Dora')
- **29** □□■□ **Ju 88 A**
- **148** □□■□ **Ju 88 Night Fighters**
- 187 ■□□□ Monoplanes ('Blechesel')

L.F.G. (see ROLAND)

MESSERSCHMITT
- **40** □□■□ †Bf 109 E ('E'—'Emil')
- **184** □□■□ †Bf 109 F ('F'—'Friedrich')
- **113** □□■□ †Bf 109 G ('G'—'Gustav')
- **23** □□■□ †Bf 110 (Day Fighters)
- 207 □□■□ Bf 110 (Night Fighters)
- 225 □□■□ †Me 163 Komet
- **161** □□■□ †Me 210/410 Series
- **130** □□■□ †Me 262 (Schwalbe/Sturmvogel)

PFALZ
- 43 ■□□□ †D III
- 199 ■□□□ †D XII (& D XIV)

PHÖNIX (see AUSTRIA-HUNGARY)

ROLAND (L.F.G.)
- 163 ■□□□ †C II ('Walfisch')

SIEMENS-SCHUCKERT
- 86 ■□□□ †D III & IV

UDET
- 257 □■□□ U-12 Flamingo

Great Britain

AIRSPEED
- 227 □□■□ Oxford Mks. I-V

ARMSTRONG WHITWORTH
- 153 □□■□ Whitley (Mks. I-VII)

AVRO
- †Avro 707 (see Avro Vulcan)
- **65** □□■□ †**Lancaster I**
- 235 □□■□ Lancaster Mk. II
- 243 □□□■ Avro (Hawker Siddeley) Shackleton Mks. 1-5
- 162 □□□■ †Vulcan (& Avro 707)
- 168 □□■□ York (Mks. I & II)

BAC/AEROSPATIALE
- 250 □□□■ BAC/Aerospatiale Concorde

B.E.
- 133 ■□□□ B.E.2, 2a & 2b

BOULTON PAUL
- 117 □□■□ Defiant (Mks. I-III)

BRISTOL
- 193 ■□□□ Bristol M.1 (M.1A-M.1D)
- **137** □□■□ **Beaufighter Mks. I & II**
- **93** □□■□ **Blenheim I**
- 218 □□■□ Blenheim Mk. IV (& R.C.A.F. Bolingbroke Mks. I-IV)
- **6** □■□□ †**Bulldog (Mks. I-IV)**
- **21** ■□□□ †**Fighter ('Brisfit')**
- 237 ■□□□ F.2B Fighter (see No. 21) (RAF: 1918-30s)
- 139 ■□□□ †Scouts C & D

DE HAVILLAND
- 91 ■□□□ †D.H.2
- 26 ■□□□ †D.H.4 (see also AMERICAN DH-4)
- 181 ■□□□ †D.H.5
- 62 ■□□□ D.H.9
- 248 ■□□□ D.H.9A (RAF:1918-30)
- 145 ■□□□ D.H.10
- 108 □□□■ †Comet Srs. 1-4 (now Hawker Siddeley Comet)
- 174 □□□■ Hornet (& Sea Hornet)
- **52** □□■□ †**Mosquito I-IV**
- 209 □□■□ Mosquito Mk. IV
- 144 □□■□ †Rapide (Dragon Rapide)

[DE HAVILLAND, cont.]
- **132** □□■□ †**Tiger Moth**
- 48 □□□■ †Vampire Mks. 5 & 9

ENGLISH ELECTRIC/BAC
- 54 □□□■ †Canberra Mks. I & IV
- 114 □□□■ †P.1 & Lightning 1

FAIREY
- 44 □■□□ Fairey III F
- 240 □□■□ Barracuda Mks. I-V
- **34** □□■□ †**Battle Mks. I-V (and Trainer)**
- 56 □■□□ Flycatcher
- 254 □□■□ Fulmar Mks. I & II
- 212 □□■□ Swordfish Mks. I-IV

GLOSTER
- **33** □■□□ †**Gamecock (Mks. I-III & Grebe Mk. II)**
- 10 □■□□ †Gauntlet (Mks. I & II)
- 98 □□■□ †Gladiator (Mks. I & II, also Sea Gladiator)
- 179 □□□■ †Javelin 1-6
- 78 □□□■ Meteor F.IV (F.4)
- **12** □□□■ †**Meteor F.8**

HANDLEY PAGE
- 11 □□■□ †Halifax B.III, VI, VII
- 58 □□■□ Hampden (Mks. I & II, also Hereford)
- 182 □■□□ †Heyford (Mks. I-III)

HAWKER
- 198 □□□■ P.1127 and Kestrel (now Harrier)
- 140 □■□□ Audax & Hardy
- **18** □■□□ †**Fury**
- 57 □■□□ †Hart (& Hart Trainer)
- 4 □□□■ Hunter F.6
- 167 □□□■ Hunter Two-Seaters
- 111 □□■□ Hurricane I (& Sea Hurricane Mk. IA)
- **24** □□■□ †**Hurricane IIC (& Sea Hurricane Mks. IC & IIC)**
- 126 □□□■ Sea Fury (& Fury)
- 71 □□□■ †Sea Hawk
- 197 □□■□ Tempest I-VI
- 81 □□■□ †Typhoon

HAWKER SIDDELEY (see AVRO & DE HAVILLAND)

MARTINSYDE
- 200 ■□□□ Elephant

R.E.
- 05 ■□□□ R.E.8

S.E.
- 103 ■□□□ S.E.5
- **1** ■□□□ †**S.E.5a**

SHORT
- 74 ■□□□ Short 184
- 84 □■□□ Empire Boats ('C' &'G'-Class; also 'Mercury-Maia' Composite)
- **142** □□■□ **Stirling (Mks. I-V)**
- 189 □□■□ Sunderland (Mks. I-V)

SOPWITH
- 121 ■□□□ †Sopwith 1½ Strutter
- **31** ■□□□ **Camel F.1**
- 169 ■□□□ †Dolphin (5.F.1)
- 13 ■□□□ †Pup
- 50 ■□□□ †7F.1 Snipe
- 73 ■□□□ †Triplane

SUPERMARINE
- 39 □■□□ †S.4-S.6B (Schneider Trophy Racers)
- 221 □□■□ Seafires (Merlins) (Mks. I-III)
- **41** □□■□ **Spitfire I & II**
- **166** □□■□ **Spitfire V Series**
- 206 □□■□ Spitfire Mk. IX (& Mk. XVI)
- 246 □□■□ Spitfire (Griffons) Mks. XIV & XVIII
- 224 □□■□ Walrus I & Seagull V (RN variants)

VICKERS (-ARMSTRONG)
- 66 □□□■ Valiant (Mks. 1 & 2)
- **5** ■□□□ †**F.B.27 Vimy (Mks. I-III)**
- 72 □□□■ †Viscount 700
- 229 □□■□ Warwick Mks. I-V
- 256 □□■□ Wellesley Mks. I & II
- 125 □□■□ Wellington I & II

WESTLAND
- 159 □□■□ †Lysander (Mks. I-III)
- 32 □■□□ Wapiti (Mks. I-VII)
- 191 □□■□ Whirlwind (Mk. I)

Italy

ANSALDO (see S.V.A.)
CAPRONI REGGIANE
123 □□■□ **Re. 2000 (Falco I)**
244 □□■□ Re. 2001 (Falco II), Re.2002 (Ariete) & Re.2005 (Sagittario)
FIAT
110 □□■□ B.R.20 (Cicogna)
22 □■□□ C.R.32
16 □□■□ †**C.R.42 (Falco)**
188 □□■□ G.50 (Freccia)
119 □□□■ G.91
MACCHI
64 □□■□ M.C.200 (Saetta)
28 □□■□ **C.202 (Folgore)**
S.V.A (ANSALDO)
61 ■□□□ Scouts (S.V.A 4-10)
SAVOIA MARCHETTI
89 □□■□ **S.M.79 (Sparviero)**
146 □□■□ S.M.81 (Pipistrello)

Japan (*Allied code names)

AICHI
241 □□■□ D3A ('Val') & Yokosuka D4Y ('Judy') Carrier bombers
KAWANISHI
233 □□■□ Four-motor Flying-boats: H6K 'Mavis' * & H8K 'Emily' *
213 □□■□ Kyofu; Shiden & Shiden KAI Variants ('Rex' *; 'George' *)
KAWASAKI
105 □□■□ †Ki-45 Toryu ('Nick' *)
118 □□■□ Ki-61 Hein ('Tony' *)
MITSUBISHI
129 □□■□ A6M2 Zero-Sen ('Zeke' * & 'Rufe' * floatplane)
190 □□■□ A6M3 Zero-Sen ('Hamp' *)
236 □□■□ †A6M5/8 Zero-Sen ('Zeke 52 *) (see Nos. 129 & 190)
160 □□■□ G3M ('Nell' * & Yokosuka L3Y 'Tina' *)
210 □□■□ G4M 'Betty' * (& Ohka Bomb —'Baka' *)
172 □□■□ Ki-21 ('Sally' * & Ki-57/MC-20 'Topsy' *)
82 □□■□ **Ki-46 ('Dinah' *)**
NAKAJIMA
141 □□■□ **B5N 'Kate' ***
46 □□■□ Ki-43 Hayabusa ('Oscar' *)
255 □□■□ Ki-44 Shoki ('Tojo' *)
70 □□■□ Ki-84 Hayate ('Frank' *)
YOKOSUKA
D4Y ('Judy') (see AICHI D3A)

Netherlands

FOKKER
87 □■□□ C.V
63 □■□□ D.XXI
134 □□■□ G.1 ('Faucheur')
176 □□■□ T.VIII

Poland

LUBLIN
231 ■□□□ R.XIII Variants
P.Z.L.
75 □■□□ P.11 ('Jedenastka')
104 □■□□ P.23 Karas
170 □■□□ P.24
258 □■□□ P.37 Los

Sweden

SAAB
138 □□■□ J 21 A & R
36 □□□■ †J 29

Yugoslavia

242 □■□□ IK Fighters (IK-1 to IK-3, & IK-5)

U.S.A.

AMERICAN DH-4
97 ■□□□ DH-4 ('Liberty Plane')
BELL
165 □□■□ **P-39 Airacobra**
BOEING
192 □□□■ Boeing 707 (& 720; C-135/VC-137)
77 □□■□ B-17E & F Flying Fortress
205 □□■□ B-17G Flying Fortress
101 □□■□ **B-29 Superfortress**
83 □□□■ †B-47 (Stratojet)
245 □□□■ B-52A/H Stratofortress
27 □□■□ †F4B-4
2 □□■□ P-12E
14 □□■□ †P-26A ('Peashooter')
BREWSTER
217 □□□■ Buffalo (Brewster F2A & Export Models 239-439)
CHANCE (& LTV) VOUGHT
47 □□■□ †**F4U-1 Corsair (also as Brewster F3A, Goodyear FG)**
150 □□■□ F4U-4 to F4U-7 Corsair (also AU-1 & Goodyear F2G)
239 □□□■ LTV A-7A/E Corsair II
90 □□□■ **F-8A to E Crusader (now LTV F-8)**
251 □□■□ OS2U Kingfisher (Vought-Sikorsky OS2U & NAF OS2N)
CONSOLIDATED
19 □□■□ **B-24J Liberator**
183 □□■□ PBY Catalina ('Dumbo'; also PBY-5A/6A Amphibian Canso)
CURTISS
37 ■□□□ †JN-4 ('Jenny')
45 □■□□ †Army Hawks (P-1 & P-6)
116 □■□□ †Navy Hawks (BFC & BF2C; F6C & F11C & F11C-2 Goshawk)
80 □□■□ **Hawk 75 (R.A.F. Mohawk)**
136 □□■□ †**P-40 Kittyhawk (Mks. I-IV; R.A.F. only, U.S.A.A.F. Warhawk)**
35 □□■□ **P-40 Tomahawk (Mks. I-II)**
124 □□■□ **SB2C-1 Helldiver (also U.S.A.A.F. A-25 Shrike)**
194 □□■□ SOC Seagull
128 ■□□□ Shrike (A-6, A-8 & A-12)
DOUGLAS
102 □□□■ †A-4 Skyhawk
202 □□■□ A-20 (7A to Boston III) (also R.A.F. Havoc; not U.S.A.A.F. models)
96 □□■□ †**DC-3 (to Dec. 1941 only)**
220 □□■□ †Dakota Mks. I-IV (1941-,70; R.A.F. & Dominion/Commonwealth air forces only)
249 □□■□ †R4D variants (U.S.N's DC-3/C-47s)
196 □□■□ †SBD Dauntless
171 □□■□ TBD Devastator
60 □□■□ **Skyraider (ex-AD-1 to AD-7 now A-1E to A-1J)**
FORD
156 □■□□ Tri-motors ('The Tin Goose' series)
GEE BEE (GRANVILLE BROTHERS)
51 □■□□ †Racers
GRUMMAN
252 □□□■ A-6A/E Intruder, EA-6A & EA-6B Prowler
92 □□■□ †F3F Series
53 □□■□ **F4F-3 Wildcat (British R.N: Martlet I only)**
107 □□■□ **F8F Bearcat**
214 □□■□ TBF Avenger (also Eastern TBM Avenger)
LOCKHEED
120 □□■□ Constellation (L-049/C-69; L-1049 Super Constellation/C-121/R7V/WV-2; L-1649 Starliner)
223 □□□■ C-130 Hercules
253 □□□■ Hudson Mks. I-IV (also U.S.A.A.F. A-28/A-29, AT-18 & U.S.N. PBO-1)
106 □□□■ **P-38J-M Lightning**
131 □□□■ †F-104G/CF-104 (U.S.A./Canadair: Starfighter)
204 □□□■ P2V Neptune (now P-2, also Kawasaki GK-210 Turboprop version)
LTV (see CHANCE VOUGHT)
MARTIN
247 □□□■ B-57 Night Intruders & General Dynamics RB-57F (U.S.A.F. Canberras)
112 □□■□ **B-26B & C Marauder R.A.F. Mks. I-II, also AT-23/TB-26 & U.S.N. JM-1)**
235 □□■□ Maryland & Baltimore (R.A.F. Maryland Mks. I-II, Baltimore Mks. I-V, U.S.A.A.F. A-30)
McDONNELL DOUGLAS
208 □□□■ †F-4 Phantom
NORTH AMERICAN
59 □□■□ **B-25 A to G Mitchell (R.A.F. Mks. I & II, also U.S.N. PBJ-1, U.S.A.A.F. AT-24, RB/TB-25)**
100 □□■□ **P-51 B & C Mustang (R.A.F. Mk. III, also U.S.A.A.F. F-6)**
8 □□■□ †**P-51 D Mustang (R.A.F. Mk. IV, F-6/-51 D, TP/TF-51 D)**
20 □□□■ †**F-86A Sabre (see also CANADAIR Sabre)**
30 □□□■ †**F-100 Super Sabre (F-100A to F & TF-100)**
42 □□□■ FJ Fury (FJ-1 to FJ-4)
155 □□□■ T-28 (Trojan, also in U.S.A., Nomad & Nomar, France as Fennec)
REPUBLIC
7 □□■□ †**P-47D Thunderbolt (R.A.F. Mks. I-II, also P/TP-47G)**
95 □□□■ †F-84F Thunderstreak (Also RF-84F Thunderflash)
226 □□□■ †F-105 Thunderchief
RYAN
158 □□■□ PT/ST Series (PT-16 tò PT-25; Sport Trainers)
THOMAS-MORSE
68 ■□□□ †Scouts (S-4 to S-9)
VOUGHT (see CHANCE VOUGHT)

U.S.S.R.

ILYUSHIN
88 □□■□ †IL-2 ('Shturmovik')
LAVOCHKIN
149 □□■□ LA-5 & 7
MIKOYAN
238 □□□■ †MiG-21 variants ('Fishbed'/'Mongol')
PETLYAKOV
216 □□■□ PE-2
POLIKARPOV
122 □■□□ †I-16 ('Mosca' or 'Rata')
YAKOVLEV
185 □□■□ †YaK-9

†Line drawings, with cross sections for accurate model making, are available for these types from 'Plans Service', Model and Allied Publications Ltd, 13-35 Bridge Street, Hemel Hempstead, Herts, England. Send 3p/25c S.A.E. for their full price list of 'Scale Aircraft Drawings'.

The S.E.5A

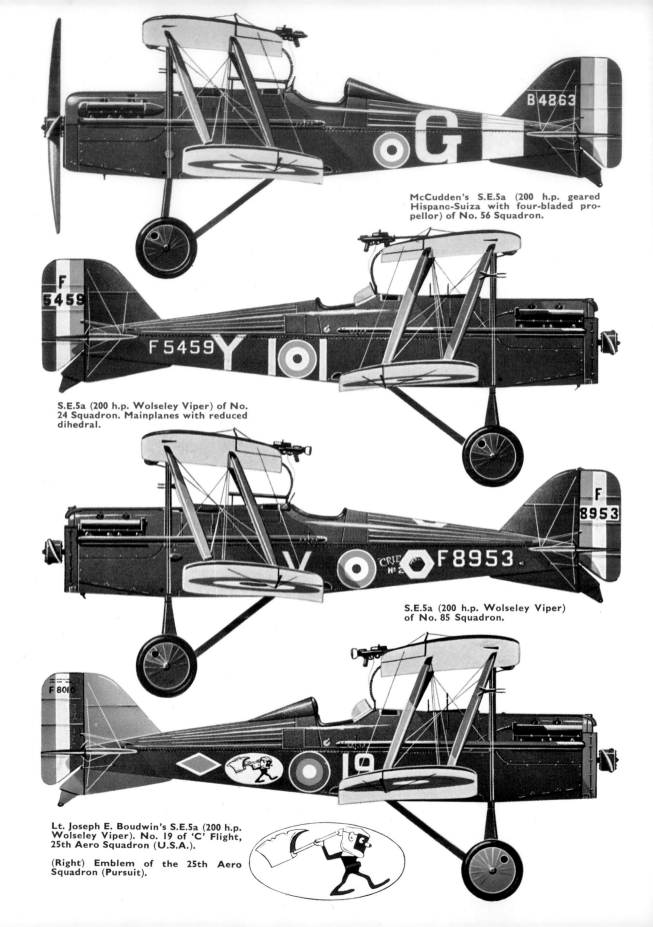

McCudden's S.E.5a (200 h.p. geared Hispano-Suiza with four-bladed propellor) of No. 56 Squadron.

S.E.5a (200 h.p. Wolseley Viper) of No. 24 Squadron. Mainplanes with reduced dihedral.

S.E.5a (200 h.p. Wolseley Viper) of No. 85 Squadron.

Lt. Joseph E. Boudwin's S.E.5a (200 h.p. Wolseley Viper). No. 19 of 'C' Flight, 25th Aero Squadron (U.S.A.).

(Right) Emblem of the 25th Aero Squadron (Pursuit).

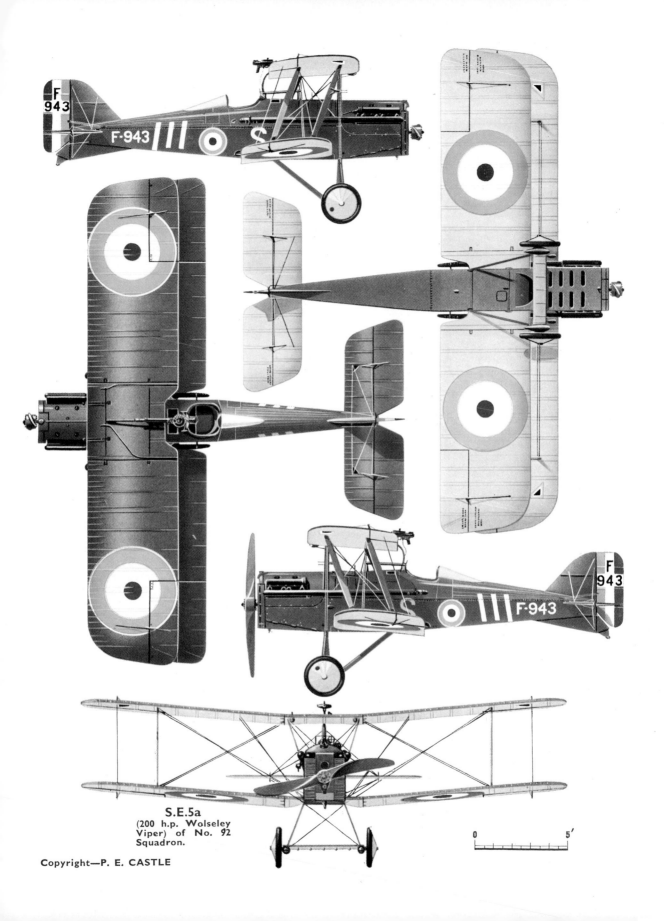

S.E.5a
(200 h.p. Wolseley
Viper) of No. 92
Squadron.

Copyright—P. E. CASTLE

0   5′

The S.E.5A

by J. M. Bruce

Photographed at Farnborough on November 17th 1917, B4897 had passed its final inspection two days previously. It was one of the first S.E.5a's to have the revised undercarriage with wooden V-struts. Just under the forward end of the exhaust manifold can be seen the number 47. This was a kind of constructor's number applied by the Royal Aircraft Factory, and indicates that this was the 47th aircraft of the batch (B4851–B4900). The engine originally fitted to B4897 was the Peugeot-built Hispano-Suiza No. 115311/ W.D.34097, airscrew 19343/T.28137, Vickers gun A.4141, Lewis gun 47202. (Photograph: Crown copyright)

IN 1916 the Royal Aircraft Factory designed two single-seat fighters powered by the 150 h.p Hispano-Suiza engine: the conventional tractor biplane, the work of H. P. Folland, was built as the S.E.5: the less conventional F.E.10 did not proceed beyond the project stage. The S.E.5 went into production at the Royal Aircraft Factory, the later aircraft having wings of slightly reduced span. The development of the S.E.5 will form the subject of a later history in this series.

The initial batch of 24 aircraft (A4845–A4868) underwent their final inspections between March 2nd and April 3rd 1917, and deliveries to No. 56 Squadron, then forming at London Colney, began. This famous fighter squadron went to France on April 8th 1917, and had on its strength most of the S.E.5s that were built; a few of the aircraft went to Nos. 40 and 60 Squadrons.

From the start of its career the S.E.5 had been intended to have the 200 h.p. geared Hispano-Suiza engine as soon as supplies could be obtained. The second prototype, *A4562*, had had an engine of this kind (No. 5193/W.D.10104). The Hispano-Suiza originally fitted to *A4563* (No. 7019/W.D.10111) may also have been of 200 h.p.; certainly by the time this, the third, prototype went to Martlesham Heath on May 29th 1917 it had the 200 h.p. Hispano-Suiza No. 7206.

By this time *A4563* was regarded as the prototype S.E.5a. It had the wings of reduced span; its engine drove a handsome four-blade left-hand airscrew (to R.A.F. Drawing T.28096); the gravity petrol tank and water header tank were built into the leading edge of the centre section; full-length shutters were fitted on either side of the airscrew hub to the one-piece radiator; and the top decking ahead of the cockpit

was deeper than that of the S.E.5. The under-fairing of the nose retained the slight curve that had characterised the S.E.5, and the L-shaped exhausts of the earlier type were fitted.

In Report M.105A Martlesham was laconically satisfied with the S.E.5a's performance: "Flying qualities good; lateral control better than S.E.5. Windscreen is now cut down and view is improved, especially for landing. Control cables and Vickers gun not easily accessible." The speed at 14,000 ft. was 123 m.p.h., that height being reached in 16 mins. 50 secs.; the ceiling was about 23,000 ft. The best recorded comparable performance by an S.E.5 was then 105 m.p.h. at 15,000 ft., with the climb to that height taking 27 mins. 6 secs.

By the standards of May 1917 the figures for the S.E.5a were good. The first production contracts had been placed at the beginning of February with Martinsyde Ltd. (Contract No. 87/A/1616, dated

The prototype S.E.5a at Martlesham Heath, May 1917.

February 1st 1917, for 200 aircraft, *B1–B200*) and Vickers Ltd., Weybridge (Contract No. 87/A/1627 dated February 6th, for 200 aircraft, *B501–B700*). These aircraft were completed as S.E.5a's, as indeed were all those built by contractors.

The Royal Aircraft Factory had not waited for Martlesham's confirmation of the S.E.5a's good performance, for at least fifteen aircraft of the second production batch (*A8898–8947*) built at Farnborough had the 200 h.p. engine. These were *A8923–A8926, A8935, A8938, A8939* and *A8941–A8947*; the engines originally installed in them were made by Wolseley or Peugeot. The first of these S.E.5a's had been completed by May 30th 1917, the day after *A4563* went to Martlesham.

Many of the aircraft of this second R.A.F. batch, including several of the S.E.5a's, went to No. 56 Squadron; the first S.E.5a received by that unit was delivered in June 1917. This may have been the prototype, *A4563*, which is known to have gone to No. 56 Squadron and was later on the strength of No. 84 Squadron. Other early S.E.5a's are known to have been used by No. 60 Squadron, a few by No. 40.

The production S.E.5a's were generally similar to *A4563*. They had long horizontal exhaust pipes, the head fairing behind the cockpit had a straight top line, and the nose underfairing was likewise given a straight-line profile. No. 56 Squadron did not at first like the long exhaust pipes, cut them off just behind the rear exhaust stubs, and welded on short pipes at an outward and downward angle. On July 13th 1917, Major R. G. Blomfield, O.C. No. 56 Squadron, reported to the Headquarters of the 9th Wing that the undercarriage was not strong enough for the 200 h.p. engine; failures had occurred at the lower ends of the struts.

As the summer of 1917 advanced, production of the S.E.5a increased steadily. Contracts placed with the Bleriot & Spad Aircraft Works (later renamed the Air Navigation Co. Ltd.) of Addlestone, and Vickers Ltd. in July 1917 were for a total of 850 aircraft; by the end of 1917 a further 1,300 had been ordered, and further large orders continued to be placed throughout 1918. By the end of 1917 over 800 S.E.5s and 5a's had been built, yet only five squadrons (Nos. 40, 41, 56, 60 and 84) were operating the type in France; of these, Nos. 40 and 41 had completed their re-equipment as late as November. Additionally, No. 24 Squadron received its first S.E.5a on Christmas Day 1917, and No. 68 Squadron was re-equipped with the type in that December.

The reason for this lay in the difficulties that had been experienced with the 200 h.p. Hispano-Suiza engine. Having one of the best power/weight ratios of the time, this engine was built in enormous numbers (in all, 28,977 were made during the war) by many

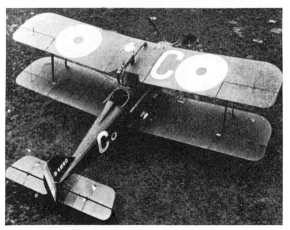

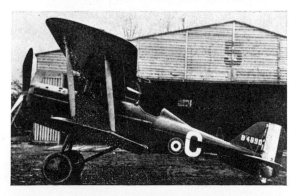

B4890 was captured intact by the Germans. This aircraft had passed its final inspection at Farnborough on October 13th 1917, at which time it had the Wolseley-built Hispano-Suiza engine No. 943/2233/W.D.8518 driving airscrew No. 21271/T.28096 and was armed with Vickers gun No. 7624 and Lewis No. 48298. It had the original steel-tube undercarriage V-struts, and an additional bracing wire was fitted to the leading edge of the fin. The aircraft may have belonged to No. 56 Squadron, and was shot down by Jagdstaffel 5. (Photos: Egon Krueger)

C1091, *photographed on April 26th 1920, with an experimental variable-pitch airscrew.* (Photo: Crown copyright)

The S.E.5a with Viper engine and underslung radiator.
(Photo: I.W.M.)

manufacturers in France, Spain, England, Italy, Russia, Japan and the U.S.A. Wolseley Motors Ltd. of Birmingham held the British licence to manufacture Hispano-Suiza engines and had begun to deliver small numbers of the 150 h.p. version early in 1917.

With admirable foresight, the Admiralty had insisted in November 1916 that the Air Board order 8,000 Hispano-Suiza engines from French manufacturers, chiefly Emile Mayen. Deliveries of Mayen-built engines did not start until early 1918, consequently engines from other manufacturers had to go into the S.E.5a's.

The Wolseley-built 200 h.p. Hispano-Suiza, later known as the Wolseley Adder, was virtually identical with the original 200 h.p. engine. It differed chiefly in having a compression ratio of 4·8 : 1 (4·7 : 1 on the French engine) and a reduction-gear ratio of 35 : 59 (24 : 41 or 21 : 28 on French engines). On test the Wolseley-made engine proved unsatisfactory: on May 7th 1917 it was reported that four successive crankshafts had failed after an average run of only four hours. Yet on May 30th the S.E.5a *A8923* was completed with the 200 h.p. Wolseley No. 782/2233/ W.D.8357, and seven other aircraft of the batch also had Wolseley geared engines.

On May 31st 1917 Lt.-Col. W. B. Caddell, then Military Aviation Director, wrote to Major-General Trenchard that the S.E.5a's *A8923* and *A8924* were fitted with 200 h.p. Wolseley Hispano-Suizas in which the crankshaft webs had been shaved down, and that these engines had been accepted on the understanding that they would not be run at speeds in excess of 1,750 r.p.m. Normal r.p.m. for the 200 h.p. engine was 2,000.

Of the engines fitted to the other 200 h.p. S.E.s of this second R.A.F.-built batch five were Peugeot-made, one was Aries-built, and one was made by Hispano-Suiza, Paris. Fifty more S.E.5a's (*B4851– B4900*) were built at the Royal Aircraft Factory

The R.A.E. hack S.E.5a, D203, with modified fin and rudder, narrow-chord ailerons, nil dihedral, and Viper radiators on a geared Hispano-Suiza engine, which has the final, short exhaust pipes. This photograph is dated August 29th 1918.
(Photo: Crown copyright)

B4885 force-landed in Holland on January 6th 1918 and was later used by the Dutch air service, in whose markings it is seen in this photograph; its Dutch number was SE214. Originally this S.E.5a had a special installation of twin Lewis guns when it was inspected on September 25th 1917, but at the time of its forced landing it had the standard single Lewis on its Foster mounting.

It had served with No. 60 Squadron, R.F.C. Like B4890 it had the steel-tube undercarriage, but its engine drove a two-blade airscrew. An S.E.5a (above) of No. 24 Squadron with reduced dihedral. The headrest has been removed and the windscreen modified. Although the engine is a Viper, the aircraft retains the higher Foster mounting that was standard on S.E.5a's with geared engines.

Apparently an early installation of a Wolseley Viper engine. The top of the radiator is not of the shape that became standard, and the under-fairing is shallower than on production Viper-powered aircraft.

The small number 98 stencilled on the side of the forward fuselage indicates that this S.E.5a is C1148. This aircraft passed its final inspection on September 28th 1918, when it had engine No. 2297/W.D.33397. In February 1919 it was fitted with a Royal Aircraft Establishment variable-pitch airscrew. This photograph is dated June 11th 1920, and shows the aircraft with standard Viper installation and fixed-pitch airscrew; it has short exhaust pipes and the wooden undercarriage.

For training purposes several S.E.5a's were modified to become two-seaters, to the considerable detriment of the aircraft's flying qualities.   (Photo: I.W.M.)

The cockpit of B4875. The three Lewis guns were 43381 (port), 43435 (centre) and 47804 (starboard), and their presence in the cockpit necessitated the redistribution of the aircraft instruments. Obviously replacing the drums of ammunition on three guns would have been difficult, and the pilot could not have escaped serious facial injury in the event of a crash.
(Photo: Crown copyright)

between July 26th and November 13th 1917; thirty-six had Wolseley-made Hispano-Suiza engines.

The general engine-supply situation had become so critical by the autumn of 1917 that Hispano-Suizas made by the French Brasier firm were passed into service with imperfect reduction gears "on the plea that engines of incomplete efficiency were better than none at all" (*The War in the Air*, Vol. VI, page 36).

In January 1918 about 400 new S.E.5a airframes were in store, engineless, owing to the failure of the engine programme. Only the delivery, starting about that time, of the 8,000 engines ordered at the insistence of the Admiralty enabled squadrons to be re-equipped and new units to go to France.

Misinterpreting an instruction to make 400 Hispano-Suizas of the 150 h.p. model (this was intended as a safety measure following the failure of the first Wolseley-built 200 h.p. engine) the Wolseley company redesigned the engine as the Wolseley Viper, a direct-drive unit with a compression ratio of 5·3 : 1 in its standard form. In August 1917 the first installation of a Viper in an S.E.5a was made in *B4862* at Farnborough (engine No. 717/2233/W.D.8292), the second in *B4899* (engine No. A21777/W.D.1877) in December. The first aircraft was tested at Martlesham in September 1917, *B4899* in December. Neither achieved outstanding results, but the Viper engine was favourably reported on.

The early experimental Viper installations retained the one-piece radiator with round-top cowling, but the production version had two radiator blocks, one for each bank of cylinders. The standard Viper installation of the late production S.E.5a was characterised by a deep nose with a squarish frontal aspect. Although the Viper was in 1918 specified in all but the Martinsyde contracts, S.E.5a's continued to be delivered with such engines as the manufacturers could obtain. The majority of these aircraft had two-blade airscrews, standard designs being A.B.8080 or T.28137M on Wolseley-built 200 h.p. geared engines or French Hispanos with 21 : 28 gears, A.B.7673 or A.D.662 on the Viper. The four-blade airscrew (T.28096) usually distinguished those S.E.5a's that had French engines with 24 : 41 gears.

In the spring of 1918 an experimental Viper installation with underslung radiator was tested. This is believed to have been an attempt to make the aircraft more suitable for operations in Mesopotamia,

where the type was in use with one Flight of No. 72 Squadron.

In January 1917 the Sunbeam Arab engine, although only partly tested, was ordered into large-scale production. It was a water-cooled 200 h.p. V-eight of about the same size and of the same configuration as the Hispano-Suiza; it was therefore natural that the Arab should be considered as a possible alternative engine for the S.E.5a when the Hispano-Suiza crisis arose. In November 1917 the R.A.F.-built S.E.5a *B4900* was completed with an Arab I in place of the standard Hispano-Suiza. In 1918, *B609*, *C1111*, *B4898*, *D7017* (which had been renumbered from *B7832* and was actually an Aeroplane Repair Depot rebuild) and *E1366* were also fitted with Arab engines, *C1111* having both the Arab I (geared) and Arab II (direct-drive). Endless troubles, especially with vibration, were experienced, and the engine was not adopted for the S.E.5a.

Apart from the continuous quest for suitable engines, much experimental work was done on S.E.5a's at Farnborough. The following table lists examples.

Aircraft	Date	Modification or Experiment
A8938	June 1917	Balanced rudder somewhat similar to that of the R.T.I two-seater. Flown in September 1917 with ailerons of 10-inch chord and narrow-chord elevators. Crashed December 1917 by Capt. (later Professor) G. T. R. Hill.
A8947	August 1917	Narrow-chord elevators.
	March 1918	Converted to S.E.5b.
B4893	November 1917	Wings of 6 ft. chord.

Aircraft	Date	Modification or Experiment
C1063	February 1918	Reduced dihedral of 2° 30'.
	September 1919	Gravity ground indicator.
D203	March-August 1918	Rounded fin and balanced rudder, narrow-chord ailerons, nil dihedral. Viper-type radiators on 200 h.p. Hispano-Suiza.
	October 1918	Balanced central rudder and twin fins.
	—	Twin fins and rudders (drawing of this tail unit is dated October 1919).
	January 1919	Spinning tests.
	—	D203 remained in use at Farnborough at least until May 1922. It was used in tests of various experimental exhaust systems.
C1134 (renumbered from C1139)	September 1918	Hart variable-pitch airscrew. (The S.E.5a's C1134 and C1139 interchanged identities at this time.)
E5696 F5278	December 1918	Parachute experiments.
D7007 D7012	December 1918 February 1919	Palethorpe landing skid.
C1148	February 1919	Variable-pitch airscrew.
C1091	April 1920	Variable-pitch airscrew.
E5927	October 1920	Major G. H. Norman's experiments with fire-extinguishing equipment.
	October 1925	Exhaust-muff cockpit heater.
	February 1926	Thermostat radiator shutter control.
E5923	1920	Fitted at Martlesham with an experimental tail unit, embodying a fin and rudder of rounded outline, a triangular tailplane of which the rear part was adjustable, and inversely tapered elevators. This aircraft was flown at Farnborough in comparative trials with S.E.5a D7018 and the S.E.5b, A8947.

Few attempts were made to change the armament of the S.E.5a, despite the seemingly peculiar arrangement of one Vickers gun offset to port, the Lewis central above the centre section, and both guns mounted at an upward angle of 5°. Of the Lewis gun, Lord Douglas of Kirtleside (who, as Major W. Sholto Douglas, M.C., was O.C. No. 84 Squadron, R.F.C., in late 1917) wrote:

Although I was all for new methods of attack, I found that pushing the Lewis gun back into the fixed position while flying in the open cockpit of the S.E.5 (*sic*) at high altitude called for an effort that was almost superhuman. We had no supply of oxygen in those days, and I found that my strength at height fell off very considerably. It was difficult enough to change the double drum of ammunition on the Lewis gun without having to man-handle the gun into position for an attack and fly the aeroplane all at the same time. There were others who had the same experience, and more often than not we had to dive down to a lower altitude before we could reload. (*Years of Combat*, page 218.)

This difficulty had probably not manifested itself as early as July 1917, when No. 56 Squadron submitted a design for a modified Foster mounting capable of carrying two Lewis guns; the Royal Aircraft Factory was instructed to fit this to an S.E.5a. This is doubtless why, in September 1917, B4885 was fitted with two Lewis guns (Nos 28743 and 47202) in addition to the usual Vickers (No. A5182). In November 1917, B4875 was extensively modified to accommodate the Eeman mounting with three Lewis guns firing upwards at an angle of 45°. Three slots were cut in the centre section, the gravity petrol tank and water header tank being necessarily moved to the leading-edge portion of the starboard upper wing. The Eeman installation was apparently intended for Home Defence anti-airship duties, but, although tried out in a Martinsyde G.102 and a Vickers F.B.26, it was ultimately abandoned.

The S.E.5a was tried on Home Defence Duties in 1918 with squadrons Nos. 37, 50, 61 and 143, but was withdrawn largely because it proved to be difficult to land at night on the small aerodromes of the period. A secondary reason was that its water-cooled engine

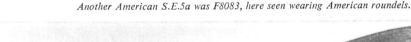

Another American S.E.5a was F8083, here seen wearing American roundels.

took too long to warm up, consequently it was unable to take off as quickly as the rotary-powered Camel.

B4875 must have been one of the first S.E.5a's to have the wooden undercarriage, which was apparently Farnborough's answer to Major Blomfield's complaint that the original steel-tube structure was not strong enough. The front leg consisted of two struts faired together with plywood.

In 1918 various minor modifications and improvements were made: the wing trailing edges were strengthened in February; a new type of oil tank with double pump was introduced in May, at which time the Lewis-gun mounting rail on Viper-powered S.E.s was lowered (but some aircraft, possibly re-engined with a Viper after having had a geared Hispano-Suiza, retained the higher mounting). In July the nose cowling for the 200 h.p. Hispano-Suiza was re-designed to facilitate manufacture. The Martinsyde company redesigned the structure of the upper fin; in September Wolseley evolved a new type of wooden undercarriage.

In the squadrons various modifications were made, often to the taste of individual pilots. Many preferred to remove the headrest; some liked to cut the cockpit lower at the sides; No. 24 Squadron reduced the dihedral of their aircraft for a time. Of more general application was the addition of stay-wires to the leading edge of the fin.

During 1918 the S.E.5a consolidated the fine reputation it had established, in spite of engine troubles, in 1917, and proved to be one of the best fighting aircraft of the war. It was stable yet light on the controls, steady in a dive and a good gun platform, structurally strong and fast enough to be able to extricate itself from trouble if need be. Many of the greatest fighting pilots—Mannock, Bishop, McCudden, Beauchamp-Proctor, McElroy, Maxwell —flew the S.E. with great distinction. Of the S.E., McCudden wrote:

G-EBVB was one of the skywriting S.E.5a's. Their extended exhaust pipes met in a single outlet, to clear which a cut-out was made in the rudder.

The S.E.5 (*sic*) which I was now flying was a most efficient fighting machine, far and away superior to the enemy machines of that period . . . Other good points of the S.E.5 were its great strength, its diving and zooming powers, and its splendid view. Apart from this, it was a most warm, comfortable and easy machine to fly . . . prisoners said that the German pilots considered the S.E.5 a most formidable fighting machine. (*Five years in the Royal Flying Corps.*)

At the time of the Armistice some 2,700 S.E.s were on the strength of the Royal Air Force, and the type was in service with twenty British, one Australian and two American operational squadrons.

Large-scale production in America was planned. Components of fifty-six S.E.5a's (including *C1115, C1119–C1121, C8740, C8746, C8749, C8750, C8752–C8754, C9081, C9087–9089, D6101, D6102, D6105, D6109–D6112*) were sent to the U.S.A., where they were assembled by the Curtiss company. Curtiss had a contract for 1,000 S.E.5a's to be powered by the 180 h.p. Wright-Martin Hispano-Suiza, but only one, S.C.43153, was completed. Its official tests began on August 20th 1918, but no more were built and the remaining 999 were cancelled at the Armistice. In October 1918 the American Expeditionary Force bought thirty-eight S.E.5a's.

An S.E.5a in American service and markings, seen at Quantico in June 1921. The upper-fairing of the nose has been removed and the structure under the fuselage may have been a bomb rack.
(U.S. Navy photo)

When peace came the S.E.5a continued in service in the air forces of Australia, Canada and South Africa. Some remained in use in the U.S.A., but they were largely supplanted by the Eberhardt conversion, the S.E.5E. Two S.E.5a's went to the U.S. Navy, however, with the designating numbers *A-5588* and *A-5589*; one was carried on a gun-turret launching platform on the battleship *Mississippi*. A few went to Poland and were used against Russia in 1920; at least one was captured and flown with the red-star insignia.

Nowhere was the type numerous, however. In Britain a few remained in service at the R.A.E. for several years, and fifty acquired civil identities. Some of the R.A.E. aircraft had a modified undercarriage with steel-tube V-struts and a separate axle for each wheel.

The civil S.E.5a is perhaps best remembered as the pioneer skywriting aircraft, and it is one of these that was rebuilt in 1959 and is flying today. Originally *F904*, subsequently *G-EBIA* and now *D7000*, it is the only surviving airworthy example of this great fighting aeroplane. In the Australian War Museum at Canberra *A2-4* is preserved; it has an oleo undercarriage. The true identity of the S.E.5a in the Science Museum, South Kensington, is *F938* (ex *G-EBIB*); and *F937* (ex *G-EBIC*) survives as one of the Nash collection.

Only one development of the S.E.5a was flown. This was the S.E.5b which had sesquiplane wings and a cleaned-up engine installation with underslung radiator. It appeared at the beginning of April 1918 and was flown experimentally at Farnborough for a few years. It was later fitted with standard S.E.5a wings of equal span.

Production: The following serial numbers for 5,489 S.E.5a's are known; they exclude the A.R.D. rebuilds. Two hundred known to be cancelled; not all of the others were delivered.

Royal Aircraft Factory, Farnborough, Hants. A8923–A8926, A8935, A8938, A8939, A8941–A8947; B4851–B4900; C1051–C1149; D7001–D7050 (only first 20 built; at least one, D7017, was merely an A.R.D. rebuild, B7832, renumbered).

Austin Motor Co. (1914) Ltd., Northfield, Birmingham. B8231–B8580; C8661–C9310; E5637–E5936; F7951–F8200.

Air Navigation Co. Ltd., Addlestone, Surrey. C1751–C1950; E5937–E6036; H674–H733.

Martinsyde Ltd., Brooklands, Surrey. B1–B200; D3911–D4010; E3154–E3253; F5249–F5348; F8321–F8420.

Grahame-White Aviation Co. Ltd., Hendon. C6351–C6500 (order cancelled and transferred to Wolseley Motor Co.).

Vickers Ltd., Crayford. C5301–C5450; D301–D450; D8431–D8580; F551–F615; F8946–F9145.

Vickers Ltd., Weybridge. C9486–C9635; D201–D300; D3426–D3575; D5951–D6200; E1251–E1400; E3904–E4103; F5449–F5698.

Whitehead Aircraft Co., Richmond. B1001–B1101 (order cancelled).

Wolseley Motors Ltd., Birmingham. C6351–C6500; D6851–D7000; F851–F950; F7751–F7800.

H5291–H5390 allotted for S.E.5a; contractor unknown, contract cancelled.

Known A.R.D. rebuilds. B733, B848, B891, B7824, B7830, B7832 (later renumbered D7017), B7870, B7881, B7901, B7913, F5912, F5924, F6276, H7162, H7165, H7261.

Armament: One fixed 0·303 in. Vickers machine-gun with 400 rounds, Constantinesco C.C. synchronising gear, Aldis and ring-and-bead sights, Hyland Type E loading handle, and Fitzgerald jam clearers. One 0·303 in. Lewis machine-gun on Foster mounting with four 97-round drums and Norman sight. Four 25 lb. Cooper bombs could be carried in racks under the fuselage.

Service use: Western Front—R.F.C. (later R.A.F.) Squadrons Nos. 1, 24, 29, 32, 40, 41, 56, 60, 64, 68 (No. 2 Squadron, Australian Flying Corps), 74, 84, 85, 92, 94; 25th and 148th Aero Squadrons, United States Air Service.

Palestine—R.F.C./R.A.F. Squadrons Nos. 111 and 145.

Mesopotamia—No. 72 Squadron. *Macedonia*—Squadrons Nos. 17, 47 and 150. *Home Defence*—R.A.F. Squadrons Nos. 37, 50, 61 and 143.

Fairly extensive modifications had to be made to B4875 in October 1917, when it was fitted with the Eeman triple mounting for three Lewis guns. The fuselage decking ahead of the cockpit was deepened, an extended windscreen was fitted, a modified centre section with three slots permitted the guns to fire upwards at an angle of 45°, and the gravity petrol tank and water header tank were installed in the leading-edge portion of the starboard upper wing. Transparent panels were let into the fuselage sides. This aircraft was originally completed in September 1917 with the Wolseley engine No. 930/2233/W.D.8505, but that engine was soon transferred to B4884 and by the time B4875 had the Eeman mounting installed its engine was No. 120007/W.D.34176 of Delaunay Belleville manufacture.

The Canadians also made a two-seat conversion of the S.E.5a. G-CYCE was originally F9117. It appears that a modified centre section, possibly containing a gravity tank between the spars, was fitted.

(Photo: K. M. Molson)

Examples of S.E.5a's used by operational squadrons :

No. 1 Sqn.—*B130, B8254* (aircraft *'O'*), *C8700* (*'P'*), *C8846* (*'M'*), *D6878, E5969* (*'A'*).

No. 24 Sqn.—*B548* (*'Z'*), *B8422, C1098* (Capt. G. E. H. McElroy), *C1938, D6918, E1293, F5459* (*'Y'*).

No. 29 Sqn.—*B8507, C9804* (*'A'*), *D5963, E5669* (*'Y'*), *F862, H7162.*

No. 32 Sqn.—*B166* (*'A'*), *B8374, C1089, D262, E1399, E4026.*

No. 40 Sqn.—*B69* (*'U'*), *B4879* (Major R. S. Dallas), *C1071* (*'Y'*), *D6197, D7000, E1318.*

No. 41 Sqn.—*B642, C5436, C8877* (Lt. W. G. Claxton), *D5959* (Capt. F. R. McCall), *E1362, E5665.*

No. 56 Sqn.—*A8923, B183* (*'4'*), *C1096, D6096, E5656, F5556, H693.*

No. 60 Sqn.—*B567, C1937, D6136* (*'Z'*), *E4095* (*'V'*), *F5471, H690.*

No. 64 Sqn.—*B2, B125, C6481, C6447, D289, D6900.*

No. 68 Sqn.—*B535, C1057* (*'C'*), *D6995, E5951* (*'Z'*), *F5465, H7165.*

No. 74 Sqn.—*B574, C1139* (Capt. K. L. Caldwell), *C9211* (*'D'*), *D276* (*'A'*, Capt. E. Mannock), *D6922, E5967.*

No. 84 Sqn.—*B682, B8233, C1794* (Lt. A. W. Beauchamp-Proctor) *D6926, F5477, H710* (*'P'*).

No. 85 Sqn.—*B7870, C6490* (Major W. A. Bishop, V.C.), *C6492, D6871, E1294* and *E1295* flown by 2nd Lt. D. C. Inglis and Major E. Mannock on July 26th 1918, when Mannock was killed.

No. 92 Sqn.—*B8430, C1142, C8896, D6925, E4024, F858.*

25th Aero Sqn., U.S.A.S.—*F8005, F8010, F8015, F8028, F8038, F8040.*

Specification

Power : 200 h.p. Hispano-Suiza 8Bb, 8Bd, 8Cb, 8Cd, 8Db, 8Dd, 8Eb, 8Ed; 220 h.p. Hispano-Suiza 8Bc, 8Be, 8Cc, 8Ce, 8Dc, 8De, 8Ec, 8Ee; 200 h.p. Wolseley W.4a Viper; 200 h.p. Wolseley W4b Adder I, II and III; 200 h.p. Sunbeam Arab I and II.

Dimensions : Span 26 ft. 7·4 in.; length 20 ft. 11 in.; height 9 ft. 6 in.; chord 5 ft.; gap 4 ft. 7 in.; stagger 1 ft. 6 in.; dihedral 5°; incidence 5°; span of tail 10 ft. 11·9 in.; airscrew diameter (T.28096, four blades) 7 ft. 9 in., (A.D.662, two blades) 7 ft. 10½ in.; wheel track 5 ft. (tyres, Palmer 700 × 100 mm.).

Areas : Wings and ailerons 245·8 sq. ft.; ailerons, each 8 sq. ft.; tailplane 14·7 sq. ft.; elevators 15·8 sq. ft.; fins, upper 4·4 sq. ft., lower 1·7 sq. ft., total 6·1 sq. ft.; rudder 5·85 sq. ft.

Weights and Performance

Aircraft	A4563	B7	B501	B4862	Production Aircraft	American-built S.C.43153
Engine	200 h.p. Hispano-Suiza	200 h.p. Hispano-Suiza (Wolseley)	200 h.p. Hispano-Suiza (Wolseley)	200 h.p. Wolseley Viper	200 h.p. Wolseley Viper	180 h.p. Wright-Martin Type E
Weights (lb.):						
Empty	1,400	1,531	—	1,406	—	—
Military load	287	287	—	286	—	—
Fuel and oil	266	230	—	248	—	—
Loaded	1,953	2,048	—	1,940	1,988	2,060
Max. speed (m.p.h.):						
At ground level	—	—	—	—	—	122·3
At 6,500 ft.	—	—	132	—	—	—
At 10,000 ft.	—	126	128	130	—	117
At 15,000 ft.	121	116·5	115·5	122·5	120	—
Climb to:	m. s.	m. s.	m. s.	m. s.	m. s.	m. s.
5,000 ft.	—	—	—	—	—	—
6,500 ft.	6 0	7 30	—	—	6 20	—
10,000 ft.	10 20	13 15	13 46	10 50	10 50	13 0
15,000 ft.	18 50	27 35	26 30	20 50	20 50	—
Service ceiling (feet)	22,000	17,000	—	—	19,500	—
Endurance (hrs.)	3	2¼	—	—	3	—

The Boeing P-12E

The Boeing P-12E

by Peter M. Bowers

A P-12E of the 27th Pursuit Squadron. See colour illustrations for details of squadron markings.

JUNE 25th 1928 can be said to have opened the final chapter in the history of the biplane fighter in service with the U.S. Army, for on that day flew the Boeing Model 83, forerunner of the most successful family of fighters to serve with America's forces between the two World Wars.

The Model 83 was developed by the Boeing Airplane Company of Seattle at company expense in the hope of succeeding with a replacement for the Army's PW-9* and the Navy's F2B and F3B fighters in service towards the end of the 'twenties. The risk involved came to be justified, for no fewer than 586 aircraft in the F4B/P-12/100 series were built in the next half dozen years. They brought the era of the biplane fighter to an end for the Army, and were in service in secondary rôles until shortly after America's entry into World War II.

The relatively long production life of the basic model and the refinement of successive variants provide a perfect example of evolution in the art of aircraft design and demonstrate the full life cycle of an aircraft "family". Some of the changes made to the basic design were the result of experience with earlier models, and some were "retro-fit" installations where the components of late models were used on early aircraft to bring them up to date. Some of these changes were initiated by Boeing or the Services to improve the efficiency of the design as a fighting aircraft. Others, especially some made by the Army Air Corps, were merely for the purpose of developing or testing powerplant or equipment for general aircraft application. In such cases the aeroplanes were frequently given experimental designations and a new series letter to indicate their change from standard fighter status. This also protected the test programme from time losses incurred by mandatory compliance with maintenance bulletins that were issued periodically for most standard service aircraft.

THE DESIGN DESCRIBED

The fuselage structure of the Model 83 was interesting in that it introduced bolted-up aluminium tubing construction. (An exactly parallel development was taking place in Britain in the evolution of the Hawker Fury—designed to replace the welded-steel Bristol Bulldog.) The fuselage of the Model 83 and early production aircraft retained welded steel tubing in the engine mounting and centre-section area, but bolted square dural tubing was used aft of the cockpit. Bolted instead of welded joints had been used in fuselage designs previously, the steel tubes being, however, bolted to tabs welded to the longerons. On the 83, the tubes were bolted directly to one another through dural gussets.

Wing design differed from previous Boeing practice in the use of straight instead of tapered planform. Construction remained unaltered—two box spars with spruce flanges and mahogany ply web. The ribs were band-sawed from mahogany ply and fitted with spruce strips. The upper wing was built up in one piece but the two lower wings, although constructed separately, were bolted together at the spar butts for installation as a single unit. The aerofoil section was the newly-developed Boeing 106 section. The entire tail unit was of semi-monocoque metal construction using the integrally stiff corrugated skinning developed for the Boeing F3B-1.

* Between 1920 and 1924 the Army used a designation system of prefixes PA, PW and PN (pursuit, air-cooled; pursuit, water-cooled and pursuit, night, respectively); subsequently the familiar "plain" P-Pursuit nomenclature was adopted.

Above: *Model 83 under test by Navy in civilian colours.* Below: *Model 89, 2nd prototype of the series, also in civil colours.*

Armament consisted of either two 0·30-cal. Browning guns (with 600 rounds per gun) or one 0·30 and one 0·50-cal. gun (with 600 rounds for the smaller gun and 200 for the larger). The guns were situated in the top of the nose, with troughs in the panelling and synchronised to fire through the propeller arc. The Pratt & Whitney R-1340-7* power-plant developed 450-h.p. at 5,000 feet in early production machines, and used a ground adjustable variable pitch two-blade metal propeller. A 55-U.S. gallon auxiliary fuel tank could be fitted between the undercarriage legs as optional equipment. Bomb-loads of up to about 700 pounds could be distributed under the lower wing and fuselage belly.

THE MODEL 83 AND 89 PROTOTYPES

Boeings produced two prototypes which, in effect,

*The engine designation denoted a radial engine with a displacement of 1340 cubic inches. The previous equivalent designation, SR-1340C, denoted a supercharged radial, the C indicating the third basic variant. This became the R-1340-7 in the new system of allocating even dash numbers for Navy, and odd dash numbers for Army engines.

sired the entire P-12/F4B range. The first, the Model 83, was first flown at Seattle on June 25th 1928 and was delivered three days later to San Diego for detailed evaluation. The Model 89 was completed the following month and transported by rail to the Navy Test Center at Anacostia, Maryland, on July 24th, flying for the first time on August 7th. The two air-craft differed in that the 83 had a spreader-bar under-carriage with diagonal strut bracing to the middle of the bar, whereas the 89 had split-axle gear. The later

Model 101 diverted from Army P-12 contract and completed as experimental XP-12A. Note full cowling and shortened landing gear.

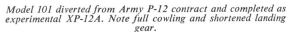

Model 102, standard Army P-12, duplicate of Navy F4B-1 except for deletion of naval gear.

Above: *XP-12G, a P-12B temporarily fitted with a turbo-supercharger.* Below: *Model 102B̊ (P-12B) using straight-chord Frise ailerons of XP-12A but retaining the divided landing gear of F4B-1 and P-12.*

aircraft was equipped with a 500-lb. bomb rack between the undercarriage legs, while the 83 was fitted with an arrester hook. Colour schemes were identical, French grey predominating; Boeing green trim appeared on the fuselage and tail, and the top surfaces of the upper wings were orange. Since both aircraft were Boeing-owned, neither bore military markings— nor, strangely, did they carry the civil registrations allocated to them. Although not Navy property, they were referred to as XF4B-1s administratively and,

while at San Diego, the 83 carried the markings "U.S. Navy" on the aft fuselage.

Both aircraft were originally powered by "long-nosed" R-1340B engines which were supposed to improve the aerodynamic shape of the nose. They were however soon replaced by the standard C (or dash-7) engines with no more than marginal effect on the performance.

THE P-12 IS ORDERED

The path of the Model 83/89 now divides, for, while the Navy had first acquired the two prototypes for evaluation, the Army now also took an active interest in the development. While at Anacostia, the Model 89 was loaned to and tested by Army pilots at Bolling Field (the Army installation across the field from the Navy facility).

As a result of the Bolling pilots' reports on the Model 89, Boeing received a contract for ten P-12s on November 7th 1928, the first nine being similar to the naval version except for the deletion of the arrester hook and other purely naval equipment. The first P-12

Model 218 with P-12B wings and empennage fitted to all-metal semi-monocoque fuselage. Was prototype for Army P-12E and Navy F4B-3. Fin shape was changed eventually.

Model 222, Army P-12C. Only difference from the P-12B is cross-axle landing gear and ring engine cowling.

completed was handed over to Air Corps Captain Ira C. Eaker on February 26th 1929 for a good-will speed flight to Central America. Named "Pan American", this P-12 was otherwise devoid of military markings, but was later returned to standard Army finish. The first flight by a standard P-12 was on April 11th 1929, although others were in process of surface shipment to the Army, the last of the nine being delivered on April 26th. (Colouring was standard Air Corps olive drab on fuselage, struts and wheels, with chrome yellow on wings and tail.)

The basic P-12 was the only model in the Army series to use the tapered ailerons, these being the only external features to distinguish it from the later P-12B. P-12s were also delivered with fairings aft of the engine cylinders, but cooling problems led to their removal soon afterwards.

Following on the first nine P-12s (29-353 to -361), the tenth and final aircraft on the first Army order, (29-362), was the XP-12A. This, the Boeing Model 101, incorporated various refinements suggested by the Army pilots and thus was regarded as the P-12 prototype proper. The differences included Frise ailerons with hinge line parallel to the wing spar, shorter undercarriage, long-chord Boeing engine cowling, redesigned elevators and a castoring tail-skid. Full armament provision was made, together with racks for five 25-lb. bombs. First flight by the XP-12A took place on April 11th 1929, but unfortunately little evaluation of the new features could be made as, with only four flying hours behind it, it was destroyed in a mid-air collision with another P-12 at Wright Field on May 18th.

Nevertheless, evaluation of the remaining P-12s sufficed to eliminate some minor snags and on June 10th 1929 Boeing received an order for 90 P-12Bs— the largest single order placed by the Army in peacetime thus far.

Top to bottom: *Model 227, Army P-12D, outwardly indistinguishable from P-12C; XP-12H, a P-12D fitted with an experimental improved version of the standard Pratt & Whitney Wasp; Model 234, P-12E with pilot's headrest modified to hold liferaft.* Below: *P-12D fitted with vertical tail surfaces of later P-12E.*

Top to bottom: *YP-12K, a standard P-12E fitted with fuel injection engine for evaluation; P-12E restored to pre-war condition in 1961. Note hand-painted registration number; same aircraft, originally of 27th Pursuit Sqdn., painted as Navy F4B-3 for Navy exhibition. Below: P-12Es of the 27th Pursuit Sqdn. See page 23 for colour scheme.*

The P-12B could be distinguished outwardly from the P-12 by the Frise ailerons and revised elevators of the XP-12, and the use of slightly larger 30 × 5-inch wheels instead of the earlier 28 × 4-inch version. The landing gear and uncowled engine were the same as on the P-12 (omitting the cylinder fairings), but later on some P-12Bs were retro-fitted with ring cowlings developed for subsequent variants.

Cost of the P-12B was $11,224 each, less engine and Government Furnished Equipment (GFE). First of the batch (*29-329* to *-341*; *29-433* to *-450*; *30-29* to *-87*) was flown on May 30th 1930, and the last was delivered on May 17th—rail delivery of dismantled airframes having started on February 1st 1930.

The first aircraft of this batch (*29-329*) was later converted by the Army (under the designation XP-12G) for installation of the experimental Y1SR-1340G and H engines equipped with turbo-super-chargers and ring cowlings of the type later adopted by the P-12C. Afterwards the aeroplane was returned to P-12B standard.

Next Army order was for the P-12C (Boeing Model 222), 136 of which were ordered on June 2nd 1930. In the event, only the first 96 (*31-147* to *-242*) were completed as P-12Cs, 35 of the remainder appearing as P-12Ds. The most obvious differences which identified the P-12C were the addition of an engine ring cowl and a spreader-bar undercarriage similar to that of the original Model 83. Performance bestowed by the R-1340-9 (or SR-1340D), which was rated at 450-h.p. at 8,000 feet, included a top speed of 175·5 m.p.h. at 10,000 feet and 176·5 m.p.h. at sea level. Amortisation had reduced the unit cost of the P-12C to $10,644 less engine and GFE. Delivery of dismantled aircraft to the Army commenced on August 30th 1930 and was completed on February 12th 1931, and the first recorded flight was on January 30th that year.

The P-12D (Boeing Model 227) followed the P-12C deliveries without interruption, beginning on February

25th 1931 and ending on April 28th, the first flight taking place on March 2nd. These thirty-five aircraft (*31-243* to *-277*) differed only internally from the P-12C—it being a common but mistaken belief that alterations to the engine cowling distinguished the two. In fact the engine cowlings were interchangeable.

The thirty-third P-12D was modified as the XP-12H by the Army to accommodate an experimental Pratt & Whitney GISR-1340E geared radial engine. Tests on *31-275* indicated that the arrangement was unsatisfactory and the aircraft was returned to P-12D standard in June 1932.

THE P-12E SERIES

On September 29th 1930 Boeing first flew its private-venture Model 218. This was initiated as a company-owned aircraft to develop new features for the P-12/F4B series, and was essentially a P-12B with semi-monocoque metal fuselage structure. As such, it came to be considered as the prototype of the P-12E and F4B-3, and was tested by both Army and Navy pilots under Bailment Contract.

Early in the test programme on the Model 218 (X66W), the vertical tail surfaces underwent modification, the change being perpetuated in subsequent production variants. Later on, the R-1340D engine was replaced temporarily by an R-1340E, but the standard engine, rated for maximum power at 8,000 feet, produced a top speed of 195 m.p.h. at that height.

After completion of testing, the sole Model 218 was sold to China and, flown by an American volunteer pilot, Robert Short, destroyed two out of three attacking Japanese fighters before being shot down over Shanghai in 1932.

The considerable promise shown by the Model 218, not least performance-wise, prompted the Army to order the type into production and, with the Boeing

designation Model 234, appeared as the P-12E—the most widely used and long-lived of the Army series. 135 P-12Es were ordered on March 3rd 1931, and 110 (*31-553* to *-586*; *32-1* to *-76*) were delivered as such between September 19th and October 15th the same year. The remaining 25 were completed as P-12Fs. The first flight by a P-12E took place on October 15th 1931.

As originally delivered, P-12Es were painted in the standard Army olive drab on fuselages, with yellow wings and tails. The fuselages were later repainted in Air Corps (pale) blue, and in 1940 the entire aircraft was painted silver—resulting from an Air Corps directive calling for all obsolescent tactical types having painted surfaces to be repainted in this colour.

The basic P-12E underwent many changes of designation after entering service, not always denoting changes in appearance or equipment. For instance, the first P-12E, *31-553*, was re-designated XP-12E on October 1st 1931 immediately after delivery; this was simply to identify a standard example of the E-series withdrawn from service for test work. Later on it resumed its P-12E title.

P-12E *32-42* became the P-12J with the installation of a Pratt & Whitney SR-1340H engine, rated at 575-h.p. at 2,500 feet, and a special bombsight at

Above: P-12E in the all-silver finish applied to obsolete fabric-covered and painted aircraft in 1940. Below: P-12E of 8th Pursuit Group—Group Commander's aircraft. 550 h.p. Wasp.

Wright Field. This machine became one of the seven YP-12Ks after yet another engine change.

The XP-12E, the P-12J and five standard P-12Es (*32-33*, *-36*, *-40*, *-46* and *-49*) became YP-12Ks when SR-1340E engines with fuel injection were installed for service trials. All reverted to P-12E standard in June 1938.

A further complication arose when the YP-12K, *31-553* (ex XP-12E), was redesignated XP-12L on January 2nd 1934, being fitted with a Type F-7 turbo-supercharger. It reverted to YP-12K in February 1937, and to P-12E in June 1938 with the other examples.

One P-12E was to have been equipped with radio controls in 1940 and tested as an unmanned target aircraft; however, the Army abandoned the proposal to use obsolete service models for this purpose and the scheme, designated A-5, did not materialise.

Nevertheless, while most P-12Es and Fs were grounded and assigned to Air Corps and contract mechanics' schools in 1941, twenty-three miscellaneous P-12s were handed over to the Navy for use as radio-controlled target aircraft on the A-5 pattern.

Although bearing different Army designations, all these P-12s* were referred to by the Navy as F4B-4As —the A denoting their former Army status.

*P-12C: *31-151*, *-154*, *-209*, *-210*; P-12D: *31-245*, *-258*; P-12E: *31-561*, *-564*, *-576*; *32-10*, *-13*, *-25*, *-33*, *-40*, *-41*, *-44*, *-46*, *-48*, *-57*, *-66*, *-69*, *-71*; P-12F: *32-85*.

One of the obsolete P-12Es (*32-17*) given to civilian schools in 1940–41 as non-flying classroom equipment, was obtained by the Ontario Air Museum, California, from the California Polytechnic Institute. It was slowly restored to display condition and had been made airworthy by 1961 under the civil registration *N3360G*. Repainted as an F4B-3, it participated in Navy celebrations of Armed Forces Day the same year. In 1962 it was restored to its correct Army configuration as a P-12E.

THE FINAL PRODUCTION VARIANT

The last 25 aircraft in the original P-12E (Model 234) order were completed as P-12Fs (Model 251). The initial difference was the installation of an SR-1340G engine, so rated as to deliver 500 h.p. at 11,000 feet instead of the 7,000 feet for the SR-1340E in the P-12E. The last ten P-12Fs were the first P-12s delivered with tailwheels, although the earlier F's and all the E's later had tailwheels by retro-fit.

Last example of the P-12F batch (*32-77* to *-101*) gave foretaste of future cockpits in having a factory-fitted sliding canopy. This was the last P-12 built (deliveries of the P-12Fs taking place between March 6th and May 17th 1932), all Army designations in the P-12 series higher than F being conversions of earlier models.

CIVIL AND COMMERCIAL VARIANTS

Commencing in 1929 Boeing produced four commercial and export variants of the Model 100 with an affinity to both the Army P-12 and Navy F4B-1. The principal differences were the deletion of standard U.S. military equipment and the installation of the fuel tank in the centre-section of the upper wing.

The first Model 100 flew on October 8th 1929 and was sold to the Bureau of Air Commerce (now the

Above: *The last P-12F fitted with an experimental closed canopy.* Below: *A second P-12F, also with closed canopy, but with clear side panels.*

Model 100, the commercial counterpart of the F4B-1/P-12.

FAA) with the Government aircraft registration *NS-21*.

The second, *NX872H*, was sold to Pratt & Whitney for use as an engine test bed; apart from the original R-1340 "Wasp", this aeroplane also flew the R-98S "Wasp Junior", the R-1535 "Twin Wasp Junior" and the R-1690 "Hornet" engines. It was then sold to stunt pilot Milo Burcham who used it for display flying between 1933 and 1941 as *NC-872H* with distinctive modifications. The space between the undercarriage legs was faired-in, low-pressure tyres fitted, and metal panelling replacing the fuselage fabric. At the time of writing (1964) the aeroplane is currently owned by Paul Mantz of Santa Ana, California.

The third Model 100 has had the most varied career and has carried every possible combination of U.S. civil registration, commencing with the plain *873H* and passing through *C, NC, NR, NX to N873H*. It was used at the factory for several years as a test machine and demonstrator, and was then sent to the Boeing School of Aeronautics at Oakland, California, for use as an advanced trainer. It was acquired about 1936 by Paul Mantz for display and movie flying and is still being used for such. It is now powered by a war-surplus Wasp Junior driving a controllable-pitch propeller.

The Model 100F was a one-off commercial equivalent of the P-12F delivered to Pratt & Whitney for engine testing. First engine fitted was the 700 h.p.

Model 100D, the fourth standard machine, used to demonstrate improved features.

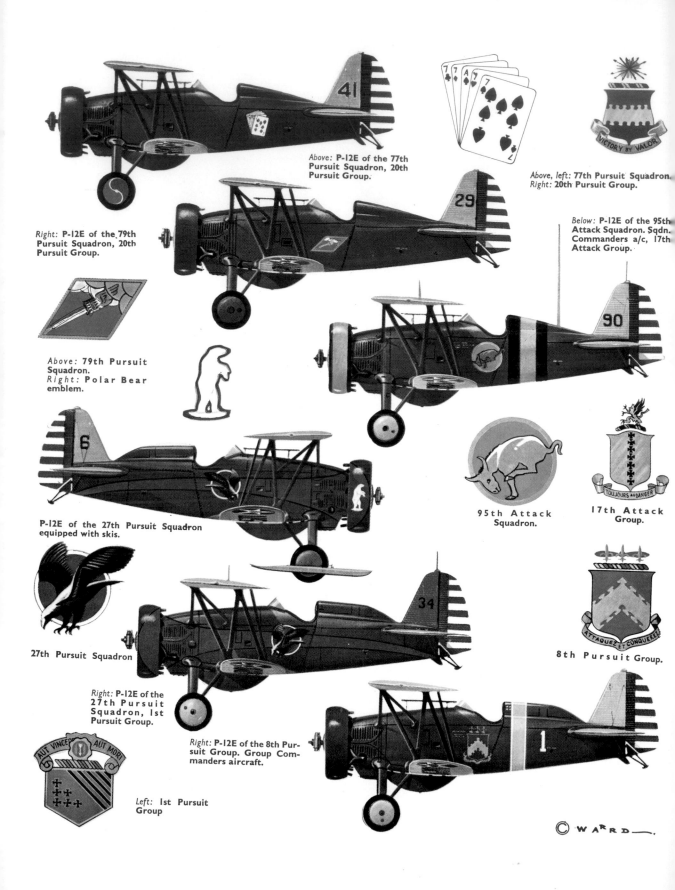

Above: P-12E of the 77th Pursuit Squadron, 20th Pursuit Group.

Above, left: 77th Pursuit Squadron.
Right: 20th Pursuit Group.

VICTORY BY VALOR

Right: P-12E of the 79th Pursuit Squadron, 20th Pursuit Group.

Below: P-12E of the 95th Attack Squadron. Sqdn. Commanders a/c, 17th Attack Group.

Above: 79th Pursuit Squadron.
Right: Polar Bear emblem.

95th Attack Squadron.

17th Attack Group.

TOUJOURS AU DANGER

P-12E of the 27th Pursuit Squadron equipped with skis.

27th Pursuit Squadron

8th Pursuit Group.

ATTAQUEZ ET CONQUEREZ

Right: P-12E of the 27th Pursuit Squadron, 1st Pursuit Group.

Right: P-12E of the 8th Pursuit Group. Group Commanders aircraft.

Left: 1st Pursuit Group

AUT VINCERE AUT MORI

© WARD

© P. ENDSLEIGH CASTLE ARAeS

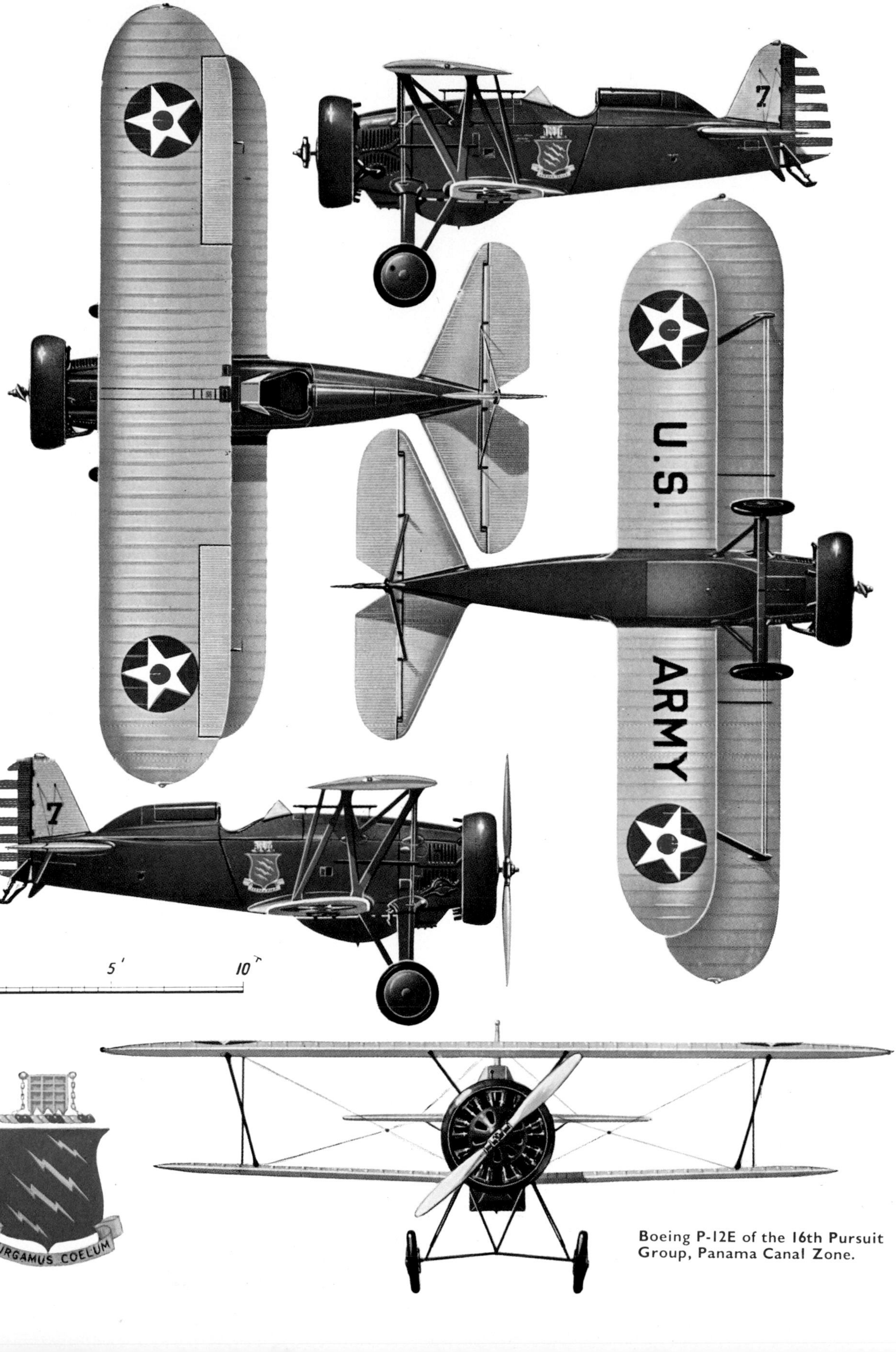

U.S. ARMY

7

7

5'   10'

PURGAMUS COELUM

Boeing P-12E of the 16th Pursuit
Group, Panama Canal Zone.

Model 251—P-12F.

R-1535 Twin Wasp Junior and with this was flown on June 20th 1932. So great was the diameter of the propeller used that both take-off and landing had to be performed in the "three-point" attitude to maintain ground clearance.

Like the Model 100, *NX872H*, the 100F also flew with the Hornet and Wasp engines. On one occasion it flew with each of the engines during the course of a single day as a demonstration of quick engine-changing techniques. Because of the different engine weights, the balance of the aeroplane was corrected during these engine changes by use of a sliding weight in the fuselage between the cockpit and tail. On a test flight the pilot lost consciousness due to a failure in the oxygen supply and the 100F fell into a spin. Not being designed to withstand the loads imposed by these gyrations, the weight broke loose and destroyed the flying controls—preventing recovery from the spin.

Last of the Model 100s, *NX874H*, was also used as

a company demonstrator and was eventually sold to the Mitsui Company of Japan.

The Model 100A was a special convertible two-seat version of the basic Model 100 built to the special order of Mr. Howard Hughes. Hughes undertook many extensive modifications before the aircraft was sold to Col. Arthur Goebel as a single seater. Registered *247K* it was destroyed in 1957.

Two Model 100Es were built for Siam (now Thailand) and were export versions of the P-12E. Owing to a ruling that export of aircraft currently in production for U.S. Forces could not be undertaken, the Boeing Model 234 designation was changed to 100E though general structure and performance was similar to that of the P-12E. Both 100Es were delivered in a dismantled state on November 10th 1931. The last surviving example (taken over by the Japanese during World War II), is currently preserved in the Thai Aeronautical Museum at Bankok.

Specification

			P-12	P-12B	P-12C	P-12E
Powerplant	...	...	450 h.p. Pratt & Whitney R-1340-7 (SR-1340C) rated at 5,000 ft.	450 h.p. Pratt & Whitney R-1340-7 (SR-1340C) rated at 5,000 ft.	450 h.p. Pratt & Whitney R-1340-9 (SR-1340D) rated at 8,000 ft.	500 h.p. Pratt & Whitney R-1340-17 (SR-1340E) rated at 7,000 ft.
Fuel Capacity	...	...	52–99 U.S. gal.	50–99 U.S. gal.	50–110 U.S. gal.	55–110 U.S. gal.
Dimensions						
Wing span	...	...	30 ft. 0 in.	30 ft. 0 in.	30 ft. 0 in.	30 ft. 0 in.
Length	...	...	20 ft. 1 in.	20 ft. 3 in.	20 ft. 1 in.	20 ft. 3 in.
Height	...	...	9 ft. 7 in.	8 ft. 10 in.	8 ft. 8 in.	9 ft. 0 in.
Wing area	...	...	227·5 sq. ft.	227·5 sq. ft.	227·5 sq. ft.	227·5 sq. ft.
Weights						
Empty	...	...	1,758 lb.	1,945 lb.	1,938 lb.	1,999 lb.
Loaded	...	...	2,536 lb.	2,638 lb.	2,630 lb.	2,690 lb.
Performance						
Max. speed	...		171 m.p.h. at 5,000 ft.	175 m.p.h. at 5,000 ft.	178 m.p.h. at 8,000 ft.	189 m.p.h. at 7,000 ft.
Cruising speed	...		135 m.p.h.	137 m.p.h.	141 m.p.h.	160 m.p.h.
Initial climb	...		2,080 ft./min.	2,040 ft./min.	1,410 ft./min.	—
Combat ceiling	...		28,200 ft.	27,450 ft.	26,200 ft.	26,300 ft.
Range	...	...	520 miles	540 miles	580 miles	580 miles

Armament: Either two 0·30-cal. or one 0·30-cal. and one 0·50-cal. machine guns on nose. Racks for light bombs under wings and between undercarriage legs.

Production
P-12: *29–353* to *–361* (9 aircraft). XP-12A: *29–362* (one aircraft). P-12B: *29–329* to *–341*; *29–433* to *–450*; *30–29* to *–87* (90 aircraft). P-12C: *31–147* to *–242* (96 aircraft). P-12D: *31–243* to *–277* (35 aircraft). P-12E: *31–553* to *–586*; *32–1* to *–76* (110 aircraft). P-12F: *32–77* to *–101* (25 aircraft). Total, 366 aircraft.

The Focke-Wulf Fw 190A

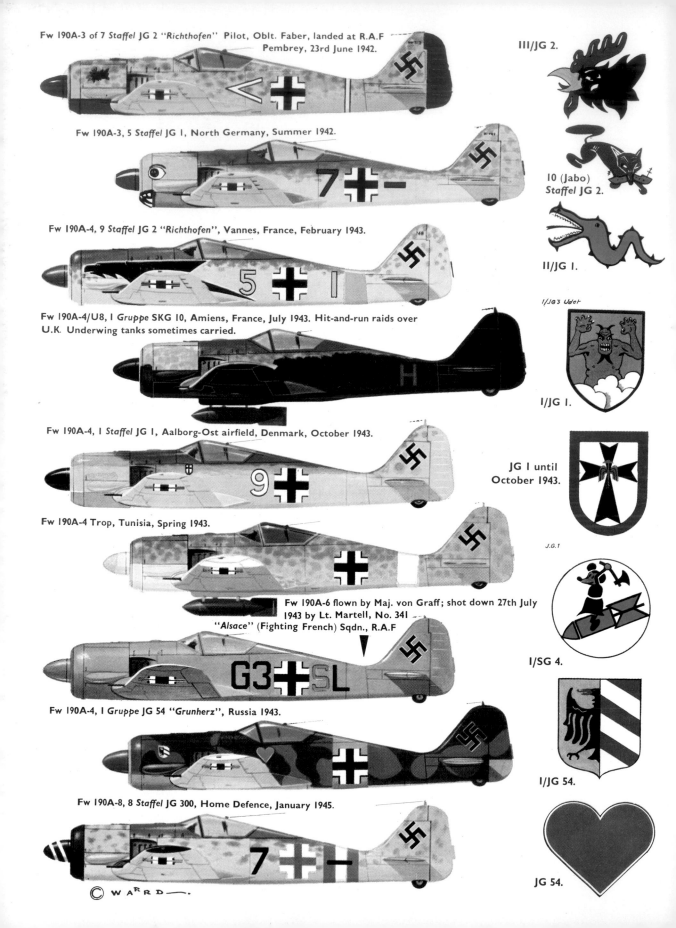

Fw 190A-3 of 7 *Staffel* JG 2 "Richthofen" Pilot, Oblt. Faber, landed at R.A.F Pembrey, 23rd June 1942.

III/JG 2.

Fw 190A-3, 5 *Staffel* JG 1, North Germany, Summer 1942.

10 (Jabo) *Staffel* JG 2.

Fw 190A-4, 9 *Staffel* JG 2 "Richthofen", Vannes, France, February 1943.

II/JG 1.

Fw 190A-4/U8, I *Gruppe* SKG 10, Amiens, France, July 1943. Hit-and-run raids over U.K. Underwing tanks sometimes carried.

I/JG3 Udet

I/JG 1.

Fw 190A-4, 1 *Staffel* JG 1, Aalborg-Ost airfield, Denmark, October 1943.

JG I until October 1943.

Fw 190A-4 Trop, Tunisia, Spring 1943.

J.G.1

Fw 190A-6 flown by Maj. von Graff; shot down 27th July 1943 by Lt. Martell, No. 341 "Alsace" (Fighting French) Sqdn., R.A.F

I/SG 4.

Fw 190A-4, 1 *Gruppe* JG 54 "Grunherz", Russia 1943.

I/JG 54.

Fw 190A-8, 8 *Staffel* JG 300, Home Defence, January 1945.

© WARD

JG 54.

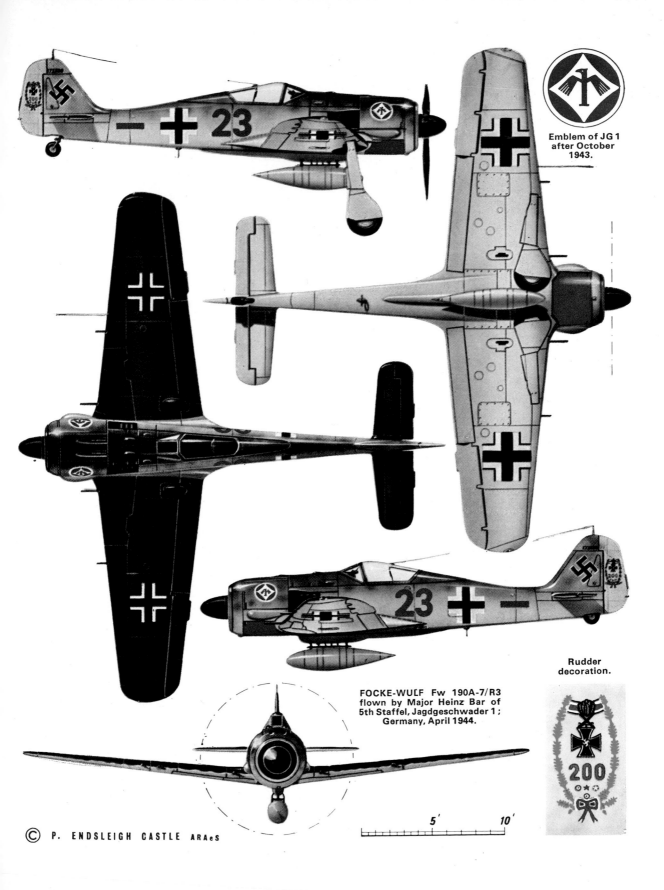

Emblem of JG 1
after October
1943.

Rudder
decoration.

FOCKE-WULF Fw 190A-7/R3
flown by Major Heinz Bar of
5th Staffel, Jagdgeschwader 1;
Germany, April 1944.

5'   10'

© P. ENDSLEIGH CASTLE ARAeS

The Focke-Wulf Fw 190A

by M. C. Windrow

Oblt. Faber's Fw 190A-3.

THE Focke-Wulf Fw 190, one of the most aesthetically attractive and functionally successful aircraft to emerge from the Second World War, was the brain-child of Dipl. Ing. Kurt Tank, technical director of the *Focke-Wulf Flugzeugbau*. The designer of many impressive projects, Tank achieved perhaps his most spectacular success with the Fw 190. Combining a bulky air-cooled engine with a slim airframe, he produced a beautifully proportioned aeroplane which completely avoided the cumbersome rotundity of most other radial-engined fighters of the period. The Focke-Wulf's appearance at the fighting front ushered in a period of heavy losses and high-level alarm in the R.A.F. Superior in many respects to contemporary British equipment, the nimble radial-engined "Butcher-bird"* forced a loss/victory ratio of at least 2/1 on Fighter Command Spitfire Vs in the first few months of its operational career.

In the autumn of 1937, the German *Reichsluftfahrt-ministerium* instructed the *Focke-Wulf Flugzeugbau*, uncommitted to any other major project, to submit a single-seat fighter design to supplement the Messer-schmitt Bf 109, which had entered squadron service with the young *Luftwaffe* eighteen months previously. Of the twin proposals put forward by Tank, one was planned around the B.M.W. 139 radial engine while the other was based on the liquid-cooled Daimler-Benz DB 601. The climate of opinion in contemporary aviation circles was in favour of the low-drag char-acteristics of in-line engines, but nevertheless the radial-engined design was accepted. Considerable demand for the Daimler-Benz powerplant was partly responsible.

Detail design work commenced in mid-1938, culminating in the completion of the first prototype, designated Fw 190V1, in the spring of 1939. Designed for production by widely-dispersed sub-contractors,

the aircraft had other features which strongly recom-mended it to the *Luftwaffe*. The wide-track under-carriage eliminated one of the weaknesses most noticeable in the Bf 109; and front-line maintenance requirements were cut to a minimum.

The Fw 190V1 was flown for the first time on June 1st 1939 by chief Focke-Wulf test pilot Hans Sander. After five flights the machine was handed over to the *Luftwaffe* for service trials at the Rechlin test establishment. Despite the lack of forward visibility while taxi-ing, which was to prove fatal to inexperi-enced pilots later in the Fw 190's career, the *Luftwaffe* pilots were extremely impressed by the new fighter. The prototype displayed superb handling qualities, well-balanced controls and brisk acceleration. By October the second prototype, the Fw 190V2, was ready for testing. Featuring a large ducted spinner instead of an engine cooling fan, it was armed with two 7·9-mm. MG 17 and two 13-mm. MG 131 machine-guns. After armament tests and some 50 hours of flight trials the machine, which had been plagued from the outset by engine overheating, was destroyed following a crankshaft failure.

Later prototypes differed in being powered by the improved B.M.W. 801C engine, offering 1,600 h.p. With strengthened engine mounts and the cockpit moved further back, these models were free from the heat and discomfort noticed by pilots of the earlier prototypes.

The flight trials of the Fw 190VA had prompted an order for 18 pre-production fighters, the first batch being ready for testing in October 1940 under the designation Fw 190A-0. The eighth and subsequent A-0s were fitted with the longer-span wing, which became standard. Hermann Goering was an enthusi-astic supporter of the new type, and preparations were made for quantity production in plants at Bremen and Hamburg, an initial order for 100 Fw 190A-1s being placed. The A-1 differed from late A-0 models only in

* The Fw 190A-1 was christened "Würger" or "Butcher-bird"

its stressed engine cowling and assisted-release cockpit hood; armament comprised two MG 17s in the cowling and two in the wing roots. In June 1941 the first 30 Fw 190A-1s were delivered to the *Luftwaffe* for operational testing. Early examples of the A-2, with two slow-firing 20 mm. MG FF cannon in the wing-root positions, were already under test at Le Bourget.

June of 1941 saw the opening of hostilities with the Soviet Union and intensive *Luftwaffe* activity in the Mediterranean, including the conquest of Crete. The only fighter units remaining in Northern France were *Jagdgeschwader 2 "Richthofen"* and *Jagdgeschwader 26 "Schlageter"*. At the close of May JG 2 replaced JG 26 in the Brest/Cherbourg sector, the latter unit moving to the Abbeville/St. Omer airfield complex near the Belgian border. In July Adolf Galland's famous JG 26 received its first Fw 190A-1s and A-2s, the more welcome because of the mauling their Bf 109F-2s had been suffering at the hands of R.A.F. Spitfire Vs.

The first operational encounter between R.A.F. fighters and Fw 190s in squadron service took place on September 27th 1941, and further combats followed with increasing frequency. A story current in R.A.F. circles at the time was that the new radial-engined fighters were ex-*Armee de l' Air* Curtiss Hawks appropriated by the *Luftwaffe*; but any pilot who encountered the Fw 190 personally could testify to the absurdity of this theory. No pre-war vintage fighter in the world could out-fly the Spitfire V, and yet the sinister-looking "Butcher-bird" could break off combat with Spitfires at will by virtue of its 10/20 m.p.h. speed advantage. Faster and more stable in the dive, and capable of magnificent aileron turns, the Focke-Wulf fighters immediately reversed the narrow margin of superiority so painfully won by the R.A.F. over the Bf 109E and Bf 109F. The *Luftwaffe* was to maintain this advantage until the arrival of the first Spitfire IXs on the squadrons in July 1942.

The first prototype was initially flown with a large ducted spinner; it is seen here after the removal of this unsatisfactory device.

The late summer and autumn of 1941 was a period of intense activity over the English Channel as the R.A.F. attempted to draw *Luftwaffe* units away from their triumphant campaign in the East, and the appearance of the Fw 190 at the front further reduced the already questionable effectiveness of this offensive.

During this period the Fw 190A-3 superseded the A-2 on the assembly lines. Powered by the 1,700 h.p. B.M.W. 801Dg engine, the A-3 carried two fast-firing MG 151 cannon in the wing roots, the MG FFs being moved outboard and the MG 17s retained in the cowling. One hundred examples of the A-3 were supplied to the Turkish Air Force, finished in the early *Luftwaffe* desert camouflage of brown/green dappling. They were preferred by Turkish pilots to the Spitfire Vb, also operated by that air force.

The first major action in which the Fw 190A participated was the "Channel Dash". On the night of 11th/12th February 1942 the German capital ships *Scharnhorst* and *Gneisenau* left Brest with escorting vessels and began a hazardous voyage through the Channel on their way to safer anchorages in Kiel and Wilhelmshaven. Galland, newly promoted to Inspector

The A-4/U8 fighter with underwing tanks fitted.

The A-5/U3 Trop sub-variant with bomb-load in place.

of Fighters on the death of his colleague Werner Molders, had the task of providing fighter cover throughout the voyage. Available to him were 252 aircraft, consisting of Bf 109Fs drawn from JG 1, JG 2, and the fighter school at Paris; 30 Bf 110 night fighters for dawn and dusk operations and the mixed strength of JG 26, operating both Bf 109F-4s and Fw 190A-2s. The Focke-Wulfs acquitted themselves well in the almost continual combats of February 12th and Operation Thunderbolt (the official German code-name) was a heartening success for the *Luftwaffe* and *Kriegsmarine*.

On March 10th 1942 Sperrle, commander of *Luftflotte 3*, ordered JG 2 and JG 26 to form a fighter-bomber (*Jagdbomber* or *Jabo*) *Staffel* within each of the *Geschwader*. Initially equipped with the Bf 109F-4/B, the two *Staffeln* began "tip-and-run" raids against England. Ten *Jabo*/JG 2, based at Caen-Capriquet, attacked Channel shipping while 10 *Jabo*/JG 26 flew missions against Dover, Worthing, Brighton and other south coast towns.

The first Fw 190A to become available for evaluation by the R.A.F. was Oberleutnant Arnim Faber's Fw 190A-3, W.Nr.313.Oblt. Faber, the adjutant of III/JG 2, landed his machine at R.A.F. Pembrey on the evening of June 23rd 1942. Although his *Staffel* (7/JG2) had been in combat with Spitfires of the Exeter-based Polish Wing returning from a strike on Morlaix airfield, Faber's Focke-Wulf was undamaged, and his reasons for landing are obscure. The most likely theory, that he mistook the Bristol Channel for the English Channel and thought he was landing at a *Luftwaffe* airfield in Northern France, is borne out by the series of victory rolls he performed before touching down. Faber's garishly-painted aircraft was immediately examined by R.A.F. and industrial experts and service pilots; their findings substantiated the reports received from aircrew on the squadrons, and seriously influenced British thinking in fighter design for the future. An example of the trend is the Hawker

Tempest II; the conception was finally perfected in the Hawker F.2/43 Fury.

By July 20th 1942, the day of the costly "reconnaissance in force" by Canadian troops at Dieppe, 10 *Jabo*/JG 26 was flying Fw 190A-4s. The A-4 subtype was powered by a B.M.W. 801D-2 engine with MW 50 fuel injection, raising the maximum speed to 416 m.p.h. Formations of JG 26 were active over the beaches and town of Dieppe during the raid.

Two views of the Fw 190A-4/R5, with overwing tank experimental installation.

30

An Fw 190A-4/U8 of SKG 10 which landed at R.A.F. West Malling on the night of 16th July 1943. A matt-black temporary finish was applied to the aircraft for night intruder sorties.

(Photo: Imperial War Museum)

Two months later, the *Jabo* units of both JG 2 and JG 26 were equipped with the Fw 190A-4/U8; armed with two MG 151 cannon in the wing roots, this variant could carry 1,100 lb. of bomb load and two 66 gallon wing tanks. The task of intercepting the *Jabo* raids became increasingly difficult. Approaching the English coast at wave-top height, pairs of Focke-Wulfs avoided the radar defences and were diving southwards again at full throttle before R.A.F. Spitfires could locate them. Fighter Command began tedious and uneconomical standing patrols and it was not until the operational appearance of the Hawker Typhoon that this threat to the morale of the population was countered. Insignificant in terms of military results, these pin-prick raids caused a reaction from the R.A.F. out of all proportion to the *Luftwaffe's* efforts.

The first raids on French targets by the 8th U.S.A.A.F.'s B-17 Flying Fortresses were carried out in August 1942, and by the end of the year the Fw 190A-equipped *Staffeln* of JG 2 and JG 26 could no longer be spared for fighter-bomber duties. In the spring of 1943 a new unit, SKG 10 (*Schnellkampfgeschwader* or Fast Bomber Wing), was formed, equipped with the Fw 190A-4/U8. Initially operating under the *Fliegerführer Atlantik* on anti-shipping strikes in the

Bay of Biscay, SKG 10 was transferred in early summer to the Amiens area, and took up the *Jabo* offensive abandoned by JG 2 and JG 26. In July II, III, and IV/SKG 10 were rushed to Sicily, and the Focke-Wulfs of I/SKG 10 continued operations over the Channel until early in 1944. The *Gruppe* even took part in night intruder missions over London and the Home Counties.

The close of 1942 saw full-scale production of the Fw 190A and the manufacture of components in many plants throughout Germany and the occupied territories; among others, some Fieseler and Ago factories were switched to this programme. The *Luftwaffe* had received over 1,900 examples of A-3 and A-4 fighters and A-4 fighter-bomber variants during the year. The Fw 190A-5 appeared early in 1943. Essentially the same aircraft as the A-4, this next production variant differed only in its improved engine mountings, which necessitated the engine being moved $5\frac{3}{4}$ inches further forward.

Of all theatres of operation where the Fw 190 was needed, North Africa presented the most pressing problem. In the early spring of 1943 Erwin Rommel's forces were fighting a hopeless rearguard action in Tunisia, and their airborne lines of communication

The Fw 190A-4/R6 was fitted with two WG 21 rocket launchers for bomber interceptor duties.   (Photo: Imperial War Museum)

Fw 190A in scheme adopted for Home Defence duties late in the war. The fuselage bands appeared variously in red/yellow, blue/white, or black/white. Blue/white was the most widely used style in 1945. Machine illustrated probably belonged to II/JG 4.

(Photo: R. Ward collection)

across the Mediterranean were being ravaged by Allied fighters. The two desert fighter formations, JG 27 and *Jagdgeschwader 53 "Pik As"*, had been reduced to a pitiable condition, and the newly-drafted JG 77 and II/JG 51 were suffering heavy losses. Units of Fw 190A-4/Trops, with desert filters and fuselage racks for a 550 lb. bomb, enjoyed a fair measure of success in operations with the *Fliegerführer Tunis*, but even so the campaign ended in costly defeat in May 1943. A quarter of a million men of the *Afrika Korps* surrendered and the Fw 190s took part in a hurried evacuation of *Luftwaffe* personnel to Sicily, carrying as many as three men per aircraft.

The Allied invasion of Sicily followed on July 10th and Fw 190A-4/U8s, A-4/Trops, and A-6/R2s (a model with 1,650 lb. bomb load capacity) were heavily committed in operations with Kesselring's *Luftflotte 2*. By the time these units (including II, III, and IV/SKG 10) were withdrawn to Italy they had suffered crippling losses.

Another type of operation in which the Fw 190A

gained good initial results was free-lance night fighting. This venture was instigated by a *Luftwaffe* ex-bomber pilot, Major (later Oberst) "Hajo" Herrmann, whose private experiments in single-seater fighter operations against R.A.F. Bomber Command's night offensive in the spring of 1943 resulted in the formation of *30 Jagd Division*, comprising JGs 300, 301, and 302. Despite complaints from orthodox night fighting formations that these *Wilde Sau* (Wild Boar) aircraft were causing serious confusion in the crowded night skies, the volunteer pilots were the darlings of Press and public as their scores mounted. Aircraft used in these operations were the Fw 190A-5/U2, with flame-dampers and anti-glare screens and the Messerschmitt Bf 109G-6/U4N. By the winter of 1943 both aircraft and pilots had been "flown to death", and losses mounted; *30 Jagd Division* was withdrawn from night operations early in 1944 and underwent conversion to various "dirty-weather" and special duties rôles.

As stated above, the 8th U.S.A.A.F. began opera-

Fw 190A abandoned at Salerno after Allied successes.

(Photo: R. Ward collection)

Exhaust detail of Fw 190A-3.   ("Flight" photo)

tions from England in August 1942 and these first insignificant raids were the forerunners of the immense formation attacks by B-17s and B-24 Liberators which during the next three years shattered the German industrial machine and German morale. At the outset of the offensive only JGs 1, 2 and 26 were available to defend the western approaches of the Reich against daylight bombing; two years later nine *Geschwader* proved inadequate, and this drain on resources seriously aggravated the situation on the Russian front.

Fw 190As equipped many first-line units of the *Reichsverteidigung* (*Luftwaffe* Home Defence Command). The rapidly increasing numbers of Allied escort fighters and their unexpected improvement in range led to a continuous series of air battles over the Netherlands, France and Germany in which the North American P-51 Mustangs and Republic P-47 Thunderbolts inexorably wore down the strength of the *Luftwaffe*. New tactics and new weapons were evolved for the *Jagdgeschwader* (an example is the WG 21 "Dodel" rocket launcher fitted to the Fw 190A-4/R6) but despite the spirited resistance of the German fighter pilots, which earned them the un-grudging admiration of the American aircrews, sheer

weight of numbers was on the side of the Allies. The output of new fighters from the factories was stepped up in an intensive effort which was a credit to the industry, but useless in the long run.

In respect of armament the Fw 190A variants were slightly superior to the Bf 109G models, but the Focke-Wulf's performance fell off badly above 21,000 feet, the height at which the bombers usually operated. Even when the escort fighters were evaded, a *Luftwaffe* pilot attacking a combat "box" of 18 B-17s had to face a combined defensive armament of more than 200 heavy machine guns, and while the Fortresses were by no means invincible, it required a fighter pilot of considerable skill and determination to press home attacks on such a formation with his four 20 mm. cannon.

In the winter of 1943/44 Fw 190As were fitted with additional armour for a new rôle—that of "storm-fighters". A Major von Kornatski had suggested to Galland that special suicide squadrons should be formed to ram the "Ami" bombers, especially the lead aircraft. Turning down this plan on principle, Galland approved the formation of an experimental *Sturm-staffel* whose task would be to press home attacks in tight formation at close range, whatever the cost. As a last resort, the pilots were to ram and bale out; an optimistic view of the results of a mid-air collision at combined speeds of up to 700 m.p.h. This volunteer unit achieved excellent results and the first *Sturm-gruppe* was formed. It was Galland's intention to add a *Sturmgruppe* to each of the *Reichsverteidigung Geschwader*, but the invasion of Normandy inter-rupted this programme. The aircraft used by the *Sturmgruppe* was the Fw 190A-5/U16.

The other major sphere of action in which the Fw 190 participated was "the Verdun of the air"—the savage fighting on the Russian front. Despite the fact that the Focke-Wulf was opposed in this theatre by aircraft of inferior design and performance, it gained for the *Luftwaffe* no lasting margin of air superiority. The cause of this failure did not lie in any technical shortcomings, it was simply part of the overall inability of the German air arm as a whole to cope with the special circumstances encountered in this campaign.

In the early hours of June 22nd 1941 the forces of the Third Reich began their massive offensive in the East on a front of more than 2,000 miles. In spite of

The A-3/U4 reconnaissance variant; camera bay is just visible under the fuselage.

Installation of racks for eight small 50-kg bombs on the Fw 190V-8.

Left: *Detail view of the A-3/U4 camera fairing.*   Right: *Heavily armoured modification to an Fw 190A cockpit canopy.*

the huge number of obsolete Soviet aircraft destroyed on the ground and in the air in the initial stages of the campaign, the elimination of the Red Air Force as an effective arm was never achieved. The main centres of aircraft production remained beyond the range of the *Luftwaffe's* bombers, and the flow of replacements continued to reach the often depleted squadrons.

The structure of the Red Air Force placed the *Luftwaffe* at a disadvantage from the outset. A tactical arm of the Soviet ground forces, it was geared to the task of supporting the Red Army on a wide front as "aerial artillery", and although equipment and standards of flying were somewhat crude by Western criteria, the MiGs, LaGGs and Ilyushins performed their task admirably.

As the area of operations in Russia constantly expanded and shifted, the type of operation most favourable to the *Luftwaffe*—the assembly of numerically and qualitively superior forces at a limited number of key points—became largely irrelevant. The physical scope of the campaign and the dauntingly primitive conditions in the field struck at the sophisticated and therefore sensitive structure of the *Luftwaffe*. The length of lines of communication, the consequent delays in supply, and the limited numbers of units available conspired to rob the *Luftwaffe's* fighter *Gruppen* of their initiative, to distort their correct employment, and to condemn them to continual sacrifice in "penny packets" on a wide front, frittering away men and machines in a horrifying war of attrition.

A fine example of the fatal incongruities forced upon the *Luftwaffe* in Russia is the fact that in 1943 JG 54 "Grunherz", a veteran interceptor unit, was equipped with the Fw 190F-8 ground attack aircraft. The suitability of the Fw 190 for fighter-bomber duties led to constant competition between fighter and fighter-bomber units for the insufficient supplies of these machines.

Fw 190A fighters first appeared on the Russian front with I/JG 51. This unit was re-equipped in time to take part in the counter-offensive of early July 1943, and distinguished itself in action against units of the 1st, 4th, and 16th Soviet Air Armies. In the ground attack rôle, the Focke-Wulf had reached *Schlachtgeschwader 1* (Ground Attack Wing No. 1) in April of that year, in the Kursk salient. From late summer Korten, the new *Luftwaffe* Chief of Staff, instituted a

vigorous programme of re-equipment in the ground attack units, replacing ageing Junkers Ju 87Ds with Fw 190 variants. Despite conflicting demands on the production lines, *Schlachtgruppen* were soon being re-equipped at a rate of about two every six weeks. Ground attack versions of the Fw 190A to appear at the front during these months were the A-5/U3 and A-5/U8, with light armament and large bomb load capacity, and the heavily-armed A-5/U11 with only 990 lb. bomb load capacity.

During 1944 the Ju 87D was largely relegated to night operations and the Fw 190 took over daylight missions, although hampered by shortages of ammunition, tyres and fuel.

By the early months of 1944, the *Luftwaffe* was in a precarious position on all fronts. The Russian "steamroller" was grinding westwards over the remains of the once-triumphant German forces. The Allied bombing offensive was causing serious shortages of synthetic fuel and components, and many *Jagdgeschwader* veterans had died in attacks on Fortress and Liberator "boxes". The training establishments were stepping up their output of raw pilots whose life expectancy could be measured in days. The ultimate collapse was still a year away, but it was already predictable. An ominous symptom was the growing number of *Luftwaffe* personnel being pressed into service as infantrymen, artillerymen, or SS troopers; and many units had disappeared entirely, to be hurriedly replaced by composite formations.

Fearful for their depleted fighter units in Northern France, the *Luftwaffe* High Command ordered the dispersal of the *Gruppen* of JG 26 away from the intensive Allied bombing of the invasion coasts in May/June of 1944. Thus it was that on the morning of June 6th the only fighter forces to launch an attack on the Normandy beaches were two Fw 190As! They were the machines of Oberst Josef "Pips" Priller, the flamboyant *Geschwaderkommodore* of JG 26, and his *rottenflieger* (wingman) Feldwebel Wodarczky. I/JG 26 had flown to Rheims, II/JG 26 to Mont de Marsan in Gascony, and III/JG 26 to Metz. The two pilots' strafing run was the only *Luftwaffe* activity over the beachhead during the daylight hours of D-Day.

The already-overstretched fighter units were immediately re-deployed to contest the Allied advance in the Cotentin peninsula; and many *Gruppen* were

decimated above the holocausts of Caen and St. Lô. III/JG 54 operated from Villacoublay, and suffered 50 per cent losses in pilots and 70 per cent losses in its Fw 190As. The Fw 190A-4/U8s of SKG 10 flew from Dreux for a few days until the unit was virtually annihilated.

Few of the *Jagdgeschwader* long survived the battles over Normandy as organised tactical units. Retreating across Europe, some formations operated from concealed bases under more or less improvised conditions, with little or no contact with higher authority. By mid-winter of 1944 Allied bombs had destroyed the last synthetic fuel refineries, and remaining stocks were jealously regulated. On New Year's Day 1945, about 650 Fw 190s of JGs 2, 3, 4, 26, and several other units took part in Operation Hermann, Goering's last ditch attempt to cripple the Allied air component in Europe by destroying their aircraft on the ground. Many *Luftwaffe* pilots were so pitifully inexperienced that they had to be guided to their targets by master-navigators in Ju 88s. The dawn raid gained good results in terms of aircraft destroyed, and increased the strain on the pilots whose machines survived, but the Allies' vast industrial capacity could quickly make good the losses, R.A.F. and U.S.A.A.F. casualties were not heavy, and the *Luftwaffe* lost more men and machines than they could afford at that stage.

Fw 190A-4 nose armament—two MG 17 machine-guns.

By mid-February 1945 the Russians had captured Fw 190 component, assembly and repair facilities at Marienburg, Sorau, Riga, Warsaw, Posen, Breslau, Liegnitz and Kreising; the Marienburg and Sorau plants alone represented 25 per cent of all Fw 190 production. In March the last stocks of fuel were issued; and the following month many brand-new examples of the *Focke-Wulf Flugzeugbau's* graceful fighter stood with dry fuel tanks on their battered dispersals, under heavy camouflage, or in tunnels beside *Autobahn*-runways. More than 20,000 had been built, the vast majority Fw 190A variants; but the other branches of *Luftwaffe* organisation broke down before many of them could be used in action.

It is an interesting comment on the versatility of this most attractive of German fighters that one of its last rôles before hostilities ceased was that of torpedo-bomber with a *Kampfgeschwader*. The three A-5/U15 torpedo-carrying Fw 190s built were operated by III/KG 200 in attacks on bridges in the winter of 1944/45; and other formations of this infamous "special duties" *Geschwader* were working-up with the "Mistel" or "Beethoven" combination weapon, with a Focke-Wulf as the carrying aircraft and a converted Ju 88A-4 as the "flying bomb". Operating from Berlin in 1945, KG 200 flew "Beethovens" against Russian bridges on the Oder.

LUFTWAFFE UNITS

The basic *Luftwaffe* tactical unit was the *Geschwader*. A fighter *Geschwader* (*Jagdgeschwader* or JG) usually comprised three *Gruppen*, each of which was in turn made up of three *Staffeln*. The operational strength of these groupings varied considerably, but a *Jagdstaffel* usually mustered between twelve and sixteen aircraft (the latter figure was official policy from 1943 onwards). The average *Jagdgeschwader* thus had an establishment of about 110/140 aircraft. *Gruppen* and *Staffeln* were numbered independently. Thus II/JG 2 (the second *Gruppe* of JG 2) comprised the fourth, fifth, and sixth *Staffeln* of JG 2; and 7/JG 2 (the seventh *Staffel* of JG 2), 8/JG 2 and 9/JG 2 together made up III/JG 2. Some *Jagdgeschwader* mustered four *Gruppen* at some time during their life (e.g. JGs 2, 27, 51, 54) but this was not the general rule.

Late-series Fw 190A displays 1944/5 colour scheme and plain white fuselage crosses.

Specification Focke-Wulf Fw 190A-8

Dimensions:	Span 34 ft. 5½ in.; length 29 ft. 4⅛ in.; height 13 ft. 0 in.; wing area 196·98 sq. ft.
Powerplant:	B.M.W. 801D-2 air-cooled fourteen cylinder two row radial engine of 1,700 h.p. (2,100 h.p. with MW 50 methanol/water injection system) at take-off.
Armament:	Two 13 mm. MG 131 machine guns in upper cowling of engine; two 20 mm. MG 151 quick-firing cannon in wing root positions; two MG 151 in outer wing positions.
Weights:	Empty, 7,000 lb.; loaded, 9,424 lb.; maximum, 10,800 lb.
Performance:	Maximum speed, 405 m.p.h. at 20,500 ft.; 355 m.p.h. at sea level; range (internal fuel), 500 miles; initial climb, 2,350 ft./min.; service ceiling, 37,400 ft.

Fw 190A Powerplant and Armament

Fw 190V1	*Powerplant* 1,550 h.p. B.M.W.139 (370 m.p.h.).	
Fw 190V2	*Powerplant* 1,550 h.p. B.M.W.139 (368 m.p.h.).	*Armament* 2 × MG17, 2 × MG131.
Fw 190V6	*Powerplant* 1,600 h.p. B.M.W.801C (391 m.p.h.).	*Armament* 4 × MG17.
Fw 190A-0	*Powerplant* 1,600 h.p. B.M.W.801C (398 m.p.h.).	*Armament* 4 × MG17.
Fw 190A-1	*Powerplant* 1,600 h.p. B.M.W.801C (388 m.p.h.).	*Armament* 4 × MG17.
Fw 190A-2	*Powerplant* 1,600 h.p. B.M.W.801C (382 m.p.h.).	*Armament* 2 × MG17, 2 × MG FF (later 2 extra MG17).
Fw 190A-3	*Powerplant* 1,700 h.p. B.M.W.801Dg (391 m.p.h.).	*Armament* 2 × MG17, 2 × MG FF, 2 × MG151.
Fw 190A-4	*Powerplant* 2,100 h.p. B.M.W.801D-2 (416 m.p.h.).	*Armament* 2 × MG17, 2 × MG FF, 2 × MG151.
Fw 190A-4 Trop	*Powerplant* 1,800 h.p. B.M.W.801D-2 (367 m.p.h.).	*Armament* 2 × MG17, 2 × MG151.
Fw 190A-4R/6	*Powerplant* 1,800 h.p. B.M.W.801D-2 (373 m.p.h.).	*Armament* 2 × MG17, 2 × MG151, 2 × MG FF 2 × WG 21 mortars.
Fw 190A-4/U8	*Powerplant* 1,800 h.p. B.M.W.801D-2 (298 m.p.h.).	*Armament* 2 × MG151. *Bomb load* 1,100 lb.
Fw 190A-5	*Powerplant* 1,800 h.p. B.M.W.801D-2 (379 m.p.h.).	*Armament* 2 × MG17, 2 × MG FF, 2 × MG151.
Fw 190A-5/U2	*Powerplant* 1,800 h.p. B.M.W.801D-2 (377 m.p.h.).	*Armament* 2 × MG17, 2 × MG FF, 2 × MG151.
Fw 190A-5/U3	*Powerplant* 1,800 h.p. B.M.W.801D-2 (298 m.p.h.).	*Armament* 2 × MG151. *Bomb load* 2,200 lb.
Fw 190A-5/U8	*Powerplant* 1,800 h.p. B.M.W.801D-2 (198 m.p.h.).	*Armament* 2 × MG151. *Bomb load* 1,100 lb.
Fw 190A-5/U11	*Powerplant* 1,800 h.p. B.M.W.801D-2 (373 m.p.h.).	*Armament* 2 × MG17, 2 × MG151, 2 × MK103., *Bomb load* 990 lb.
Fw 190A-5/U15	*Powerplant* 1,800 h.p. B.M.W.801D-2 (310 m.p.h.).	*Armament* 2 × MG151.
Fw 190A-5/U16	*Powerplant* 1,800 h.p. B.M.W.801D-2 (380 m.p.h.).	*Armament* 2 × MG17, 2 × MG151, 2 × MK108.
Fw 190A-6	*Powerplant* 1,800 h.p. B.M.W.801D-2 (398 m.p.h.).	*Armament* 2 × MG17, 4 × MG151.
Fw 190A-6/R2	*Powerplant* 1,800 h.p. B.M.W.801D-2 (310 m.p.h.).	*Armament* 2 × MG17, 2 × MG151. *Bomb load* 1,650 lb.
Fw 190A-7	*Powerplant* 1,800 h.p. B.M.W.801D-2 (395 m.p.h.).	*Armament* 2 × MG131, 4 × MG151.
Fw 190A-7/R2	*Powerplant* 1,800 h.p. B.M.W.801D-2 (390 m.p.h.).	*Armament* 2 × MG131, 2 × MG151, 2 × MK108.
Fw 190A-7/R3	*Powerplant* 1,800 h.p. B.M.W.801D-2 (394 m.p.h.).	*Armament* 2 × MG131, 4 × MG151.
Fw 190A-8	*Powerplant* 2,100 h.p. B.M.W.801D-2 (405 m.p.h.).	*Armament* 2 × MG131, 4 × MG151.
Fw 190A-8/R1	*Powerplant* 2,100 h.p. B.M.W.801D-2 (391 m.p.h.).	*Armament* 2 × MG131, 6 × MG151.
Fw 190A-8/R3	*Powerplant* 1,800 h.p. B.M.W.801D-2 (370 m.p.h.).	*Armament* 2 × MG151, 2 × MK103.
Fw 190A-8/R11	*Powerplant* 1,800 h.p. B.M.W.801D-2 (398 m.p.h.).	*Armament* 2 × MG131, 2 × MG151, 2 × MK108.
Fw 190A-8/U1	*Powerplant* 1,800 h.p. B.M.W.801D-2 (394 m.p.h.).	*Armament* 2 × MG131.
Fw 190A-8/U11	*Powerplant* 1,800 h.p. B.M.W.801D-2 (311 m.p.h.).	*Armament* 2 × MG131, 2 × MG151 *Bomb load* 990 lb.
Fw 190A-9	*Powerplant* 2,000 h.p. B.M.W.801F (416 m.p.h.).	*Armament* 2 × MG131, 4 × MG151.
Fw 190A-9/R11	*Powerplant* 2,000 h.p. B.M.W.801TS (420 m.p.h.).	*Armament* 2 × MG131, 4 × MG151.
Fw 190A-10	*Powerplant* 2,000 h.p. B.M.W.801T (310 m.p.h.).	*Armament* 2 × MG151. *Bomb load* 3,860 lb.

Fw 190A Dimensions, Weights and Remarks

Fw 190V1	*Span* 31 ft. 2 in.	*Length* 28 ft. 6½ in.	*Loaded weight* 3,968 lb.	
Fw 190V2	*Span* 31 ft. 2 in.	*Length* 28 ft. 6½ in.	*Loaded weight* 4,410 lb.	
Fw 190V6	*Span* 34 ft. 5½ in.	*Length* 28 ft. 10½ in.	*Loaded weight* 7,055 lb.	*Ducted spinner.*
Fw 190A-0	*Span* 31 ft. 2 in.	*Length* 28 ft. 10½ in.	*Loaded weight* 6,170 lb.	*First seven with short span eleven with long.*
Fw 190A-1	*Span* 34 ft. 5½ in.	*Length* 28 ft. 10½ in.	*Loaded weight* 7,065 lb.	*100 built.*
Fw 190A-2	*Span* 34 ft. 5½ in.	*Length* 28 ft. 10½ in.	*Loaded weight* 7,716 lb.	
Fw 190A-3	*Span* 34 ft. 5½ in.	*Length* 28 ft. 10½ in.	*Loaded weight* 8,377 lb.	
Fw 190A-4	*Span* 34 ft. 5½ in.	*Length* 28 ft. 10½ in.	*Loaded weight* 8,380 lb.	*Fitted with booster MW 50.*
Fw 190A-4/Trop	*Span* 34 ft. 5½ in.	*Length* 28 ft. 10½ in.	*Loaded weight* 8,820 lb.	
Fw 190A-4/R6	*Span* 34 ft. 5½ in.	*Length* 28 ft. 10½ in.	*Loaded weight* 9,480 lb.	
Fw 190A-4/U8	*Span* 34 ft. 5½ in.	*Length* 28 ft. 10½ in.	*Loaded weight* 10,803 lb.	*FuG 16ZE, FuG 25A, two 66 gallon drop tanks.*
Fw 190A-5	*Span* 34 ft. 5½ in.	*Length* 29 ft. 4⅛ in.	*Loaded weight* 9,480 lb.	*New engine mountings.*
Fw 190A-5/U2	*Span* 34 ft. 5½ in.	*Length* 29 ft. 4⅛ in.	*Loaded weight* 9,655 lb.	*Anti-glare screen, flame-dampers.*
Fw 190A-5/U3	*Span* 34 ft. 5½ in.	*Length* 29 ft. 4⅛ in.	*Loaded weight* 10,580 lb.	
Fw 190A-5/U8	*Span* 34 ft. 5½ in.	*Length* 29 ft. 4⅛ in.	*Loaded weight* 10,800 lb.	*Similar to Fw 190A-4/U8.*
Fw 190A-5/U11	*Span* 34 ft. 5½ in.	*Length* 29 ft. 4⅛ in.	*Loaded weight* 9,920 lb.	
Fw 190A-5/U15	*Span* 34 ft. 5½ in.	*Length* 29 ft. 4⅛ in.	*Loaded weight* 10,800 lb.	*Torpedo fighter, three built.*
Fw 190A-5/U16	*Span* 34 ft. 5½ in.	*Length* 29 ft. 4⅛ in.	*Loaded weight* 9,744 lb.	
Fw 190A-6	*Span* 34 ft. 5½ in.	*Length* 29 ft. 4⅛ in.	*Loaded weight* 8,600 lb.	*Lighter structure.*
Fw 190A-6/R2	*Span* 34 ft. 5½ in.	*Length* 29 ft. 4⅛ in.	*Loaded weight* 10,360 lb.	
Fw 190A-7	*Span* 34 ft. 5½ in.	*Length* 29 ft. 4⅛ in.	*Loaded weight* 8,818 lb.	*Strengthened oleo legs.*
Fw 190A-7/R2	*Span* 34 ft. 5½ in.	*Length* 29 ft. 4⅛ in.	*Loaded weight* 9,215 lb.	
Fw 190A-7/R3	*Span* 34 ft. 5½ in.	*Length* 29 ft. 4⅛ in.	*Loaded weight* 9,039 lb.	*One 66 gallon belly tank.*
Fw 190A-8	*Span* 34 ft. 5½ in.	*Length* 29 ft. 4⅛ in.	*Loaded weight* 9,424 lb.	*Improved internal fuel capacity.*
Fw 190A-8/R1	*Span* 34 ft. 5½ in.	*Length* 29 ft. 4⅛ in.	*Loaded weight* 10,360 lb.	*GM 1 boost or further 25 gallon internal fuel.*
Fw 190A-8/R3	*Span* 34 ft. 5½ in.	*Length* 29 ft. 4⅛ in.	*Loaded weight* 10,140 lb.	
Fw 190A-8/R11	*Span* 34 ft. 5½ in.	*Length* 29 ft. 4⅛ in.	*Loaded weight* 9,920 lb.	*FuG 16ZE and FuG 25A.*
Fw 190A-8/U1	*Span* 34 ft. 5½ in.	*Length* 29 ft. 4⅛ in.	*Loaded weight* —	*Two-seat trainer type. Two prototypes, one production model.*
Fw 190A-8/U11	*Span* 34 ft. 5½ in.	*Length* 29 ft. 4⅛ in.	*Loaded weight* 10,538 lb.	*Saw action in mixed units with Ju87.*
Fw 190A-9	*Span* 34 ft. 5½ in.	*Length* 29 ft. 4⅛ in.	*Loaded weight* 9,700 lb.	
Fw 190A-9/R11	*Span* 34 ft. 5½ in.	*Length* 29 ft. 4⅛ in.	*Loaded weight* 9,920 lb.	*Similar to Fw 190A-8/R11.*
Fw 190A-10	*Span* 34 ft. 5½ in.	*Length* 29 ft. 5⅛ in.	*Loaded weight* 11,050 lb.	*Three 66 gallon drop tanks, strengthened oleo legs.*

The Hawker Hunter F.6

The Hawker Hunter F.6
by Francis K. Mason

A standard Armstrong Whitworth-built Hunter F6 with 100-gal. drop tanks and 24 rocket projectiles. Wing leading edge extensions, extended cartridge case chutes, gun blast deflectors and store jettison guns are fitted (note absence of drop tank fins).

(Photo: Cyril Peckham)

REPRESENTING the design and production climax of the basic Hawker P.1067 Hunter concept, which had originated in the F.3/48 Specification for a transonic interceptor, the Hunter Mark 6 was built in larger numbers than any other version. Following the Avon-powered Hunter Mark 1 and Sapphire-powered Mark 2—which had both suffered Service criticism for their limited range and endurance—the Mark 4 and 5 (also with Avon and Sapphire respectively) introduced increased internal fuel capacity and external store provision, including the carriage of up to four 100-gallon drop tanks.

While production of these early Hunters had been getting under way, Hawker Aircraft had been pursuing the development of a "second generation" Hunter, a re-heated Avon-powered version with a 50° swept wing. Designated the P.1083, this version carried high hopes and boded well to become the first truly supersonic fighter in R.A.F. service, and construction of a prototype (*WN470*) was well advanced by mid-1953. At the same time the original P.1067 prototype (*WB188*) was flying with a re-heated Avon R.A.7R engine as part of the powerplant development programme. (This aircraft established an Absolute World Speed Record in September 1953 at 727·7 m.p.h.).

Radical changes, however, were seen in 1953 in Air Staff fighter policies. Believing the air-to-air missile-armed supersonic fighter to be no more than four years away, the Air Staff saw in the Hunter a promis-

ing interceptor *and* ground attack fighter which would remain at operational status for a further six to eight years. Almost overnight the only marginally supersonic P.1083 was abandoned, and with it went the re-heated Avon in the Hunter context. Greater emphasis was to be laid on the new generation of Avon 200-series turbojets which were initially rated at 10,000 lb. thrust without reheat.

During the late summer of 1953 the Hawker design team prepared proposals for a "straight" Hunter, powered by the Avon 203, but in most other respects similar to the Hunter 4 and 5 (which were not due to fly until the autumn of 1954). Designated the P.1099, the project was accepted and a prototype completed within three months by the simple expedient of using the centre fuselage sub-assembly of the defunct P.1083 to match the new Avon.

The only known "roll-out" picture of the prototype Hunter 6, seen here during initial engine running tests.

A nosewheel-up landing by a C.A. Trial Hunter 6 caused by fatigue failure of the operating mechanism during intensive gun firing trials.

The prototype Hunter 6 *XF833*, was first flown by Sqdn. Ldr. Neville Duke on January 22nd 1954 from Dunsfold and, after preliminary flight trials, was delivered to the A. & A.E.E. at Boscombe Down the following month. After blade failures in the engine had led to a couple of forced landings, the Avon 203 was down-rated to 10,000 lb. thrust, and Service and manufacturers' trials—including handling, gun firing and performance measurement—proceeded satisfactorily. The aircraft was subsequently painted glossy pale green for an appearance at the 1954 Farnborough display and was eventually delivered to Rolls-Royce for trials with a thrust reverser in the tailpipe.

The 30% greater power from the Avon 203 of course permitted a considerable increase in take-off weight as well as reduced take-off runs and times to height. Promise of early deliveries of Avon 203s prompted the issue of production contracts for the Hunter 6, and, to meet the inevitable demand for development and trial installation aircraft, Contract No. 7144 (which had originally called for ten Hunter 4s) was changed to include seven Mark 6s (*WW592–WW859*). The first of these was flown by A. W. ("Bill") Bedford on March 25th 1955 and commenced a series of trials at Dunsfold in parallel with those being conducted on *XF833* at Boscombe Down. By the end of 1955 all seven development aircraft had flown and embarked on the C.A. release programme in the hands of Neville Duke, Bill Bedford, Hugh Merewether, Frank Bullen, Duncan Simpson, David Lockspeiser and Don Lucey.

The first true production aircraft, *XE526*, was flown by Merewether on October 11th 1955, and although deliveries to R.A.F. Maintenance Units started in the following January, acceptance for Squadron service was delayed by the R.A.F. for a further nine months. The delays were occasioned on three counts: (i) The investigation of aerodynamic "pitch-up" tendencies at high altitude and high indicated Mach numbers; (ii) the investigation of "pitch-down" when firing the guns at high altitude, and (iii) the development of a full-power elevator. (In connection with the last of these, there was a proposal to fit later Hunter 6s with slab tailplanes and although flight trials with the associated ram air turbine commenced during 1956, the plan was dropped in favour of the fully-powered elevator with spring-feel.)

To overcome the pitch-up tendency, Hawker had already proposed the addition of an extended wing leading edge (increasing the wing area from 340 sq. ft. to 349 sq. ft.) to the outer sections of the wings. On the gun-firing pitch-down problem, a concentrated programme of trials—in which one Hunter fired 40,000 rounds in flight at full throttle—led to the development of muzzle blast deflectors.

Though both these expedients brought solution to their respective problems, the first hundred or so production Hunters were delivered to the M.U.s without modification, and by the autumn of 1956 the R.A.F. had agreed to accept the aircraft, albeit with temporary restrictions. In the meantime, modification kits were produced and issued to the Service.

Thus, although the existence of the powerful new Hunter had been known since 1954, the first R.A.F. Squadron was not so equipped until late in 1956. It is a point worth recording here that the Maintenance Unit principally concerned with the Hunter was No. 5 M.U. at Kemble, assisted to a lesser extent by Nos. 19 (St. Athan), 33 (Lyneham) and 45 (Kinloss).

First Squadron to receive the Hunter 6 was No. 74 (F) Squadron at Horsham St. Faith, Norwich. This airfield had also been the location of a field working party responsible for the preparation of Hunters to full R.A.F. standard and handed over the first Hunter 6s (most of them built by Sir W. G. Armstrong Whitworth Aircraft Ltd., Coventry) to No. 74 before the Squadron's move to nearby Coltishall.

By March 1957 the build-up of Hunter 6 squadrons had achieved the planned rate of two per month, Nos. 43, 54, 63, 65, 66, 74, 92, 247 and 263 either equipped

A late standard Hunter 6 equipped with two 230-gal. drop tanks and 24 rockets outboard.   (Photo: Hawker Siddeley Aviation)

XK161 fitted with 1,000-lb. bombs on the inboard pylons and 24 rockets outboard.   (Photo: Hawker Siddeley Aviation)

or completing delivery of their new aircraft. By the end of the year No. 111 Squadron had converted and the initial deliveries to home-based Fighter Command squadrons were complete. With production of the new aircraft reaching around forty per month from the factories early in 1957, it was also possible to commence replacing the Hunter 4s on the 2nd Tactical Air Force Squadrons based in Germany.

The Hunter 6 gained immediate popularity with the Squadrons and in tactical exercises proved itself an excellent ground support aircraft. There was a short period towards the end of 1957 when 2nd T.A.F. Squadrons found that the serviceability of the Hunter 6 left something to be desired—at least when compared with the Hunter 4—but this was found to be due to the non-arrival of modification kits from the U.K.

The Hunter 6 arrived in R.A.F. service too late to participate in "hostilities" during the Suez Crisis of late-1956 and it was left to the Hunter 5s of Nos. 1 and 34 Squadrons to reinforce the Middle East fighter

force. Nevertheless 1957 saw the start of Hunter 6 squadron "rotation" to bases in the Mediterranean and the Middle East.

Also a product of 1957 was the Duncan Sandys' White Paper on Defence which purported to fore-shadow the end of the manned interceptor, and which brought cancellation of the last 150 Hunter 6s on order for the R.A.F. The result was that Hunter 6 production for the R.A.F. was completed on July 9th 1957 with the flight of *XK156* by Duncan Simpson. This aircraft was in fact the very last single-seat Hunter built for the R.A.F., all subsequent versions

Right and below: Two views of a standard "clean" Hunter 6 showing the camouflage pattern and underside markings. XE588 was later flown for evaluation in Switzerland and was ultimately destroyed during the course of spinning clearance trials.

being converted from aircraft built before that date.

By December 1957, 210 Hunter 6s were at first line strength with the R.A.F., the remaining 159 being held in reserve at the M.U.s. Fourteen had crashed and been written off.

HUNTER 6s OVERSEAS

Ever since the early nineteen-fifties foreign interest in the Hunter had been vigorous and in 1953 negotiations had resulted in its choice to equip the N.A.T.O. air forces of Holland, Belgium and Denmark. The two former countries had arranged to manufacture the aircraft under licence and thirty Mark 4s were delivered to Denmark. Production of the Mark 4 commenced at Fokker and Avions Fairey during 1956 and in 1958 transferred to the Mark 6.

In the meantime other countries evinced interest in the Hunter 6. N.A.T.O. pilots evaluated early production aircraft in 1956, but in view of plans to introduce the Lockheed F-104G Starfighter into European air forces it was considered unnecessary to replace the Republic F-84 Thunderjet and Hunter 4. Moreover, the Fiat G-91 represented new ideas on the subject of battlefield support aircraft.

Switzerland, on the other hand, being uncommitted to N.A.T.O. policies, issued a fighter requirement to which the Hunter seemed ideally suited. Preliminary evaluations eliminated such aircraft as the Canadair Sabre, the Folland Gnat and the Swiss P-16, with the result that it only remained to decide on a standard of preparation for the Hunter 6 and the size of the order. Demonstrations of bombing and gun-firing were performed by *XE587* and *588* during 1957 in Switzerland (*XE587* being equipped with a tail parachute) and in January 1958 an order for 100 aircraft was signed with the Swiss Government. In order to speed deliveries, the first twelve aircraft were to be released from R.A.F. stocks. Subsequently termed Hunter Mark 58s and equipped with tail parachutes, the Swiss Hunters were nonetheless basically Mark 6s—rather than Mark 9s—and seem likely to remain in service in Switzerland until towards the end of the nineteen-sixties.

After the commencement of the Swiss negotiations, but before their conclusion, an Indian defence delegation had visited Britain and showed interest in the Hunter 6. In the course of three short months during the summer of 1957 Indian pilots evaluated the Hunter and an order was signed for 160 aircraft on September 1st that year. Once again the British Government released aircraft to speed deliveries, twelve Hunters being returned from M.U.s and thirty-two of the cancelled R.A.F. order (*XK157–176* and *XK213–224*) being completed to the Indian standard, in Indian

R.A.F. Hunters. Top to bottom: *XF526 of No. 56 Squadron; XG225 (S) of No. 92 Squadron ("The Blue Diamonds"), XG157 (Sqdn. Ldr. Wood's aircraft) of the Central Gunnery School; XF418 of No. 111 Squadron ("The Black Arrows"). The latter aircraft was part of the Squadron's initial equipment and was not fitted with extended wing leading edges.*

(Photos: J. M. G. Gradidge)

insignia. After having completed a short conversion course at Benson, Indian Air Force pilots started ferrying their Hunters (equipped with four 100-gallon drop tanks each) out to Karachi, thereafter joining Nos. 7, 14, 17, 20 and 27 Squadrons of the I.A.F. at Poona and Ambala. Some of these aircraft subsequently went into action against ground targets during the brief campaign against Portuguese Goa.

In the R.A.F., Hunter 6s of Fighter Command demonstrated their control precision through the medium of formation aerobatics, their greater reserve of power making them obvious and worthy successors to the Hunter 4. Without doubt the most famous R.A.F. aerobatic team of all time was that of No. 111 (F) Squadron—the Black Arrows, so named after then all-black Hunters—led by Sqdn. Ldr. Roger Topp. Year after year this team performed with more and more aircraft in the formation, culminating with a formation roll with twenty-two Hunters. When 111's turn came to re-equip with Lightnings, its place was taken by No. 92 Squadron's team, the Blue Diamonds.

The first "aerodynamic" P.1109A, WW594.

41

Turning now to the Middle East (for it is likely to be in this theatre that the Hunter will eventually serve longest), it was in 1958 that the R.A.F. started trials to select a replacement for the ageing Venom fighter-bomber. Under the general direction of the Central Fighter Establishment and A. & A.E.E., Folland Gnats, Percival Provosts and Hunter 6s were subjected to "eliminating trials" to decide on the R.A.F.'s future standard tropical ground attack fighter. Considerable experience in warm climates had been achieved with the Hunters in Cyprus, and it was not surprising that the Hunter was selected from the trials at Aden. The first squadron, No. 208, was in fact formed and equipped at Tangmere under Sqdn. Ldr. John Granville-White, before being transferred to the Middle East. When, a year or so later, Iraq threatened the sovereignty of Jordan, No. 208 Squadron flew escort flights for the Blackburn Beverley carrying supplies from Cyprus into the blockaded country.

WW598, a P.1109, as used by the High Speed Flights section of the R.A.E. for tropical low-level gust investigation.

Prior to the *coup* which had overthrown King Feisal of Iraq, that country had received from Britain a present of fifteen Hunter 6s (five in April and ten in December 1957) from R.A.F. Middle East stocks. It is almost certain that these aircraft, in the hands of rebel pilots flying from Mosul, were the first Hunters ever to fire their guns in anger, being used in rocket attacks on royalist encampments in South Iraq.

Shortly afterwards further presents of Hunters were given to the Governments of the Lebanon and Jordan.

The Hunter 6 remained the R.A.F.'s principal first-line fighter until, in 1960, its place at home started being taken by the English Electric Lightning. Nevertheless as late as 1964, Hunter 6s remained on strength with two squadrons of No. 38 Group, while many others, modified as Ground Attack Mark 9s and Fighter Reconnaissance Mark 10s are likely to remain in service until towards the end of the nineteen-sixties.

Of course, Hunter 6s came to be used by a host of non-operational R.A.F. units, among them Nos. 229 and 233 Operational Conversion Units at Chivenor and Pembrey respectively, the Fighter Weapons School, the Central Flying School, the Central Fighter Establishment and the Empire Test Pilots School.

Numerous trial installations were performed on Hunter 6s, perhaps the most important being the application of de Havilland Firestreak infra-red-seeking air-to-air missiles. This, the Hawker P.1109, resulted in considerable lengthening of the nose to accommodate the associated radar, deletion of two of the four 30-mm. Aden guns and mounting of two Firestreaks on the inboard underwing pylons. Two versions were built; the 1109A was no more than an aerodynamic "shape", and the 1109B with full weapon installation. Four such aircraft were completed, one of which took part in firing trials (and proved entirely successful), and although the project was abandoned one aircraft, *WW598*, was subsequently used by the R.A.E. for high-speed low-altitude gust investigation in the Middle East in preparation of gust data for the BAC TSR-2 project.

Another project involved the carriage of wing-tip fuel tanks on *XG131* in connection with a two-seat night/all-weather fighter version of the Hunter (the P.1114 and P.1115). This project remained stillborn and the tip-tanks, although demonstrated at the 1956 Farnborough display, produced quite unacceptable buffet conditions, and the aircraft was returned to standard for delivery to the Service.

Perhaps the most important development carried out on the Hunter 6 was that of the Hawker 230-gallon steel drop tank, although this was not introduced

R.A.F. Hunters. Top to bottom: XJ691 of No. 14 Squadron; XE647 (E) of No. 63 Squadron; XF447 of No. 65 Squadron; XF449 (squadron not identified); XK139 (at Dunsfold) of No. 66 Squadron. (Photos: J. M. G. Gradidge, excluding XK139)

Experimental lateral dive brakes fitted to XF379. These were later abandoned in favour of the now standard ventral dive brake.

removed, provision for 230-gallon tanks and an associated increased pilot oxygen capacity. The Mk.6/ Interim Mk.9 did not include the tail parachute, but, for reinforcement purposes only, could accommodate the large drop tanks. By 1961 almost all the interim aircraft had been advanced to full Mark 9 standard.

The final version was the Jordanian F.R. Mark 6, of which only one was delivered. This aircraft, *712* of the Royal Jordanian Air Force, was a standard Mark 6 but equipped to mount three cameras in the nose. In this respect the aircraft was similar to the R.A.F.'s F.R.Mk.10 Hunter, but the Jordanian example lacked the tail parachute.

By 1961 Hunter 6s in Belgium and Holland were being replaced in service and in anticipation of further export orders from Britain, the parent company acquired about 30 ex-Belgian aircraft, most of them being flown to Dunsfold with SBAC registration numbers and Belgian insignia removed. Minutely overhauled and brought up to Mark 9 standard, some of these were re-exported to Kuwait and Iraq in 1963–64.

THE HUNTER DESCRIBED

The Hunter structure was conventionally built in five main sections: front fuselage, centre fuselage, rear fuselage with tail unit, port and starboard wings. The nose section contained the radar ranging equipment, cockpit, gun armament and magazine and nosewheel gear. The centre fuselage, incorporating the wing stubs, contained the powerplant, engine intakes and main fuselage fuel tanks, the rear fuselage, detachable to expose the engine for maintenance, supported the tailpipe, included the tail controls and surfaces, and the ventral airbrake. The wings incorporated the mainwheel units, the wing fuel tanks, ailerons, flaps and

into service until much later. Originally proposed by Hawker Aircraft shortly before the Suez Crisis, the 230-gallon tank was intended to enable the Hunter 6 to reinforce Middle East units, flying non-stop from the U.K.; dummy tanks were flown on a Mark 4, and on October 2nd 1958 Hugh Merewether flew *XF374* from Dunsfold to El Adem, Libya, non-stop in 3 hours 19 minutes—a distance of 1,588 naut. miles. His aircraft carried the prototype pair of 230-gallon tanks and two 100-gallon tanks outboard.

Two other versions of the Hunter 6 should be mentioned. The first is the Mark 6/Interim Mark 9; the full-standard Hunter 9 (with which we are not concerned here in detail) was a developed version equipped with braking parachute, gun blast deflectors

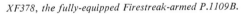

XF378, the fully-equipped Firestreak-armed P.1109B.

First Hunter 6 in Swiss national markings; later all Swiss Hunters were designated Mark 58s.

provision for a pair of store pylons on each side; these were built up on a front and rear main spar which attached through heavy forgings to the main spar frames in the stub wings.

Armament. The fixed armament consisted of four 30-mm. Aden guns each with up to 150 rounds. The gun barrels remained fixed to the aircraft structure, and the gun bodies and magazine tank were incorporated in a removable pack which could be winched down to facilitate re-arming. External weapons could be carried on detachable wing pylons, up to 1,000-lb. bombs or 230-gallon drop tanks on the inboard pylons, and 100-gallon tanks on the outboard pylons. Alternatively up to twenty-four rocket projectiles could be attached under the outer wings in place of the pylons. Equivalent loads of Napalm tanks, practice bombs, rocket batteries or target-towing gear could be carried.

Flying the Hunter. The Hunter came to be developed so that no restrictions existed in its flying. At normal all-up weight and in zero wind it would be airborne in well under 1,000 yards and, using Maxaret anti-skid wheel brakes but no parachute, land in the same distance. It possessed a considerable initial rate of climb (for its day) of over 17,000 feet per minute and would climb to over 50,000 feet in little over twelve minutes from wheels rolling. It would "go super-sonic" in only a shallow dive at altitude without noticeable effects on the controls and recovery was straightforward by reducing the throttle and easing back on the control column. Aerobatics could be performed with the utmost precision and use of the airbrake was

positive at all speeds without adverse trim effects. Stalling was clean without tendency to drop a wing and there were no restrictions on spinning—either erect or inverted. A maximum true airspeed of Mach 0·95 was attainable at the Tropopause, and 621 knots at sea level.

Production

A total of 383 Hunter 6s was built for the R.A.F., of which 264 were manufactured by Hawker Aircraft Ltd., at Kingston, and 119 by Sir W. G. Armstrong Whitworth Aircraft Ltd., at Baginton, Coventry. 32 aircraft, originally ordered for the R.A.F., were also completed but were sold as Mark 56s to India.

Hawker Aircraft Ltd., Kingston-upon-Thames, Surrey:
Contract No. 10032: *XF833*, prototype. Contract No. 7144, 7 aircraft: *WW592–WW598*, 2nd Batch, 100 aircraft: *XE526–XE561, XE579–XE628, XE643–XE656.* 3rd Batch, 91 aircraft: *XG127–XG137, XG169–XG172, XG185–XG211, XG225–XG239, XG251–XG274, XG289– XG298,* 4th Batch, 45 aircraft: *XJ632–XJ646, XJ673–XJ695, XJ712–XJ718.* 5th Batch, 21 aircraft: *XK136–XK156.* 32 aircraft sold to India as Hunter 56s: *XK157–XK176, XK213–XK224* (registered in I.A.F. as *BA201– BA232*) 100 aircraft cancelled in 1957: *XK225–XK241, XK257–XK306 XK323–XK355.*

Sir W. G. Armstrong Whitworth Aircraft Ltd., Coventry:
1st Batch (sub-contracted from Hawker), 19 aircraft: *XG150– XG168.* 2nd Batch, 100 aircraft: *XF373–XF389, XF414–XF463, XF495– XF527.* 50 aircraft, ordered from Hawker Aircraft (Blackpool) Ltd., cancelled in 1957: *XJ945–XJ959, XJ971–XJ997, XK103–XK111.*

Specification

Powerplant: One 10,000-lb. s.l.s.t. Rolls-Royce Avon Mk. 203 (R.A.28 rating) axial-flow turbojet.

Dimensions: Span 33 ft. 8 in.; Length, 45 ft. 10½ in.; Height, 13 ft. 2 in.; Wing area, 349 sq. ft.

Weights: Empty, 12,760 lb. Normal all-up weight (clean), 17,750 lb. Max. overload weight, 24,000 lb.

Hunters of the Indian Air Force (believed to be No. 5 Squadron) displaying rear fuselage and nose insignia.

An Iraqi Hunter 6 equipped with practice bomb carriers and 3-inch rockets.

(Photo: David Lockspeiser)

The sole Jordanian Hunter 6 reconnaissance fighter. Unlike R.A.F. Mark 10s the 230-gal. drop tanks were not stressed for combat loads.

An ex-Belgian Hunter 6 (previously LF-41) after purchase by Hawker Siddeley Aviation in 1962. The temporary registration G-9-80 was allotted for the ferry flights to Dunsfold on November 13th 1962, the pilot being Duncan Simpson. Note obliteration of Belgian markings.

Below: *An Avions Fairey-built Hunter 6 of No. 9 Wing, Belgian Air Force.*

(Photo: *via* Hawker Siddeley Aviation)

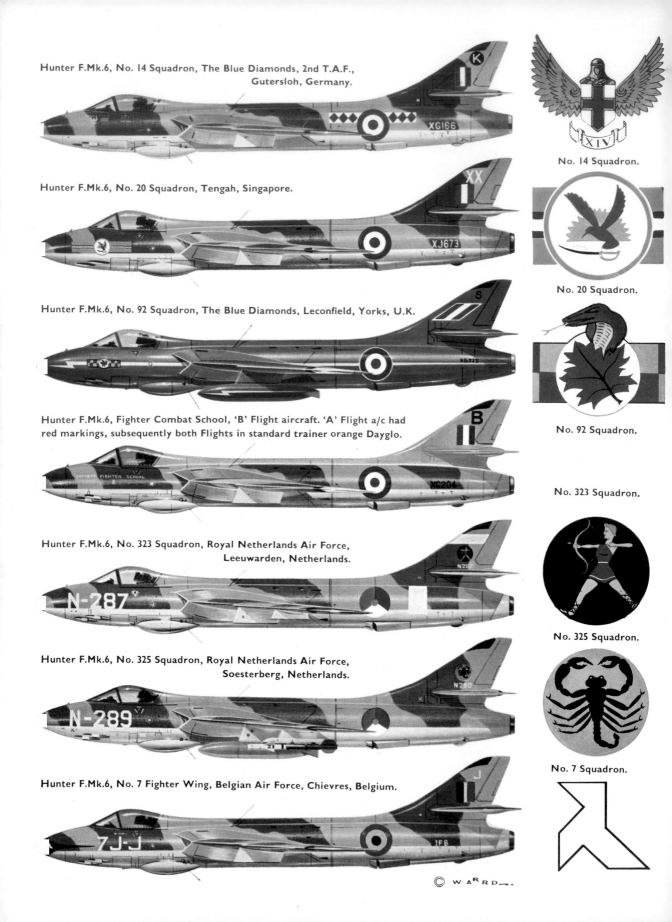

Hunter F.Mk.6, No. 14 Squadron, The Blue Diamonds, 2nd T.A.F., Gutersloh, Germany.

No. 14 Squadron.

Hunter F.Mk.6, No. 20 Squadron, Tengah, Singapore.

No. 20 Squadron.

Hunter F.Mk.6, No. 92 Squadron, The Blue Diamonds, Leconfield, Yorks, U.K.

No. 92 Squadron.

Hunter F.Mk.6, Fighter Combat School, 'B' Flight aircraft. 'A' Flight a/c had red markings, subsequently both Flights in standard trainer orange Dayglo.

No. 323 Squadron.

Hunter F.Mk.6, No. 323 Squadron, Royal Netherlands Air Force, Leeuwarden, Netherlands.

No. 325 Squadron.

Hunter F.Mk.6, No. 325 Squadron, Royal Netherlands Air Force, Soesterberg, Netherlands.

No. 7 Squadron.

Hunter F.Mk.6, No. 7 Fighter Wing, Belgian Air Force, Chievres, Belgium.

© WARD.

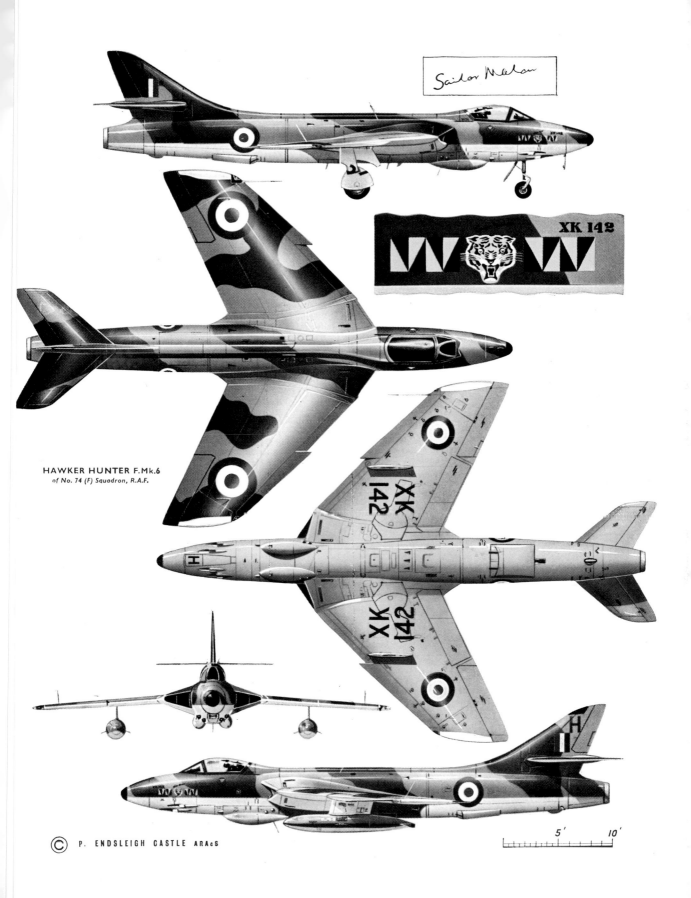

Sailor Malan

XK 142

HAWKER HUNTER F.Mk.6
of No. 74 (F) Squadron, R.A.F.

© P. ENDSLEIGH CASTLE ARAeS

5'   10'

The Vickers Vimy
by J. M. Bruce

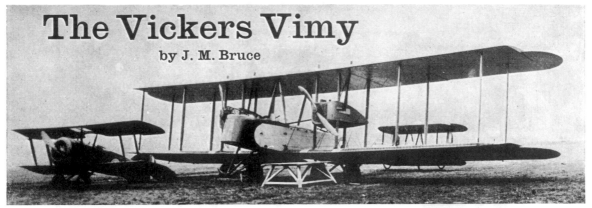

The first prototype, B9952, with enlarged radiators.

ON 23rd July 1917, less than six weeks after German bombers had attacked London in daylight, killing 162 people and injuring 432, the Air Board took the extraordinary decision that all orders for experimental heavy bombers should be cancelled. The incensed protest of the Controller of the Technical Department led to a further discussion a week later, when wiser second thoughts persuaded the Air Board to order 100 Handley Page 0/400s for night bombing and prototypes of new experimental heavy bombers from Handley Page Ltd. and Vickers Ltd.

The Vickers contract, No. A.S.22689/1/17, dated 16th August 1917, was for three aircraft, numbered *B9952–B9954*. Vickers' chief designer was the young Reginald Kirshaw Pierson, who roughed out a preliminary layout of the new bomber during a discussion with Major J. C. Buchanan at the Air Board.

Detailed design work and construction of the first prototype occupied less than four months; the Vickers type number F.B.27 was allotted to the aircraft. It was intended to power the F.B.27 with two 200-h.p. R.A.F. 4d or two 200-h.p. Hispano-Suiza engines. The R.A.F. 4d was an air-cooled V-twelve, the Hispano-Suiza a water-cooled V-eight. By the late autumn of 1917 the R.A.F. 4d had not been developed to the point where it could be installed in the F.B.27, consequently the first aircraft was built with two 200-h.p. Hispano-Suizas. It made its first flight at Joyce Green on 30th November 1917, piloted by Captain Gordon Bell.

The Vickers F.B.27 was designed to accommodate a crew of three and twelve bombs. There were gunners' cockpits, each with a Scarff-mounted Lewis gun, in the nose and behind the wings; the pilot's cockpit was just ahead of the wings. The bombs were stowed vertically within the fuselage between the spars of the lower centre section.

When it first appeared *B9952* had horn-balanced ailerons, elevators, and 1° of dihedral on the mainplanes. Long vertical pipes led the exhaust gases through the upper wing to discharge above it. Fuel capacity totalled only 92 gallons in a single tank, ten in a gravity tank that formed the central leading-edge portion of the upper centre section. The petrol pipes were protected with nickel-steel tubing.

The first Vickers F.B.27 went to Martlesham Heath for official trials in January 1918. It is reported to have created a minor sensation by lifting a greater load than

the Handley Page 0/400, which had almost twice as much power. Unfortunately, persistent engine troubles were experienced while the aircraft was at Martlesham. It returned to Joyce Green on 12th April 1918, by which time its exhaust stacks had been replaced by shorter horizontal pipes.

Later in 1918, *B9952* was extensively modified. Two 260-h.p. Salmson water-cooled radial engines replaced the Hispano-Suizas; a tail unit similar to that of the later prototypes was fitted; the mainplanes were rigged with 3° of dihedral and the leading-edge gravity tank was of the 15-gallon size introduced on *B9954*. Small transparent panels were let into the nose, and the plywood covering of the fuselage sides was extended to the rear of the pilot's cockpit.

In this modified form *B9952* survived the Armistice. It was allotted, but probably never wore, the civil

Above, top. *First prototype F.B.27 in its original form.* Above: *B9952 at Martlesham Heath, doped khaki-green, and fitted with horizontal exhaust pipes replacing original upright stacks.* Below: *B9952, final form with Salmson engines and revised tail unit with plain elevators.*

The second prototype, B9953, with Maori engines and inversely tapered ailerons.

registration G-EAAR. With a Vickers identification, C-105, painted on its fuselage, it flew from Brooklands to Amsterdam in August 1919 to form part of the Vickers exhibit at the E.L.T.A. exhibition. Its civil registration was cancelled in May 1920.

The second prototype, B9953, appeared early in 1918. It differed from the first aircraft in having plain elevators and plain ailerons that were inversely tapered. The tips of the wings and tailplanes also differed from those of B9952, and the plywood covering on the fuselage nose was differently disposed.

Defensive armament was improved by the provision of a lower rear gun position. On a cross rail between the third and fourth bays of the rear position of the fuselage was a mounting for a Lewis gun that could be fired rearwards and downwards through an aperture in the underside of the fuselage. This gun was supposed to be fired by the rear gunner, who would have had to be a man of considerable agility to use both guns effectively in combat. A small transparent panel was let into each side of the fuselage, level with the rear ventral gun position. This additional gun position was standardised on all subsequent aircraft of the type.

Power for the second F.B.27 was provided by two 260-h.p. Sunbeam Maori engines driving four-blade left-hand airscrews. The main radiators had shutters, and engine instruments were carried on the inboard sides of the nacelles; each dial was provided with an individually externally-mounted lamp.

The Maori-powered F.B.27 was tested at Joyce Green in April 1918. The cooling system proved troublesome at first, but the aircraft was sent to Martlesham Heath on 26th April and underwent some official tests in the following month. It was not extensively tested, however, for it crashed on an early flight owing to engine failure.

Some weeks later the third prototype, B9954, appeared. This machine had two 300-h.p. Fiat A-12bis engines and was the first F.B.27 to have nacelles of the same general shape as those that characterised the later production Vimy. These nacelles were roughly octagonal in cross section, and the radiators were provided with shutters. The tops of the engines projected above the nacelles, and each had a long, massive exhaust pipe to starboard, just above the top of the nacelle. Two centrifugal petrol pumps were fitted to the front spar of the lower centre section directly under the engines; these pumps were driven by small four-blade airscrews on the leading edge. The water header tank for each radiator was fitted in the

centre section immediately behind the front spar, the water pipe running down the front inboard strut on each side. Two wind-driven electric generators were fitted, one on the inboard side of each inner rear engine-nacelle strut, for B9954 was equipped with navigation lights and was reported to have landing lights.

The nose of the fuselage was re-designed. Seen in side elevation, the front was vertical, whereas on B9952 and B9953 it had a backwards rake. Three vertical transparent panels were fitted, and the bomb sight was mounted externally. The area of plywood covering was increased, extending as far aft as the rear of the pilot's cockpit. On the rear gunners' cockpit there was a Scarff twin-gun mounting for a pair of double-yoked Lewis guns.

No further change was made in the design of the tail unit, which was identical with that of B9953; but B9954 appeared with two different sets of mainplanes and ailerons. Its original surfaces were like those of B9953. It had been decided in June 1918 that all production aircraft were to have the balanced ailerons of the first prototype, and it is probable that B9954 did not keep its plain ailerons for long. By the time it went to Martlesham Heath on 15th August 1928 it had been fitted with balanced ailerons. With both sets of wings B9954 had greater dihedral than its two predecessors: the angle was increased to 3°, which remained standard on production aircraft. In this form B9954 was fitted with external bomb racks under the fuselage and lower centre section.

At Martlesham, performance tests were held up owing to delays in replacing the original airscrews, both of which cracked in flight. In fact, B9954 did little flying at Martlesham, for it was destroyed there on 11th September 1918. According to *Flight* of 12th June 1919, the crash occurred ". . . owing to the pilot stalling shortly after leaving the ground. Unfortunately it had been loaded with live bombs, which exploded on reaching the ground, causing fatal injuries to the pilot".

The fuel capacity of the Vickers F.B.27 had been more than doubled since the appearance of B9952. On B9954 the two main tanks held 86 gallons and 140 gallons of petrol, and the gravity tank had been enlarged to hold fifteen gallons.

The worth and potential of the F.B.27 had been convincingly demonstrated by B9952 in its original form, and contracts for its production were let before the development and evaluation of the later prototypes was carried out. The first contract, for 150 aircraft, was dated 26th March 1918; the aircraft were

53

B9954 in its original form with inversely tapered ailerons.

to be numbered *F701–F850*, and production was to be undertaken at Vickers' Crayford works.

Production by several other manufacturers was envisaged. In May 1918 contracts were given to Clayton & Shuttleworth, Morgan & Co., and the Royal Aircraft Establishment at Farnborough; and in June a further 200 aircraft were ordered from Vickers, the production to be undertaken at Weybridge. More than 1,000 Vimys were ordered under wartime contracts.

By this time the name Vimy had been allotted to the F.B.27 design under the first official system of aircraft nomenclature. It was regarded as being within the category of R.A.F. Type VII, Short Distance Night Bomber. Several types of engine were to be fitted to the production aircraft, and Mark numbers were to be used to distinguish sub-types. The maker's designation was now F.B.27A which, according to one official document, was first applied to the second prototype.

The wide range of engines tried in and envisaged for the production Vimys provides an interesting commentary on the aero-engine supply situation as it was in 1918. The official list of contracts mentions the Fiat A-12bis, 230-h.p. B.H.P. and 400-h.p. Liberty engines only; there is no mention of the Rolls-Royce Eagle, but this is scarcely surprising. For a variety of reasons*, the output of Rolls-Royce engines fell considerably short of the demand for them, and there can be no doubt that the large British orders for the American Liberty engine were placed because it promised to be a possible alternative to the Rolls-Royce Eagle.

Much statistical forecasting was done in 1917 immediately after the decision to increase the strength of the R.F.C. to 200 squadrons. In September 1917 it was forecast that enough engines would be available to equip fifteen of the additional bombing squadrons and eighteen fighter squadrons. The bomber units would be equipped with B.H.P. or Fiat engines, of which it was estimated there would be a surplus of 1,183 by June 1918. Two thousand Fiat engines had been ordered in August 1917 for delivery between January and June 1918, half for America, half for use in D.H.9s. But by the end of June only 311 had been handed over to the British services, and there was a deficit of 558 B.H.P. and Fiat engines in June 1918 instead of the expected surplus. Only the first few production Vimys had Fiat engines; these aircraft had two main tanks each of 77-gallons capacity only.

It was intended to fit the 300-h.p. high-compression Siddeley Puma version of the B.H.P. engine to some

Vimys and full detail drawings were prepared. This idea was abandoned, however, and no Vimy was fitted with the Puma engines.

At the request of the United States of America authorities, two 400 h.p. Liberty 12 engines were installed in one Vimy at Bexley Heath; one document indicates that the aircraft had been built to the order of the U.S. Air Service. The Liberty nacelles were somewhat similar to those of the Fiat engines but each had two rather high-set exhaust pipes. The frontal radiators were distinguished from all other Vimy engine installations by having vertical shutters.

The Liberty-Vimy never flew: while being erected at Joyce Green it was destroyed by fire. The Liberty engine was specified for a number of Vimys on order for the R.A.F., but the decision to fit the American engine was cancelled in January 1919.

With so many changes of power unit and so much uncertainty over engine availability, it is perhaps not surprising that there are conflicting official records of the allocation of Mark numbers to Vimy variants.

An A.I.D. report printed in December 1918 implies that the designation Vimy Mark II applied alike to the aircraft with Liberty, Fiat and Salmson engines. This is largely supported by the official handbook on the engine installations of the Vimy. Dated May 1919, this book applies the designation Vickers F.B.27A Vimy Mk II to aircraft fitted with the Fiat A-12, Fiat A-12-*bis*, Rolls-Royce Eagle VIII, Siddeley Puma and Liberty engines; this appears to indicate that the Mk II designation was intended to apply fundamentally to the airframe, regardless of power units. A Vickers drawing of the Vimy with Eagle VIII engines dated September 1920 also bears the designation F.B.27A Vimy Mark II; so does an official description of equipment, dated October 1920. However, other official sources give different information.

Technical Department Instruction No. 538A, which is dated January 1919 and therefore originated between the dates of the A.I.D. report and the engine-

B9954 with standard wings, increased dihedral and horn-balanced ailerons.

* See *The War in the Air*, Vol. VI, pages 45-51.

F9569, first Vimy to have Rolls-Royce engines. In this view the shape of original radiators can be seen. Below: F9569 had enlarged rudders and pointed side fairings on engine nacelles.

Below: This photograph was made at Bircham Newton, and the Vimy is believed to be the one that left that aerodrome for Egypt in September 1919, flown by Capt. C. H. Darley, D.S.C., D.F.C., with his younger brother Capt. C. C. Darley as navigator. After a forced landing near Lake Bracciano in Italy the Vimy struck a telegraph pole when attempting take-off and crashed. Capt. C. H. Darley was burned to death, his brother surviving and reaching the rank of Air Commodore in the R.A.F. Note exhaust pipes of Vimy are inboard of interplane struts.

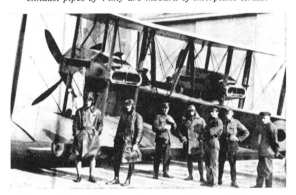

Below: Vimy with 37-mm. Coventry Ordnance Works gun.

Below: Vimy J7451 at R.A.E., Farnborough, with smoke-producing apparatus. (Photo: Crown Copyright)

installation handbook, states that the Vimy Mk I was the Maori-powered version; Mk II was the Fiat version; Mk III was to have B.H.P. (Siddeley Puma) engines; and that Mk IV had Rolls-Royce Eagle VIII engines. This document gives no Mark number to the Hispano-Suiza prototype, and indicates that the Maori and B.H.P. variants had been abandoned.

Yet another allocation of Mark numbers appears in an official record of performances of British aeroplanes, drawn up in February 1921. This calls the Hispano-Suiza version the Mk I, the Maori version the Mk II, the Fiat-powered variant the Mk III, and gives no Mark number to the Eagle-powered Vimy. The designation Vimy IV has come to be generally applied to this last-named sub-type, but its authenticity seems to have been, at best, only partial. Officially, it was comparatively short-lived, for the Vimy Mark numbers were revised and rationalised in the mid-1920s. This is discussed further on page 58.

In the Fiat-powered production aircraft there was provision for carrying up to eighteen bombs: two 520-pounders under the fuselage and four 230-pounders under the lower centre section on external racks; the internally-carried load could consist of four 112-lb. bombs and eight 250-lb. bombs.

The Vimy was also being developed in another rôle. By 1918 a good deal of experimental work with torpedo-carrying aircraft had been done, and official requirements for such aircraft had been divided into two categories: a fast, manoeuvrable machine carrying a light torpedo for close-range attack, and a heavier aircraft for long-range attack. The Sopwith Cuckoo was regarded as fulfilling the first requirement, with the Short Shirl and Blackburn Blackburd in prospect. The development of the long-range aircraft was less urgent, but the Vimy was selected as suitable and an A.I.D. description of the aircraft states "Two torpedoes may be carried instead of the two 520-lb. bombs",

In August 1918 consideration was given to the installation of flotation gear in the Vimy, but it is not known whether any aircraft was so equipped.

To quote again from Flight of 12th June 1919, the Air Board intimated "that the machines delivered during 1918 were to be utilized for anti-submarine work, and that subsequent deliveries were earmarked for night bombing in France." It is uncertain whether the torpedo-carrying version of the Vimy was intended for the anti-submarine rôle, but it seems unlikely. Early in 1918 a new policy had been laid down for the use of aircraft in the anti-submarine campaign, and one of its most striking features was the great increase in the number of landplanes required for the task. In November 1917 the estimated requirements of aircraft were for 525 seaplanes and 66 landplanes, but under the new policy 459 seaplanes and 726 landplanes would be required. These figures were never realised, but no doubt the Vimys would have constituted part of the total of 726 landplanes. In 1920 F9186 underwent ditching trials, but it is not known whether there was any connection with the proposed wartime duty.

It was probably intended that the Vimy should replace the Blackburn Kangaroo on anti-submarine work. It is indicated in Technical Department Instruction No. 538A that the Fiat-powered Vimy was to be the anti-submarine version.

On 11th October 1918 a fourth prototype Vimy flew from Joyce Green to Martlesham for its official trials. This aircraft, *F9569*, was powered by two 360-h.p. Rolls-Royce Eagle VIII engines housed in nacelles generally similar to those of the Fiat-powered *B9954*, but distinguished by their twin exhaust pipes and four-blade left-hand airscrews. As on *B9954*, the water header tanks were in the centre section, but they were located centrally above the engines and their water-supply and vapour-release pipes were midway between the struts.

The prototype Eagle-Vimy had enlarged rudders of a slightly modified shape; otherwise the airframe was virtually identical with that of *B9954*. The fuel capacity was greatly increased, however, at the expense of the internal bomb compartment: there was tankage for 452 gallons of petrol.

At Martlesham the Eagle-Vimy proved its excellence by flying at over 100 m.p.h. near the ground at an all-up weight of 12,500 lb. (not with a load of 12,500 lb., as has been incorrectly stated in some reports: with full crew and 3,650 lb. of fuel aboard, the military load was only 1,209 lb., some of which would be accounted for by the Lewis guns and their ammunition). The service ceiling at that weight was only 7,000 ft., but presumably that was of small account as the Vimy was intended to be a night bomber. The fuel load of 3,650 lb. gave an endurance of eleven hours.

By this time, large-scale production of the Vimy had begun. Vickers, Morgan, Westland and the Royal Aircraft Establishment were all active Vimy builders, but the type was not available in quantity before the war ended. On 31st October 1918 the R.A.F. had only three on charge: two were with experimental units; the other, despite the official decree that Vimys built in 1918 were to go to anti-submarine squadrons, went to a unit of the Independent Force at Nancy. It was intended that the Vimy should make long-range raids deep into Germany, as far as Berlin. The Armistice intervened, however, and no Vimy was ever used operationally.

The Eagle-powered Vimy went into production also, and indeed most of the production aircraft were of this variant. They differed from *F9569* in having fin surfaces incorporated in the tail unit, the rudders reverting to the shape and area of those of the earlier prototypes; their radiators were enlarged and had cowlings that were more nearly regular octagons; the exhaust pipes were carried lower on the sides of the nacelles and shortened; the pointed tails of the nacelle sides that had appeared on *F9569* were not reproduced: the generators were fitted near the bottom of each forward inboard engine-nacelle strut. Some production Eagle-Vimys had their exhaust pipes enclosed within the engine nacelles instead of lying outboard of the engine-supporting interplane struts.

By the end of 1918 Vickers Ltd. had built only thirteen Vimys, seven at Crayford and six at Weybridge. Production continued after the Armistice, and the final total of Vimys built by Vickers under their wartime contracts was 112. This total comprised twelve of the batch *F701–F850* (of which *F701* had Fiat engines), the complete batch *F8596–F8645*, and fifty of the batch *F9146–F9295*. It is known that *F8619* was at Farnborough on 17th September 1919, and that *F8631* was there on 10th November 1919.

Trainer version of the Eagle Vimy with modified nose. Below: *JR7444 of No. 4 F.T.S., Abu Sueir, with Armstrong-Siddeley Jaguar engines.* (Photo: Air Ministry)

It seems probable that most, if not all, of the Vimys ordered from Morgan & Co. were completed. On 23rd May 1919, *F3151* went to Farnborough from Hendon; *F3172* was at the R.A.E. on 10th November 1919; and *FR3185* crashed at Ramleh in Palestine several years later.

The Westland Aircraft Works built twenty-five of the seventy-five Vimys ordered under Contract No. 35A/2388/2689. It is known that *H5081* was at the R.A.E. Farnborough on 12th December 1919, whence it went to Orfordness on 16th January 1920. The Westland-built aircraft were tested by Squadron Leader Rollo de Haga Haig, who on one occasion succeeded in looping a Vimy.

The history of the Vimys built at the R.A.E. itself is a remarkable one. Two batches, numbered *F2915–F2934* and *H651–H670*, were ordered. Only two aircraft, *F2915* and *F2916*, were completed in 1918; both were originally powered by Fiat engines. Official records indicate that *F2917* was in existence on 14th March 1919, but it is uncertain whether it was completed, at least with this identity.

It appears that Farnborough had at least partially completed *F2918–F2920* but then ceased to use serial numbers of the first batch. The reason for this is not clear, but possibly the change to Rolls-Royce engines led to the abandonment of the *F2915–F2934* range of serials.

After the Armistice, Farnborough's later Vimys seemed to be built, partly at least, on a kind of make-do-and-mend system. According to official records, by 21st July 1919 Vimy *H651* had had Eagle engines Nos. 5186 (port) and 5508 (starboard) installed. This Vimy flew for the first time on 7th August 1919 and by 13th October it had racks for eight 112-lb. bombs under the wings and four under the fuselage. It was tested with six 112-lb. bombs in the front internal bomb bay and two 230-pounders under each lower wing. The 230-lb. bomb ribs and carriers were subsequently removed and fitted to the Vickers-built Vimy *F8610*. To replace them, *H651* was fitted with the 230-lb. bomb ribs and carriers taken from *F8619*.

This last-mentioned Vimy was a Vickers-built aircraft that had been sent to Farnborough on 12th September 1919 because the R.A.E. had complained about the stability of the Vimy and wanted to compare a Vickers-built machine against one constructed at Farnborough (possibly *F2915* which, as will be mentioned later, had an experimental tail unit). On 3rd October, F8619 collided with a field ambulance that was laying flares on the aerodrome, damaging its nose and lower centre section. It was thereafter dismantled, its parts finding various uses; F8619 itself was written off on 3rd November 1919. The rear fuselage and tail unit were used for strength tests; the engines (nos. 4478 and 4602) and many other components were installed in the R.A.E.-built Vimy H656; the 230-lb. bomb racks went to H651, as already noted, its controls, spars and brackets were installed in H655; and the countershafts for operating the radiator shutters were fitted to H658.

A direct product of the change to Rolls-Royce Eagle engines was H652. This Vimy was originally the Fiat-powered F2916, which apparently flew only twice before being converted at Farnborough to have Eagles. Minor additional modifications were the replacement of the standard carburettor controls by R.A.E. Positive Controls, and the replacement of the Vickers fuel system by a Bush system.

It is not known whether H653 and H655 were renumbered aircraft; both were apparently built with Eagle engines. A note under 30th October 1919 states that H653 had parachute gear (type unspecified) fitted; the first mention of H655 occurs on 8th December 1919. On 15th November 1919, H654 was complete or nearly so. This aircraft was originally built for Fiat engines and may have undergone renumbering; it was later used by No. 70 Squadron in Iraq.

There is no doubt about H656 and H657; they were renumbered from F2919 and F2920 respectively. The former flew to Orfordness on 13th January 1920; H657 ultimately found its way to Egypt, where it was flown at No. 4 F.T.S., Abu Suier, until about 1933.

The last three R.A.E.-built Vimys, H658–H660, were completed in January and February 1920. It is recorded that H658 had the red-and-blue night roundels on the fuselage, and was the first aircraft to be doped with the new Nivo finish. H659 had to make do with second-hand engines (1962/W.D.40223 and 1190/W.D.39837); H660 had one second-hand (2342/W.D.40413) and one new (5152/W.D.53300) engine.

It has been mentioned that the R.A.E. was dissatisfied with the Vimy's stability, and that F2915 had experimental fins and rudders. By 1st May 1919 it had been fitted with a centre fin and rudder, and its side fins had been removed. In July 1919 the Morgan-built Vimy F3151 was fitted with experimental rudders and a central fin. When the R.A.E. conducted its experiments on the rudder control of twin-engine aeroplanes* the aircraft concerned were a Vimy (apparently F3151) and the D.H.10, E6042.

In the period after the Armistice the R.A.F. began to contract rapidly, consequently the introduction of the Vimy into the Service was a slow process. In July 1919, No. 58 Squadron in Egypt received Vimys as replacements for its Handley Page 0/400s. When the unit was renumbered as No. 70 Squadron on 1st February 1920 it kept its Vimys until they were replaced by Vernons late in 1922. In 1921, Squadrons Nos. 45 and 216, also in Egypt, had been equipped with Vimys. Those of No. 216 are well remembered

for the part they played in operating the air-mail service between Cairo and Baghdad until August 1926.

At home, the Vimys of "D" Flight of No. 100 Squadron were, in 1922, the only twin-engine bombers then in service with the R.A.F. in the U.K. On 5th July 1923 this Flight provided the nucleus of No. 7 Squadron, which flew the Vimys until they were replaced by Virginias in 1925. On 1st April 1924, Nos. 9 and 58 Squadrons were re-formed, both with Vimys, and the R.A.F.'s home-based heavy-bomber strength was trebled.

Although withdrawn from the front-line squadrons from 1924 onwards the Vimy served until January 1929 with No. 502 (County of Ulster) Squadron.

Apart from its use by full squadrons, the Vimy also served with the Night-Flying Flight at Biggin Hill. This unit was formed on 1st July 1923 for co-operation flying with anti-aircraft units; its equipment consisted of three Vimys and one Bristol Fighter. During the General Strike of 1926 the Vimys of the Night-Flying Flight helped to distribute the Government's emergency news-sheet, the British Gazette.

Vimys figured in several experiments in the years following the war. One was fitted with a 37-mm. Coventry Ordnance Works recoilless gun on a special mounting on the nose; the bow cockpit had to be modified, and the massive pivoting support for the gun was mounted externally to starboard.

At the R.A.E., Farnborough, H651 was used in experiments connected with the automatic landing of aeroplanes.* An iron weight of 1 lb. 7 oz. was suspended on fifty feet of strong waxed linen thread of 1/32-in. diameter; the other end of the thread was attached to a spring balance in the nose cockpit. The aircraft was flown light, at a weight of 9,000 lb. with the rear tank empty in order to bring the centre of gravity forward. The Vimy was trimmed at stalling speed with the controls free, and was then glided down at a constant air speed. A constant air speed was the ideal aimed at but, says the Report, "It is practically impossible to fly a Vimy at a constant air speed as hunting takes place as soon as the steady speed is approached". When the spring balance indicated that the weight had struck the ground the observer signalled to the pilot, who released the controls (an adjustable spring had been fitted to the control column) and allowed the Vimy to land itself. The words of the Report are probably something of an understatement:

In the earlier part of the experiment considerable nerve and judgment were required on the part of the pilot to leave the aeroplane free long enough to determine what would happen, and take charge again in time before it did happen. Credit is due to Flight Lieut. Scholefield, who successfully carried the experiment through this stage.

About twenty-five landings were made by this method and although some were very bad, no serious damage was done to the aeroplane. In nearly every case the aeroplane landed with the tail some height up, but this did not appear to cause any serious bounce.

The Vimy H651 was also used to test the Kennedy Cable Lock in October and November 1920. This

* See Aeronautical Research Committee Reports & Memoranda No. 908, *Experiments with rudders on two twin-engine aeroplanes*, December 1923.

* See Aeronautical Research Committee Reports and Memoranda No. 909: *Automatic Landing of Aeroplanes*, by F. W. Meredith of the R.A.E., December 1923.

device was a kind of irreversible mechanism that allowed the pilot to move the controls as he wished but prevented the air forces acting on the controls from moving them when the stick was released.

Other R.A.E. experiments included an installation of smoke-producing apparatus (in *J7451*) and an experimental attachment to the undercarriage.

It seems that even the modest requirements of the post-war R.A.F. called for more Vimys than the curtailed wartime production had provided, for a further thirty were built, possibly from spares, by Vickers Ltd. under three small contracts given to them in 1923, 1924 and 1925. The Mark-numbering system was revised but, in the absence of adequate confirmatory detail, remains obscure. What seems certain is that, in the revised scheme, the basic Eagle-powered aircraft was designated Vimy Mk I, and the machines of the batches *J7440–J7454* (and possibly *J7701–J7705*) were designated Vimy Mk III. Apparently the Mk II was applied to some of the aircraft that were reconditioned by Vickers Ltd. The designations Vimy Reconditioned I, Vimy Reconditioned II, Vimy Reconditioned II School, and Vimy Production School all existed, but it is doubtful whether there was any discernible difference between the first two at least.

Between 1923 and 1931, Vickers Ltd. reconditioned at least forty-eight Vimys originally built under war-time contracts. Many of these were reconditioned more than once: some, like *F9634*, *F9147* and *F9168* came back three times; *F9176* was reconditioned four times. By the time these aircraft came in for overhaul the Vernon troop-carrier was in production, and the reconditioned Vimys were fitted with Vernon-type engine mountings, engine cowlings, exhaust manifolds, service tanks and tail-skids. Certain parts of the electrical system were revised. In all Vimys from the Reconditioned Mk II onwards the engines had Rolls-Royce hand starters, and the Production School and Mk III variants had metal tail-skids.

Many Vimys were used for training purposes. Of the aircraft reconditioned by Vickers Ltd., at least thirty were converted to dual control, including five of the Vimys Mk III, which had their dual control installed in October and November 1928. Some Vimys, possibly the batch *J7238–J7247*, were initially built as trainers; this variant was known, to the manufacturers at least, as the Vimy Production School type. It had an extended nose, a modification that was made to other Vimys (e.g., *JR7444*) used as trainers.

With training units the Vimy soldiered on until the early 1930s. Apart from its use as a flying trainer at such units as No. 4 F.T.S., Abu Sueir, Egypt, it served as a parachute trainer at Henlow. For this purpose the Vimy had a ladder fitted on the port side of the fuselage beside the rear gunner's cockpit, and a small platform was built about the base of the outermost rear interplane strut on each side. The aircraft took off with a parachutist standing on each strut platform, facing rearwards and therefore pressed against the strut by the airstream. At a signal from the pilot, the parachutist moved round to the rear of the strut, pulled his parachute release, and had then no option about leaving the aircraft. The Vimy's upper and lower ailerons were interconnected by three cables: on the parachute trainers the middle cable was moved one

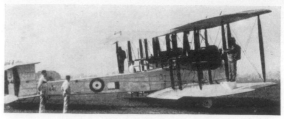

J7441 in use as a parachute trainer.

rib-space inboard to increase the clearance for the parachutist on his rearward departure. The ladder on the fuselage side was for free-fall parachute descents; part of the trailing edge of the port lower centre section was cut away to facilitate its use.

The useful life of a number of Vimys, including some of the parachute trainers, was extended by replacing their Rolls-Royce Eagles with Bristol Jupiter IV or Armstrong-Siddeley Jaguar IV radial engines. At least one Vimy (*F9168*) is known to have had Jupiter VI engines, but these were replaced by Jupiters IV in August 1929. It may be that *F9168* was the first Vimy to have Jupiter engines, the initial conversion being made at Martlesham Heath. The fact that all other known conversions had Jupiters IV was doubtless a reflection of the economy-ridden condition of the R.A.F. at the time, for there can be little doubt that the engines had already seen service in Hawker Woodcocks. From the spring of 1929 onwards, most Vimys coming in to be reconditioned were given Jupiter or Jaguar engines, and Jupiter conversion sets were provided by Vickers Ltd. to facilitate engine changes at R.A.F. stations.

Both radial installations were characterised by stark simplicity and a total absence of any kind of cowling. The struts supporting the engines had to be modified and re-arranged: the rear struts formed an X-shaped support for the rear of the convergent engine-bearers, and the forward struts converged towards the engines.

Although the Vimy's R.A.F. career was unspectacular, it gained immortality by its successes in early long-range flights. The Vimy's first achievement in this field, the first Atlantic direct crossing, was of such a magnitude that it almost eclipsed the other two major flights.

The aircraft in which Captain John Alcock, D.S.C., and Lt. Arthur Whitten-Brown covered the 1,890 miles between Lester's Field, St. Johns, Newfoundland, and Clifden, Co. Galway, Ireland, was specially built for the Atlantic flight. Its engines were two 360-h.p. Rolls-Royce Eagles VIII; additional tanks increased its fuel capacity to 865 gallons and gave the aircraft a range of

The Vimy of Alcock and Brown after assembly in Newfoundland.

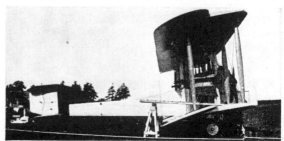

2,440 miles. The nose cockpit was faired over, and the pilot and navigator sat side-by-side in the main cockpit; behind them an enlarged turtle-back fairing extended over the fuel tanks. In place of the nose skid a wheel was fitted, but it and the tailplane skids were removed for the Atlantic flight.

At Vickers there was at one time some division of opinion as to whether one or two special Vimys should be built. The pressing need to make haste settled the matter, however, and only one was constructed. Such was the simplicity and speed of aircraft design work at the time that Rex Pierson wrote on 21st February 1919: "At present I am getting out drawings of (1) New oil tanks, (2) New water tank of increased capacity, (3) Petrol system, and I hope to let Muller have these by tomorrow morning."

Alcock made the first test flight in the Vimy on 18th April 1919, and he and Brown made several flights in it before it was dismantled and shipped to Newfoundland. After overcoming many difficulties, not the least of which was the finding of a field suitable for the take-off, the Vimy was airborne at 4.13 p.m. (G.M.T.) on 14th June 1919, and crossed the Newfoundland coast fifteen minutes later. At 8.40 a.m. (G.M.T.) on the following day it landed in Derrygimla Bog, Clifden, damaging the lower wings and the forepart of the fuselage. The Vimy was repaired and presented to the Science Museum, South Kensington, in December 1919; it can still be seen there.

In November 1919 another Vimy began another historic long-distance flight. A prize of £10,000 had been offered in March 1919 by the Australian Government for the first flight made by Australians from Britain to Australia in a British aircraft. It was stipulated that the flight must be accomplished within 720 hours, and the take-off was to be made from Hounslow aerodrome or Calshot seaplane station.

In view of the Vimy's recent Atlantic conquest it was natural that Vickers should enter an aircraft of the same type for the Australian flight. The Vimy selected was *F8630*, which was given the civil identity G-EAOU; this registration was irreverently interpreted as meaning "God 'elp all of us". The pilot was Captain Ross Smith, the redoubtable "Hadji" of No. 1 Squadron, Australian Flying Corps, and a Bristol Fighter pilot of distinction; his brother Lt. Keith Smith, was navigator; and their mechanics were Sgts. J. M. Bennett and W. H. Shiers.

SPECIFICATION

Power: First prototype, two 200 h.p. Hispano-Suiza, later two 260 h.p. Salmson 9Zm; second prototype, two 260 h.p. Sunbeam Maori; third prototype, two 300 h.p. Fiat A-12bis; fourth prototype, two 360 h.p. Rolls-Royce Eagle VIII. Production Vimy, two 300 h.p. Fiat A-12bis or two 360 h.p. Rolls-Royce Eagle VIII; one experimental installation of two 400 h.p. Liberty 12. Post-war trainer versions had two 450 h.p. Bristol Jupiter VI, two 420 h.p. Jupiter IV, or two 420 h.p. Armstrong-Siddeley Jaguar IV.

Dimensions: Span (B9952) 68 ft. 4 in., (B9953 and original form of B9954) 67 ft. 2 in., (B9954 modified and production Vimy) 68 ft.; length 43 ft. 6½ in.; height 15 ft.; chord 10 ft. 6 in.; gap 10 ft.; stagger, nil; dihedral, (B9952 and B9953) 1°, (all other Vimys) 3°; incidence 3° 30′; span of tail 16 ft.; chord tailplane and elevators 6 ft.; airscrew diameter (Hispano-Suiza) 9 ft. 3 in. (Fiat) 9 ft. 5 in. (Eagle) 10 ft. 6 in.

Areas: Wings and ailerons 1,300 sq. ft. (1,376 sq. ft. on B9953 and original form of B9954); ailerons, each 60·5 sq. ft. (58·75 sq. ft. on B9953 and original form of B9954); tailplanes (B9952) upper 37 sq. ft., lower 31 sq. ft. (all others) upper 61·3 sq. ft., lower 53·1 sq. ft.; elevators, total (B9952) 74 sq. ft. (all others) 63 sq. ft.; fins, each (production Eagle Vimy only) 13·5 sq. ft.; rudders, each 10·8 sq. ft.

Production

Contractor	Serial Nos.	Notes
Vickers Ltd. (Aviation Dept.), Imperial Court, Basil Street, Knightsbridge, London, S.W.	B9952–B9954	Prototypes built at Bexley Heath.
	F701–F850	Built at Crayford; only twelve completed. Fiat B.H.P. or Liberty engines specified.
	F8596–F8645	Full batch built at Weybridge. Contract specified ten should have Fiat engines, remainder B.H.P. Most, if not all, had Eagles.
	F9146–F9295	Only 50 completed at Weybridge.
	F9569	First Vimy with Rolls-Royce Eagle engines.
	H9963	Single aircraft only; believed Vickers-built.
	J7238–J7247 J7440–J7454 J7701–J7705	Vimy III.
Clayton and Shuttleworth, Lincoln.	F2996–F3095 J251–J300	Of all the Vimys ordered from this firm, 124 were to have B.H.P. engines, the remainder Fiats. Doubtful whether any was completed.
Morgan & Co., Leighton Buzzard	F3146–F3195	B.H.P. engines specified, Eagles fitted. At least 40 aircraft completed.
	J1941–J1990	Contract cancelled.
Royal Aircraft Establishment, Farnborough, Hants.	F2915–F2934	Fiat engines specified. No production beyond F2920 known; most completed aircraft were renumbered in H651–H670 batch.
	H651–H670	Fiat engines specified, Eagles fitted. Apparently only H651–H660 allotted.
Westland Aircraft Works, Yeovil, Somerset.	H5065–H5139	Liberty engines specified, Eagles fitted. Twenty-five only built.
Boulton & Paul Ltd., Riverside, Norwich	H4046–H4195	Contract cancelled 30.8.18.
Metropolitan Waggon Co., Birmingham	H4725–H4824	Contract cancelled.
Ransomes, Sims & Jeffries, Ipswich	H9413–H9512	Contract cancelled 1.11.18.

Armament: Bomb load of the Fiat-powered Vimy could consist of two 250 lb. bombs under the fuselage, four 230 lb. bombs under the lower centre section, and eight 250 lb. and four 112 lb. stowed internally. The internal bomb compartment could hold twelve 250 lb. bombs when necessary. Alternatively, two torpedoes could be carried. The Eagle-powered Vimy had provision for carrying twelve 112 lb. or twelve 250 lb. bombs internally, eight 112 lb. bombs under the lower wings, four 112 lb. bombs under the fuselage, and two 230 lb. bombs, one under each lower longeron. These two last bombs were carried on 520 lb. Skeleton Bomb Carriers Mk III converted to take the 230 lb. bomb. Standard equipment, two Michelin Flare Carriers Mk I and High Altitude Drift Bomb Sight Mk 1a.

Defensive armament consisted of four Mk III Lewis 0·303 in. machine guns: two, with 4½ in. Neame No. 1 Sight, were on a Scarff No. 2 Ring Mounting on the front cockpit; one could be carried on a Scarff mounting on the rear cockpit, but in post-war service this mounting was not usually fitted; one, with 2 in. Neame No. 2 Sight, was on a pivot mounting in the rear ventral position. There was provision for carrying four spare drums of ammunition in the front cockpit, six in the rear.

Service use: One Vimy was with the Independent Force, R.A.F., at the end of October 1918. After the war the Vimy was flown by R.A.F. Squadrons Nos. 7, 9, 45, 58, 70, 99, 100 ("D" Flight) and 216 and by the Night-Flying Flight at Biggin Hill. For training purposes the type was used at Cranwell; the Home Aircraft Depot, Henlow; and at No. 4 F.T.S., Abu Sueir, Egypt.

Examples of Vimys used by R.A.F. units:
No. 9 Sqn.—F8631 (later used at No. 4 F.T.S.). No. 58 Sqn.—F3184, F9161, F9187, J7238, J7246, J7441, J7449, J7450. No. 70 Sqn.—F8643, F9190. No. 216 Sqn.—H653, HR5089, J7443. No. 502 Sqn.—F9146, J7247. No. 4 F.T.S.—F8631 (ex No. 9 Sqn.), F8632, H657, JR7444, J7448, JR7454.

© J. M. Bruce 1965

Ross Smith took off from Hounslow at 8 a.m. on 12th November 1919, and G-EAOU had an adventurous journey before reaching Darwin at 4.10 p.m. on 10th December. The 11,130 miles from Hounslow had been covered in just under twenty-eight days elapsed time, 135 hrs. 55 mins. flying time.

Vickers Ltd. presented G-EAOU to the Australian Government. It was allotted the Australian serial A5-1, but it is doubtful whether the aircraft ever bore this marking. It was exhibited in the Australian War Memorial at Canberra until 1957, when it was moved to Adelaide to form the centre of a memorial to the four men who had made the first flight to Australia. Although severely damaged by fire on 3rd November 1957 while in transit from Canberra, the Vimy was carefully restored and installed in the memorial.

The third long-distance flight undertaken by a Vimy began on 4th February 1920, when Lt.-Col Pierre van Ryneveld, D.S.O., M.C., and Major C. J. Quintin Brand, D.S.O., M.C., D.F.C., with two mechanics, took off from Brooklands bound for Cape Town. The flight was sponsored by the South African Government; the aircraft was Eagle-powered, registered G-UABA and named *Silver Queen*: the prize was again £10,000, put up by the *Daily Mail* for a flight from Cairo to Cape Town. The *Silver Queen* had as competitors the Handley Page 0/400 G-EAMC and the Vickers Vimy Commercial G-EAAV.

On 10th February 1920 van Ryneveld and Brand left Heliopolis after dark; next day, when they were 530 miles from Cairo and still eighty miles short of Wadi Halfa, the radiator tap on the starboard engine opened, the engine soon stopped, and an emergency landing was made at Korosko. The Vimy was wrecked on the boulder-strewn ground, but the crew unhurt.

At the request of the South African Government the Royal Air Force placed another Vimy at the disposal of van Ryneveld and Brand. The engines and instruments of *Silver Queen* were salvaged and returned to Cairo for installation in the replacement aircraft, which was named *Silver Queen II*. The new Vimy took off from Heliopolis on 22nd February; Bulawayo was reached one week later, but there *Silver Queen II* was wrecked while taking off for Pretoria, her take-off performance having been greatly reduced by heat and the altitude of the aerodrome at Bulawayo. Again van Ryneveld and Brand were unhurt, and they completed their flight to Cape Town in the D.H.9 *H5648*, reaching their destination on 20th March.

For Service use the Vimy Ambulance and Vernon were developed via the Vimy Commercial of 1919 (to which the spurious type numbers F.B.27B and F.B.28 have been wrongly attributed: the last number in Vickers F.B. series was the F.B.27A Vimy); production of all Vimy variants ended in 1925. In the R.A.F. the Vimy outlived its descendants and did not disappear until 1933. Although denied the opportunity of proving itself in the war for which it was designed, the Vimy had a great and varied career that Rex Pierson can hardly have envisaged when, in 1917, he made his first rough sketches in Major Buchanan's office at the Air Ministry.

Weights and Performance

Engines	Hispano Suiza	Maori		Fiat		Eagles			Salmson	Jaguar
No of Trial Report	M.177A	M.199		Mfr's Trials	M.229	M.241			Mfr's Trials	—
Date of Trial Report	April 1918	May 1918		—	Sept. 1918	October 1918			—	—
Load	—	No bombs	2,000 lb. of bombs	—	2,000 lb. of bombs	No bombs	With bomb load	With increased fuel load	—	—
Weights (lb.):										
Empty	5,420	6,735	6,735	6,625	6,934	7,101	7,101	7,101	5,560	6,550
Military load	2,353	108	2,118	2,043	2,124	Nil	1,650	1,209	1,992	1,200
Crew	540	360	360	540	360	360	360	540	540	540
Fuel and oil	807	1,087	1,087	1,092	1,390	2,539	3,389	3,650	1,508	3,110
Loaded	9,120	8,290	10,300	10,300	10,808	10,000	12,500	12,500	9,600	11,400
Performance—Maximum speed (m.p.h.):										
At ground level	90	—	—	—	98	—	103	—	—	112
At 5,000 ft.	87	—	89	96	—	—	98	98	94	105
At 6,500 ft.	85	96	85	—	—	100	95	—	—	101
At 10,000 ft.	—	89·5	—	90	—	96	—	—	—	—
Climb to (m. s.):										
5,000 ft.	23 35	— —	19 20	13 30	— —	— —	21 55	21 55	13 30	10 15
6,500 ft.	36 10	13 10	28 30	— —	30 00	14 00	33 00	33 00	— —	15 00
10,000 ft.	— —	24 25	— —	45 00	— —	25 55	— —	— —	— —	32 30
Ceiling (ft): Service	6,500	14,000	8,000	—	6,500	14,000	7,000	7,000	—	10,500
Absolute	9,500	—	10,500	11,000	—	—	10,500	10,500	11,500	12,300
Endurance (hours)	3½	4¼	4¼	3½	—	—	—	11	5¾	5

Acknowledgements: The author gratefully acknowledges the contributions made to this history by the assistance and researches of C. F. Andrews, Bruce Robertson and H. E. Scrope.

The Bristol Bulldog

The Bristol Bulldog

by C. F. Andrews

Bulldog IIA, K2227, c/n 7446, pictured during its last flight on 13th September 1964. Was originally a demonstration aircraft and registered G-ABBB on 12th June 1930, and powered by a Gnome-Rhône 9ASB engine. See page 64 for original G-ABBB and original K2227.

(Photo: Cyril Peckham)

THE Bristol Bulldog was designed by Captain Frank S. Barnwell as a single-seat, interceptor fighter at a time when British air strategy was undergoing radical change. During the seven years that followed the end of World War I, great reliance had been placed on standing patrols of radio-equipped fighters such as the Gloster Gamecock and the Armstrong Whitworth Siskin, which were able to deal adequately with the lumbering bombers of the period.

These obsolescent fighters served long after they should have been replaced, but the fault did not all lie at the Air Ministry's door, for extreme government economy had forced them to rely upon versatility and serviceability at the expense of performance. A succession of fighter specifications had produced some excellent ideas, but lack of money resulted in the majority remaining as drawing-board designs.

But a change, long overdue, was about to take place. The advent of the private venture Fairey Fox in 1925 brought home the need for a change in air defence. The Fox was a formidable two-seat bomber based on the Curtiss D.12 in-line, liquid-cooled

engine, housed in a low-drag, streamlined cowling, driving a Fairey-Reed metal propeller complete with spinner. The Fox could outpace and outclimb contemporary fighters and caused a major upheaval in military aeronautics. It was a stark reality confronting the architects of British defence policy.

The Bristol Aeroplane Company had, during this period, produced several promising single-seat fighter designs, none of which had achieved the distinction of service. Frank Barnwell's first effort in this class was the Scout F of 1918. Powered by the Cosmos Mercury air-cooled, radial engine, it was ancestor of a number of Bristol designs which culminated in the successful Bulldog.

When the Cosmos aero-engine design was acquired by Bristols along with its designer, Mr. A. H. R. Fedden (later Sir Roy), soon after the first World War, an engine division of the Company was created to exploit the air-cooled radial type. Consequently Bristol aeroplane designs thereafter embodied as far as possible Bristol engines, a combination for the British aircraft industry, obviously of great advantage

Left: Prototype Bulldog I, c/n 7155, with Jupiter VII. First flew on 17th May 1927, with Cyril Uwins at the controls. Right: 7155 with long-span (50 ft. 0 in.) wing and enlarged rudder. Was to be used for an attempt on the high-altitude record in December 1927.

62

Left: *Prototype Bulldog II, c/n 7235, serial J9480. First flew on 21st January 1928.* Right: *11th production Bulldog II, c/n 7332, serial J9576, in No. 3 Squadron colours. No. 3 was the first squadron to operate Bulldogs. Note amended fin shape.*

Left: *Bulldog II, c/n 7399, SBAC number R.1. Test bed for Mercury III engine fitted with four-blade propeller.* Right: *R.1 with Gnome-Rhône Jupiter VI engine. Registered G-ABAC on 30th May 1930 and destroyed on 4th June.*

to the parent Company and indeed to the Air Ministry and other customers.

This was the situation in which Bristols were placed when in 1924 the Air Staff decided on a replacement for the obsolescent Siskin in the form of an interceptor fighter, powered with the Rolls-Royce Falcon X liquid-cooled, in-line engine, to Specification F.17/24. Barnwell and Fedden disagreed on the choice of engine for a proposed Bristol submission to this specification, as the latter naturally wanted to use his radial type. The project was shelved until April 1926, when Barnwell resumed work on a single-seat fighter design to meet either Specification F.9/26 (Type 102A) for a day-and-night fighter, or navalised Specification N.21/26 (Type 102B) for a ship-borne fighter. This design was based on Bristol Type 99, the Badminton racing biplane of 1925.

In the meantime, the interceptor requirement was revived and at the beginning of 1927 Barnwell submitted schemes for a design using the Rolls-Royce F.XI in-line engine or the Bristol Mercury radial. This was in addition to the revised F.9/26 design with a Mercury engine (Type 105) and both offered such promise that mock-ups were constructed for official inspection. Both layouts were similar with equal span wings, but early in the project stage the lower wing of both was reduced in span and chord, thus introducing one of the characteristics of the finalised Bulldog design, the reasons for which change are detailed later. The interceptor was intended to meet Specification F.17/24, but Bristols were then asked to revise the scheme to comply with the later interceptor Specification F.20/27, with the geared Mercury III, then under development by their engine division. This interceptor

Bulldog II, J9591, c/n 7397, as used for flight testing the geared Mercury IV with cylinder-head helmets. Registered G-AATR on 13th January 1930 but reverted to original serial in January 1931 for tests with Mercury IVA. Entered R.A.F. service in September 1931 with normal Jupiter VIIF as on standard R.A.F. Bulldogs.

Bulldog 11A, G-ABBB, R-11, c/n 7446, with Aquila I engine in September 1935. Became K2227 in 1961 (see photo page 62). Originally with Gnome-Rhône 9ASB. Stored at Filton until 1939, when presented to Science Museum. Returned to Filton for reconditioning 1957; crashed 13th September 1964. Below: *The original K2227 of No. 56 Squadron. Only two Bulldogs had this engine cowling—see side-view colour drawings on page 70.*
(*Crown copyright*)

layout found favour and one prototype was ordered as Type 107 (constructor's number 7178, serial number *J9051*). At the same time, the Air Ministry ordered four competitive prototypes to F.20/27, one each from the Gloster, Hawker, Vickers and Westland aircraft companies. The Bristol design became the Bullpup.

The parallel project, Type 105, showed just as much promise for Specification F.9/26 and Bristols decided to build a private venture prototype (constructor's number 7155), with a Bristol Jupiter VII radial engine, although, as previously stated, preference was intended to be given to designs embodying the Rolls-Royce F series in-line engine. Although an offer in March 1927 to the Air Ministry to build 50 aircraft

if some contribution towards the cost of development was made was declined, the Ministry did agree to test the prototype at Martlesham Heath, where the Aeroplane and Armament Experimental Establishment was located up to 1939.

THE BULLDOG IS BORN

The third layout of the Jupiter powered Type 105 closely followed that of the Mercury powered Type 107, the chief difference being that it was larger. Both were drawn in detail and built concurrently. Bristol's suggestion for the names Bulldog and Bullpup respectively was readily accepted, both conforming to official nomenclature. The supply of the new Mercury engine was limited so the Bulldog was quickly completed with the Jupiter installation and no delay was experienced on account of official decisions, the project being a private venture. As a consequence, the Bulldog first flew, at Filton, on 17th May 1927 in the hands of Capt. Cyril F. Uwins, Bristol's chief test pilot, whose first prototype flight for the Company had been appropriately in the Cosmos-engined Bristol Scout F.1 way back in 1918. The Bulldog proved very satisfactory in early test flights and went to Martle-

Left: *Prototype Bulldog IIA, K1603, c/n 7459. Delivered to Martlesham Heath as D.T.D. installation aircraft.* Right: *Bulldog IIA, c/o's aircraft, No. 19 Squadron. Note camera-gun on top wing and wing-tip pennants.*
(*Flight* photo)

Prototype Bulldog T.M., two-seat trainer, K2188, originally constructed as single-seat fighter.

sham in June, making its first public appearance at the Royal Air Force Display at Hendon in July.

Wind tunnel tests had established the advantage of the unequal area wing arrangement, a configuration inherited a long way back from the French Nieuport and German Albatross D.III of World War I, the main purpose in those early designs being to give the pilot a good view downwards. In the Bulldog this desirable attribute still applied, but in the meantime it had been found that advantage could be taken of the arrangement in the introduction of an upper and lower aerofoil of different aerodynamic characteristics. The upper wing of the Bulldog was a special section known as the Bristol IA, jointly evolved by L. G. Frise, Bristol's chief aerodynamicist, and the Royal Aircraft Establishment. From it was later developed more advanced sections leading to the R.A.F. 34. The lower wings of decreased span and chord were of the Clark YH section—the Clark Y so popular with flying model makers but with a reflex trailing edge. Frise-type ailerons, in which the hinges were set back from the rear spar fixings to provide a measure of aerodynamic balance, were fitted to the top wings only. The dihedral angle of both wings, upper and lower, was five degrees. In a general sense, the provision of upper and lower wings of different aerofoil sections enhanced lift/drag characteristics over a wider speed range, although possibly involving spinning problems, which affected the Bulldog and similar types, a phenomenon then becoming the subject of intense investigation.

THE BULLDOG DESCRIBED

The Bulldog was of high tensile steel strip construction, as developed by H. J. Pollard at Bristol and first used in the Bristol Boarhound two-seat fighter of 1924. Metal airframes were rapidly becoming a priority requirement and from 1926 onwards were mandatory for all new orders from the Air Ministry. In the Bristol system, high tensile steel strips were

rolled into cusped and flanged sections, riveted together lengthways to form longerons and struts, the joints being made by gusset plates, thus avoiding costly machined end-fittings. The spars were fabricated

Above: *Bulldog IIIA, R-5, c/n 7560, prototype. Built as private venture and first flown 17th September 1931. Mercury IVA engine and spats.* Below, top: *R-5 with Mercury IVS.2 engine, June 1932.* Bottom: *R-5 without cowling and spats and with Mercury IVS engine.*

The second Bulldog IIIA, R-7, c/n 7745, private venture aircraft. Registered G-ABZW on 3rd October 1932 but never carried marks. Narrow-chord ailerons on upper and lower wings as standardised on Marks IV and IVA.

from rolled section booms and diaphragms following the Boulton and Paul method, in the evolution of which Pollard had been associated with J. D. North, its originator, before joining the Bristol Company in 1921. Following contemporary practice, the whole airframe, with the exception of the aluminium sheet front fuselage, was fabric covered. All the metal components were dipped and stove enamelled to prevent corrosion. Steel construction of aircraft prevailed until the advent of new light alloys capable of controlled heat treatments and of the American Alclad plate which enabled stressed skin surfaces to be developed. Anodising and later processes superseded stove enamelling for the corrosion protection of light alloys, but that came after the day of the Bulldog, which represented in its time sophisticated metal construction in steel, a system claimed to be lighter and stronger than equivalent structures in drawn steel tubes. It was certainly much cheaper.

Apart from its all-steel strip construction, the Bulldog was conventional in its detail design. Fuel was carried in two gravity tanks housed in the upper planes outboard of the centre section, and the lubricating oil tank was located behind the fireproof engine bulkhead and embodied a surface oil cooler. Two Vickers guns were located low on each side of the cockpit firing through the propeller by control of the hydraulic synchronisation gear. A short-wave two-way radio was mounted in a small compartment just aft of the cockpit. The undercarriage was of the long

stroke type, to enable the aeroplane to operate from rough airfields, with oleo damped rubber compression spring legs attached to the top longerons. The interplane struts were steel tubes faired with balsa, and the centre section cabane was steel tube strutting.

Although the Bullpup was designed for the pure interceptor rôle, its counterpart the Bulldog was intended as a day-and-night fighter Specification F.9/26. The Bulldog was entered to take part in the competition for the latter requirement. This was held in the summer of 1927 at Martlesham and the Bristol entry was matched against the Armstrong Whitworth Starling, the Boulton and Paul Partridge, the Gloster Goldfinch and the Hawker Hawfinch, all prototype products of reputable stables. After the competition had been in progress for some time, the Bulldog and Hawfinch emerged as rivals on the short list, the Hawker machine being superior in spin recovery only. The manoeuvrability of the Bulldog and its well-harmonised controls earned full marks and it could be dived to its terminal velocity of 270 m.p.h. without damage to surfaces or structure. The fabric covering remained intact in this flight case, a critical condition in aircraft at that time, and no flutter distortion in any flight case appears to have been reported, another phenomenon then becoming apparent with the gradual increase of aircraft performance. The ease of repair of local damage to the structure, without removing fittings or members, also gained the Bulldog a good mark.

Left: *R-7, K4292, with Perseus long-chord cowling. two-blade propeller and tail wheel.* Right: *K4292 with Mercury VIS-2 in long-chord cowling and Hamilton three-blade, variable-pitch propeller, July 1934.*

R-7, in its intermediate form with Mercury VIS.2 engine, short-chord cowling and Hamilton variable-pitch, three-blade propeller. Note twin aileron wires instead of strut.

The second Bulldog IVA, R-8, c/n 7808. Registered G-ACJN and built to test Mercury VIS.2 engine. Later fitted with this engine, but first used for testing Perseus IA. Seen here painted ready for the 1934 SBAC Show.

An attempt was made to improve the spin recovery characteristics of the Bulldog by fitting a larger fin and rudder but this introduced "weathercocking" in a cross-wind during landings and ground handling. In consequence a different solution was sought by lengthening the fuselage in order to increase the control exercised by the original, small vertical tail surfaces. The Air Ministry ordered another prototype with this and other minor modifications in November 1927 as the Bulldog Mark II, Bristol Type 105A, constructor's number 7235, serial number *J9480*.

THE BULLDOG II
The Bulldog II first flew at Filton on 21st January 1928, piloted by Capt. Uwins. Soon after it went to Martlesham where it was so closely matched by the Hawker Hawfinch that the A. and A.E.E. reserved their judgment until both had been sent for Service trials by the R.A.F. Fighter Squadrons at Biggin Hill, Kenley, Northolt, Upavon and North Weald. By June 1928 no decision had been reached although the Bulldog was found to be slighter faster. The final choice was therefore made on ease of maintenance, in which the Bulldog scored because of its single bay wing cellule as contrasted with the two-bay structure of the Hawfinch, and the fact that its wing-mounted tanks could be changed twice as quickly as the front fuselage tank of its competitor. This was an important consideration during operation in the field.

The F.9/26 competition was, therefore, won by the Bulldog II and a contract was placed for 25 production aircraft to Specification F.17/28, revised according to special Service requirements from F.9/26. In addition an extra airframe was built to serve as a demonstration machine. Deliveries to the R.A.F. began in May 1929 and were completed the following October, the first 18 going to No. 3 Squadron and the rest to No. 17, both

of these units having specialised in night fighting with Hawker Woodcocks, which the Bulldogs replaced.

Constructor's numbers for the first batch of Bulldogs were 7322 to 7347, serial numbers *J9576* to *J9591*, machine 7331 being the Company's demonstrator. It was fitted with a Jupiter VIA engine instead of the standard Jupiter VI and registered G-AAHH. Its finish was silver with a green decking and a green stripe along the sides of the fuselage, similar to No. 3 Squadron's markings. Number 7341 was taken out of the Air Ministry contract and sent to Bristol's agents in Japan for prospective sales promotion. It was replaced by 7397, serial number *J9591*, which was retained at Filton to serve as a test bed for the geared Mercury IV engine.

The immediate success of the Bulldog in R.A.F. service soon attracted foreign attention and in September 1929 five aircraft, constructor's numbers 7353 to 7357, were delivered to Latvia, changes being the installation of French-built Gnome-Rhône Jupiter VI engines and Oerlikon guns. In October 1929 Bulldog Mark II, 7358, with a Jupiter VIIF, was sent to the United States Navy for evaluation as a dive bomber but during a terminal velocity dive an aileron failed and the machine crashed, killing the pilot, Lt. Cuddihy, well known as a Schneider Trophy pilot. A modified Bulldog, 7398, was sent out as a replacement, American serial *A-8607*, and was one of a new batch of 40 Bulldogs produced at Filton.

Of these 40, 23 were delivered to the R.A.F. in 1930, constructor's numbers 7364 to 7386, serials *K1079* to *K1101*. Nine went to No. 17 Squadron and the rest to No. 54. Numbers 7387 and 7388 were sold to the Royal Siamese Air Force. The next eight went to the Royal Australian Air Force in January 1930, powered with Jupiter VIF engines. These were C/N's 7389 to 7396, Australian serials *A12–1* to *A12–8*. Three Bulldog IIs were delivered to the Royal Swedish Air Force in August 1930, their serial numbers being *1201, 1202, 1203* (C/N's 7400 to 7402).

A third production batch of 20 aircraft was laid down and from this seven were delivered to Latvia (C/N's 7439 to 7445) in July 1930. The first five had the Jupiter VI but the other two were fitted with Gnome-Rhône 9ASB supercharged engines, the French equivalent of the Jupiter VII. The same engine was fitted to the next airframe, 7446, which was built as a second demonstrator. It was registered as G-ABBB* and finished silver overall except for the royal blue decking. The remaining 12 Bulldogs of this third batch, numbers 7447 to 7458, were sold to Estonia fitted with the French Jupiter VI engines.

THE MARK IIA

Although all the users of Bulldogs in the various air forces were completely satisfied with the aeroplane, it was inevitable that after a period in service various improvements in detail should be indicated. These were developed on the Company machine, G-ABBB and included standardising the Jupiter VIIF engine, revising wing spars and ailerons and other details and increasing the all-up weight to 3,530 lb. In this form the Bulldog was redesignated Mark IIA and Bristols

---

* This particular aeroplane is referred to later in the section dealing with special Bulldogs.

received a contract for 92 aircraft in May 1930 to the revised Specification F.11/29. Production of 100 airframes was planned for parallel lines, one for 36 complete aircraft and the other for 64 airframes less engines, although engines were fitted to the latter for half an hour's test flying. Delivery of 92 aircraft (7459–7550, serials *K1603–K1694*) was completed in a year, most of them going to Nos. 32, 54 and 111 Squadrons. The remaining eight were purchased by Sweden as a repeat order, constructor's numbers 7582 to 7589 (Swedish serials 5211 to 5218). The Swedish Bulldogs gave satisfactory service and three survivors were given by Sweden to Finland at the end of 1939 as advanced trainers.

Meanwhile the attributes of the aeroplane were still attracting foreign interest and Denmark ordered four Bulldog IIAs to their special requirements while the production mentioned above was proceeding. Airframe numbers of these were 7564 to 7567 and their original Danish serial numbers were *J-151* to *J-154*. They differed from the R.A.F. Mark IIAs with their unblown, high compression Jupiter VIFH engines, their Viet gas starters, and their Madsen machine guns, which were installed lower in the fuselage body than the Vickers guns in the British Bulldogs.

While Bulldog production at Filton was still continuing, the Air Ministry placed a further contract for 100 Mark IIAs*. Of these No. 19 Squadron received *K2155* to *K2169* and No. 41 Squadron *K2176* to *K2187*—while the rest were sent, after flight test and less engines, to stores depots. Bulldog *K2188* was retained for conversion into a dual control prototype and *K2476* to *K2495* were followed in production by *K2858* to *K2872* to the end of 1932. The two-seat *K2188* had been evaluated by the Central Flying School to their satisfaction as an advanced trainer and an order was placed for an initial 17 aircraft named Bulldog Type TM to Specification T.12/32. Increased rudder area and slight swept-back wings were incorporated to improve spin recovery. A further 38 Bulldog IIA fighters were produced at Filton for the R.A.F., serials *K2946* to *K2963* and *K3504* to *K3513*; *K3512* was modified before completion with a wide

* At this stage the airframe numbers became involved and reference should be made to the tabulation at the end.

Cockpit of Bulldog IIA. Legend on dash states: "engine revolutions normal full speed 1775. Max. permissible for not more than 5 minutes 1950".

Bulldog II prototype with lengthened fuselage, experimental engine helmets and head-rest.

track undercarriage, Dunlop disc wheels and Bendix brakes. At Martlesham the tail skid was found wanting and a castoring tail wheel was substituted, while the fin area was increased to improve directional stability. The gross weight by then was 3,660 lb. These modifications were applied retrospectively to all R.A.F. Bulldogs during 1933.

In the early nineteen thirties Bulldog Mark IIAs were the standard equipment of 10 of the 13 fighter Squadrons forming the Air Defence of Great Britain. These Home Fighter Squadrons were No. 3 (Upavon and Kenley), No. 17 (Upavon and Kenley), No. 19 (Duxford), No. 23 (Kenley and Biggin Hill), No. 29 (North Weald), No. 32 (Kenley and Biggin Hill), No. 41 (Northolt), No. 54 (Hornchurch), No. 56 (North Weald) and No. 111 (Hornchurch and Northolt). This was a small force indeed but the Bulldogs performed with great credit by day and by night in the annual Air Exercises of the Home Command of the Royal Air Force and in addition earned a popular reputation at public air shows. The coloured smoke trail formation aerobatics of Nos. 3, 19 and 54 Squadrons were especially memorable.

The final Air Ministry order for Bulldogs was for 42 two-seat trainers, *K3923* to *K3953*, *K4566* to *K4576*, the first 18 for the R.A.F. College Cranwell and Nos. 3 and 5 Flying Training Schools. The last Bulldogs built in quantity were 17 Mark IVAs for Finland with Bristol Mercury VIS.2 engines. They were the only Bulldogs to fire their guns in anger and that was in the Russo-Finnish war of late 1939. They were operated with ski undercarriages as well as with wheels and put up a gallant show in the early stages of those little-remembered hostilities. Their Finnish serial numbers were *BU59* to *BU75* and the first of these has now the distinction of being the only Bulldog surviving since the crash of the Shuttleworth Trust's Mark IIA G-ABBB (*K2227*) at the Farnborough Air Display of 1964. *BU59* rests in the museum of the Finnish Air Force at Vesivehmaa.

Mark IVA Bulldogs were the only Mercury-engined variants of the basic Bulldog/Bullpup design to be produced in any quantity. Although the Bullpup with a Mercury IIA put up a reasonable show in the F.20/27 interceptor competition at Martlesham in 1929 nothing further came of it as regards production contracts. A Mark I airframe 7399 served as a test bed for the Mercury III under the SBAC markings *R-1* and had a four blade propeller. The geared Mercury IV was tested in number 7397 airframe (serial *J9591*) later registered as G-AATR for cowling trials, including drag-reducing cylinder helmets, reverting to its Service serial marking for testing the Mercury IVA.

THE BULLDOG IIIA

Although the Mercury-powered Bulldogs failed to achieve any success comparative with that enjoyed by the Jupiter-engined types, the history of the two Mark IIIAs built is of interest.

In 1931 the improved Mercury IV engine went into production as the Mercury IVS.2 and a new Mark of Bulldog was developed to take advantage of the increased power. The rear fuselage was stiffened by increased depth at the sternpost and the gauge of the steel strip longerons was made heavier. The Bristol IA section of the upper wings was changed to the R.A.F. 34, which apart from better aerodynamic efficiency facilitated the enclosure of the wing tanks within its biconvex profile. Pilot's view was improved by reducing the lower wing chord by seven inches, and other improvements included the fitting of a short-chord Townend ring around the engine and a new exhaust collector ring of low back pressure. This effort to improve performance with the Mercury IVS.2 raised the speed at 15,000 feet from 175 m.p.h. for the Mark IIA to 208 m.p.h. for the Mark IIIA, as this variant was identified.

The private venture Mark IIIA with R.A.F. roundels and the S.B.A.C. identification *R-5* was flown by R.A.F. pilots in 1932 in extended trials against the Gloster SS19B (production name Gauntlet) to decide on a successor to the Bulldog IIA as a

Line-up of Swedish Bulldog IIAs, c/ns 7582 to 7589, May 1931. Serials 5211–5218.

Left: *Estonian Bulldog II, August 1930. Twelve delivered c/ns 7447 to 7458.* Right: *Latvian Bulldog, c/n 7439, with Jupiter VI. Delivered July 1930.*

Left: *Bulldog IIA, Danish Air Force. Note gun blister under cockpit and position of trough (0·300 Madsen m/gs).* Right: *Finnish Bulldog IVA, BU59, Mercury VIS.2 engine, similar to R-7, page 66.*

Siamese Bulldog II, delivered January 1930, c/ns 7387/8. Right: *Bulldog Type 105J, first machine built by Nakajima for Japanese Navy (J.S.S.F.) with helmets on Jupiter VII engine.*

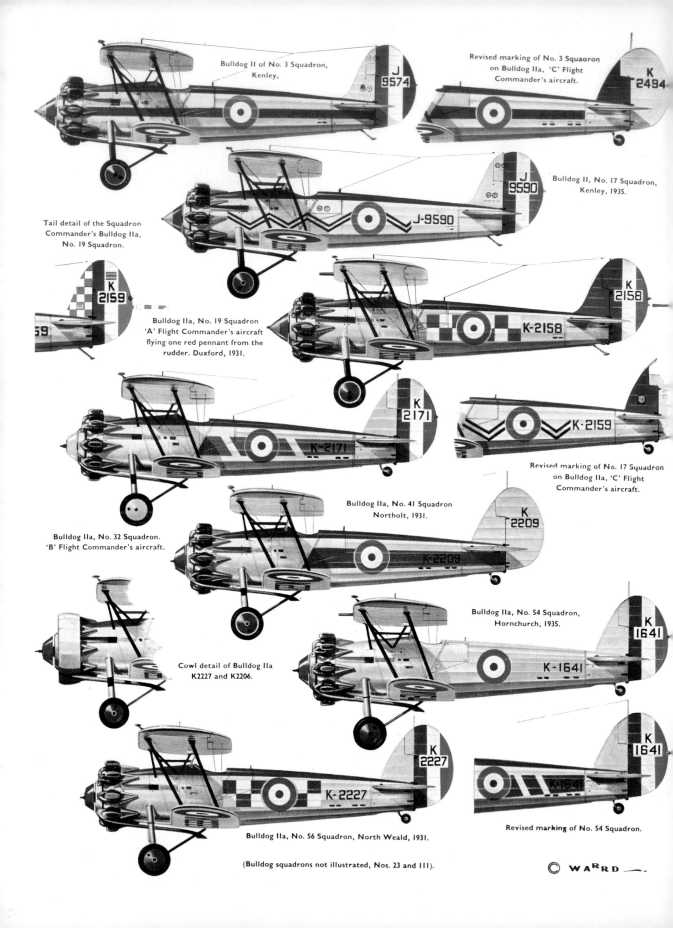

Bulldog II of No. 3 Squadron, Kenley,

Revised marking of No. 3 Squadron on Bulldog IIa, 'C' Flight Commander's aircraft.

Bulldog II, No. 17 Squadron, Kenley, 1935.

Tail detail of the Squadron Commander's Bulldog IIa, No. 19 Squadron.

Bulldog IIa, No. 19 Squadron 'A' Flight Commander's aircraft flying one red pennant from the rudder. Duxford, 1931.

Revised marking of No. 17 Squadron on Bulldog IIa, 'C' Flight Commander's aircraft.

Bulldog IIa, No. 32 Squadron. 'B' Flight Commander's aircraft.

Bulldog IIa, No. 41 Squadron Northolt, 1931.

Cowl detail of Bulldog IIa K2227 and K2206.

Bulldog IIa, No. 54 Squadron, Hornchurch, 1935.

Bulldog IIa, No. 56 Squadron, North Weald, 1931.

Revised marking of No. 54 Squadron.

(Bulldog squadrons not illustrated, Nos. 23 and 111).

© WARRD

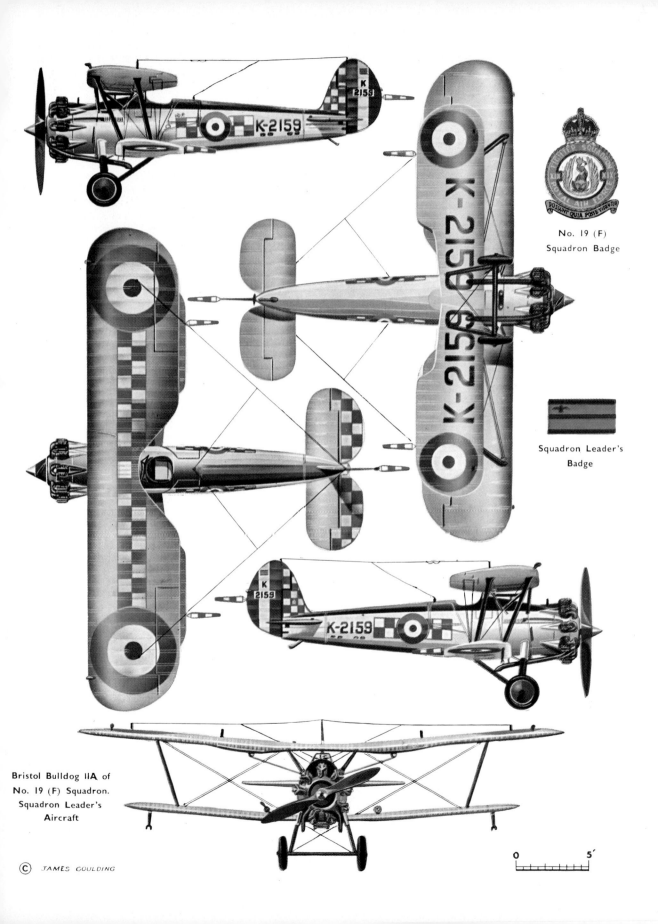

No. 19 (F)
Squadron Badge

Squadron Leader's
Badge

Bristol Bulldog IIA of
No. 19 (F) Squadron.
Squadron Leader's
Aircraft

© JAMES GOULDING

0   5'

day-and-night fighter. The Gauntlet was superior in performance, largely as a result of Harry Folland's extreme attention to reduction of drag in detail design and it received the contract.

A second Bulldog IIIA was built for the Paris Show in 1932 and eventually was converted to a new standard, the Mark IVA, to meet the F.7/30 Specification, in which it had to compete with its Gloster rival, the Gladiator, which had 26 m.p.h. advantage in speed. Various engine trials were carried out with this Bulldog and ultimately it finished up as a trial horse for the Hamilton three-blade variable pitch metal propeller, and was equipped with a short-chord N.A.C.A. cowling.

Among the many variants and conversions of the Bulldog, mention must be made of the high altitude Mark I with high aspect ratio wings of 50 feet span.

It was intended for attempts on the height and climb-to-height records in 1927 which were frustrated by a successful Italian attack by Donati. One airframe, 7744 (K4189) was constructed in stainless steel which proved inferior to the standard high tensile steel and was abandoned.

The two Japanese variants labelled J.S.S.F. (Japanese Single Seat Fighter) were built by Nakajima in Tokyo, who were manufacturing Bristol Jupiter engines under licence. Nothing came of this attempt to acquire business except that Bulldog features appeared in subsequent Nakajima designs.

Bulldogs remained the foremost front line fighters in the R.A.F. until 1937 when they were replaced by Gladiators. One of their final services was when No. 3 Squadron's Bulldogs were sent to the Sudan during the Abyssinian crisis to act as watchdogs!

Acknowledgment is made to Chris Barnes and the wealth of material from his book Bristol Aircraft since 1910 (*Putnam*).

Type	102	105A Bulldog I	Bulldog (High Altitude)	105A Bulldog II	105A Bulldog IIA
Power plant	Jupiter VI	Jupiter VII	Jupiter VII	Jupiter VII	Jupiter VIIF
Span	30 ft.	34 ft.	50 ft.	33 ft. 10 in.	33 ft. 10 in.
Length	21 ft. 7 in.	23 ft.	24 ft.	25 ft. 2 in.	25 ft. 2 in.
Height	8 ft. 8 in.	8 ft. 9 in.	10 ft.	8 ft. 9 in.	8 ft. 9 in.
Wing area	290 sq. ft.	307 sq. ft.	480 sq. ft.	307 sq. ft.	307 sq. ft.
Empty weight	1,815 lb.	1,987 lb.	2,000 lb.	2,200 lb.	2,222 lb.
All-up weight	2,720 lb.	3,250 lb.	3,000 lb.	3,490 lb.	3,530 lb. (later 3,660 lb.)
Max. speed	—	173 m.p.h.	150 m.p.h.	178 m.p.h.	178 m.p.h.
Service ceiling	—	27,000 ft.	40,000 ft.	29,300 ft.	29,300 ft.
Accommodation	1	1	1	1	1
Production	nil	2	(1)	92	268
Constructor's Airframe Nos. ...	nil	7155 7267	(7155)	7235 7322–7347 7353–7358 7364–7403 7439–7445 7447–7458	7446 7459–7550 7564–7567 7582–7589 7691–7710 7713–7726 7744 7746–7773
Serial Nos.	—	—	—	J9480 J9567–J9591 K1079–K1101 America A–8607 R.A.A.F. A12-1–A12-8 Sweden 1201–1203	K1603–K1694 K2135–K2234 K2155–K2169 K2176–K2187 K2475 K2476–K2495 K2858–K2872 K2946–K2963 K3504–K3513 K4189 Sweden 5211–5218 Denmark J-151–J-154

Type	105A Bulldog IIIA	105A Bulldog IV	105A Bulldog IVA	105J J.S.S.F.	Bulldog TM
Power plant	Mercury IVA	Mercury IVS 2	Mercury VIS 2	Nakajima Jupiter VII	Jupiter VIF H
Span	33 ft. 8 in.	33 ft. 8 in.	33 ft. 8 in.	33 ft. 8 in.	34 ft. 2 in.
Length	25 ft. 4 in.	25 ft. 4 in.	25 ft. 4 in.	25 ft. 6 in.	25 ft. 3 in.
Height	9 ft 1 in.	9 ft. 1 in.	9 ft. 1 in.	9 ft.	8 ft. 9 in.
Wing area	294 sq. ft.	294 sq. ft.	294 sq. ft.	300 sq. ft.	309 sq. ft.
Empty weight	2,800 lb.	2,810 lb.	2,690 lb.	2,400 lb.	2,200 lb.
All-up weight	4,000 lb.	4,100 lb.	4,010 lb.	3,350 lb.	3,300 lb.
Max. speed	208 m.p.h.	218 m.p.h.	224 m.p.h.	196 m.p.h.	168 m.p.h.
Service ceiling	31,000 ft.	31,700 ft.	33,400 ft.	30,000 ft.	28,000 ft.
Accommodation	1	1	1	1	2
Production	2	(1)	18	2	59
Constructor's Airframe Nos. ...	7560 7745	(7745)	7808 7810–7826	—	7727–7743 7777–7807 7828–7837
Serial Nos.	—	—	Finland K4292 BU59–BU75	—	K2188 K3170–K3186 K3923–K3953 K4566–K4576

The Republic P-47D Thunderbolt

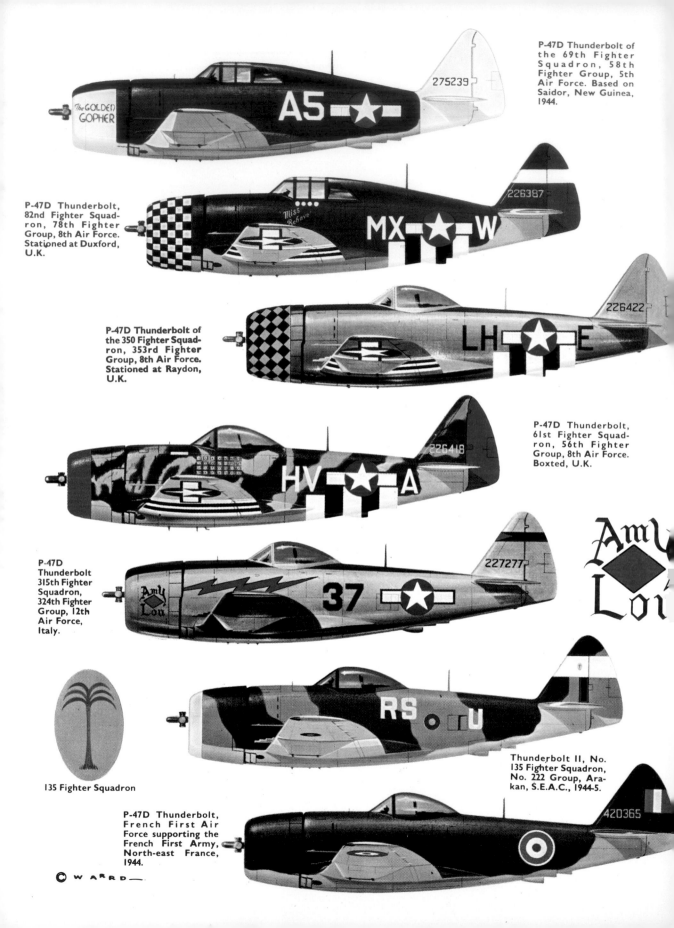

P-47D Thunderbolt of the 69th Fighter Squadron, 58th Fighter Group, 5th Air Force. Based on Saidor, New Guinea, 1944.

P-47D Thunderbolt, 82nd Fighter Squadron, 78th Fighter Group, 8th Air Force. Stationed at Duxford, U.K.

P-47D Thunderbolt of the 350 Fighter Squadron, 353rd Fighter Group, 8th Air Force. Stationed at Raydon, U.K.

P-47D Thunderbolt, 61st Fighter Squadron, 56th Fighter Group, 8th Air Force. Boxted, U.K.

P-47D Thunderbolt 315th Fighter Squadron, 324th Fighter Group, 12th Air Force, Italy.

135 Fighter Squadron

Thunderbolt II, No. 135 Fighter Squadron, No. 222 Group, Arakan, S.E.A.C., 1944-5.

P-47D Thunderbolt, French First Air Force supporting the French First Army, North-east France, 1944.

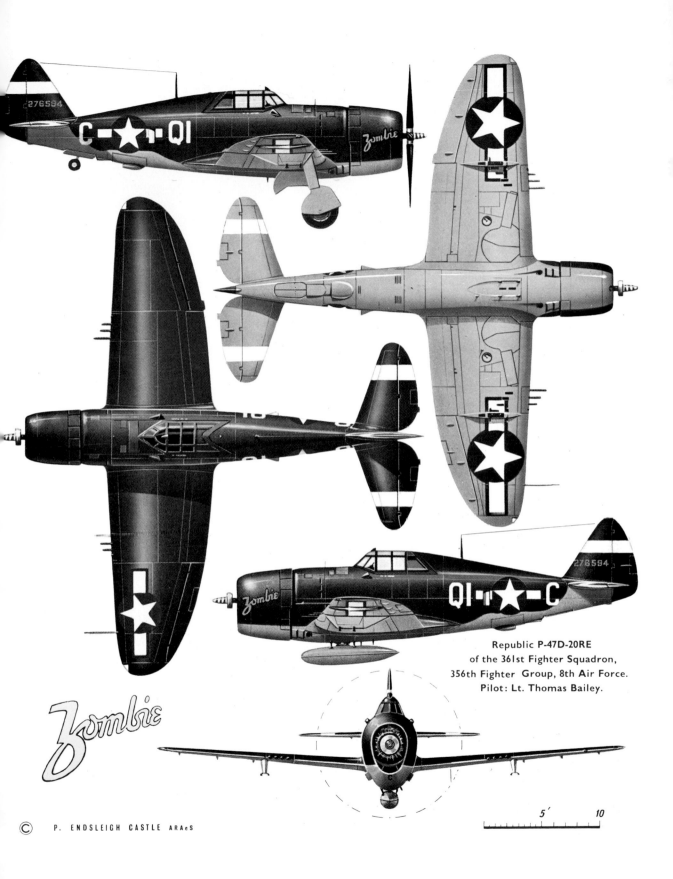

Republic P-47D-20RE
of the 361st Fighter Squadron,
356th Fighter Group, 8th Air Force.
Pilot: Lt. Thomas Bailey.

276594

C-★-QI

QI-★-C

Zombie

5′   10

© P. ENDSLEIGH CASTLE ARAeS

The Republic P-47D Thunderbolt

by Edward Shacklady

Thunderbolt Mark II (P-47D-25) of No. 135 Squadron, Royal Air Force, in Arakan, Burma, 1944. Serialled HD298, code U-RS, it was one of the first batch of 120 aircraft delivered. (Photo: Imperial War Museum)

BEAUTY or beast, that was the Republic P-47 Thunderbolt, and there were no two ways about it. Pilots either loved or loathed designer Alexander Kartveli's corpulent fighter. And yet this aeroplane, conceived during the opening months of World War II, was to become one of the most outstanding fighters of its generation and a legend in its own time. A legend that was written around the exploits of the numerous "Ace" pilots who flew it, men like Lt.-Col. F. S. Gabreski, whose total of thirty-one confirmed victories put him at the head of the high scoring list, and Captain R. S. Johnson (28) and Colonel H. Zemke (20).

Like all new and untried aeroplanes the Thunderbolt was plagued with teething troubles and it was a constant battle to overcome them. The prototype XP-47 suffered from many deficiencies including excessive control loads at high altitude, and the first production batches of the P-47B and 47C developed faults that were patiently eradicated.

By the time the P-47D began leaving the production lines most of the major snags had been overcome, and this variant was eventually to be produced in greater numbers than any other type. It represented about 80 per cent of the entire P-47 production programme with a grand total of 12,602 machines built.

The U.S.A.A.F. first ordered the P-47D in October 1941, and despite its "D" suffix it differed little from its immediate predecessor the P-47C-5-RE. But as production mounted the modifications multiplied so rapidly that the late model "D"s were a different breed of aeroplane.

Initial sub-batches amounting to a total of 3,962 aircraft, ran from the P-47D-1-RE to the P-47D-22-RE and were produced at Republic's Farmingdale, New York, factory. Demand for the fighter was so great that a second production line was started at a new Republic facility at Evansville, Indiana, where a total of 1,461 P-47D-2-RA to P-47D-23-RAs were built.

The Curtiss Aircraft Corporation was brought into the Thunderbolt programme and they constructed just 354 P-47G-1-CU to P-47G-15-CU machines, these being identical to the Republic aircraft.

These 5,777 aeroplanes were fitted with the original metal-framed sliding cockpit canopy as fitted to the early Thunderbolts, and all-round view was extremely restricted. The U.S.A.A.F. had been conducting experiments with the new clear-view hood, then standard on the Hawker Typhoon, and had actually fitted one of these to a P-47D, redesignating the aircraft XP-47K. Tests proved that the hood provided a 360-degree view for pilots and the modification, together with a cut-down rear fuselage, was introduced on the three production lines.

The first sub-batches to feature all modifications were the P-47D-25-REs produced at Farmingdale, and the P-47D-26-RAs built at Evansville. Existing P-47s serving with the U.S.A.A.F. in Great Britain were retro-fitted with the new hood at the U.S. Air Service Command bases with canopies supplied by the British aircraft industry. All subsequent Thunderbolts featured the clear-view hood.

Early production P-47D-11-RE showing old razor-back fuselage and metal-framed cockpit canopy. Built at Farmingdale, 6th production batch. (Republic Aviation photo)

P-47D with R.A.F. Malcolm hood over Europe. Combination of this hood and airframe was extremely rare. (U.S.A.F. photograph)

P-47D-25-RE of the 1° Grupo de Aviacao de Caca of the Brazilian Air Force, Italy, 1942. Note three-tier rocket tubes. Aircraft built by Republic, Farmingdale, 15th production batch.

The P-47D-6-RE to P-47D-11-RE and the P-47G-10-CU to P-47G-15-CU had ventral bomb shackles which were stressed to carry one 500 lb. bomb. Later series had a strengthened wing and shackle to accommodate three 500 lb. bombs, or a combination of bombs or fuel tanks. With a full ordnance load the number of rounds of ammunition for the six Browning machine-guns was reduced from a maximum of 425 to 267 r.p.g.

Later production batches from the P-47D-20-RE onwards were fitted with the universal wing, an idea copied from the standard British practice of producing a wing that could carry a multitude of loads. A single Pratt & Whitney R-2800-59 or -63 air-cooled piston engine incorporating water-methanol injection was standard. The water injection added several hundred horse-power for emergency use and to absorb this increase a four, paddle-bladed airscrew of 13 ft diameter was installed. It added 400 feet per minute to the climb, but pilots learned to be wary of such a large airscrew for when the Thunderbolt was taking-off or landing with the tail wheel up, the blade tips were a scant six inches off the ground. Other improvements included a jettisonable cockpit canopy, operated by pulling a ring, the slipstream then pulling it clear, a flat, bullet proof windscreen and increased fuel capacity that raised the radius of action to 637 miles.

The last production batches of this range were fitted with strengthened fuselage shackles capable of supporting a 91 gallon fuel tank, and the bomb load was increased from two 500 lb. to two 1,000 lb. and one 500 lb. bomb. Three auxiliary fuel tanks could be carried on the same fittings, and various combinations of bombs and tanks could be carried to suit tactical requirements.

Like the P-51D fitted with the clear-view canopy the P-47D suffered from some loss of lateral control due to decreased keel area resulting from the cut-down rear fuselage, and all Thunderbolts from the P-47D-27-RE batch onwards were fitted with a dorsal fin strake. Improvements in design also produced the underwing, zero-length launching stubs for rocket projectiles, that had been previously stored in bazooka-type tubes in groups of three.

Farmingdale produced a total of 2,547 P-47Ds fitted with the clear-view canopy, and Evansville built 4,632. The former facility sent an enormous total of 6,509 P-47Ds into battle, while the latter was runner-up with 6,093. This enormous rate of production brought the cost of the basic Thunderbolt down drastically, the average price of each aircraft reached a low of 83,001 dollars by the time production ceased.

77

Eighth Air Force P-47D-25-RE, 15th production batch, Republic, Farmingdale, England, 1943. (Photo: via Roger Freeman)

Thunderbolt II, P-47D-25, of No. 81 Squadron, R.A.F., at Batavia, 1945. No. 81 was re-formed from No. 123 Squadron in June 1945.

R.A.F. THUNDERBOLTS

The P-47D was the first version of the Thunderbolt to serve with the U.S.A.A.F. in the Pacific, where it was delivered to the 248th Fighter Squadron in quantity and operated from Brisbane, Australia, as a long range escort fighter.

Next to the U.S.A.A.F. the largest operator of the P-47D was the Royal Air Force, to whom a total of 830 were delivered. In R.A.F. service the 47D was designated the Thunderbolt Mark I and Mark II. The former, of which 240 were delivered, had the old metal-framed cockpit canopy, while the latter (590 aircraft) featured the clear-view bubble canopy.

Two batches of Mark Is were delivered and serials ran from *FL731* to *FL850* (120 aircraft) and *HB962* to *HD181* (120 aircraft). The Mark Is were evaluated in Europe, but shipped immediately afterwards to South East Asia Command, where they were used against the Japanese.

The Thunderbolt Mark II was the equivalent of the P-47D-25 and four main batches were delivered. Serials ran as follows: *HD182* to *HD301* (120 aircraft), *KJ128* to *KJ367* (240 aircraft), *KL168* to *KL347* (180 aircraft), *KL838* to *KL887* (50 aircraft). A few aircraft of the last two batches had the dorsal fin strake.

One of the first R.A.F. squadrons to operate the Thunderbolt was No. 5, based in Burma and previously operating Mohawks and Hurricanes. They flew the cab-rank patrol under the direction of visual ground control posts, and with their three 5,050 lb. bombs and eight machine-guns caused tremendous damage amongst Japanese troops and supply lines. R.A.F. squadrons operating the P-47D were:—Mark I, Nos. 5, 34, 113, 123, 135, 146. Mark II, Nos. 5, 30, 34, 42, 60, 79, 81, 113, 123, 131, 134, 135, 258, 261 and 615. Soon after VJ-Day they disappeared from R.A.F. squadrons which were either disbanded or re-equipped with British aircraft.

Despite its exclusive use with the R.A.F. in the Far

Another 8th Air Force P-47D-22-RE, photographed during an attack on Berlin, 7th May 1944. Produced at Farmingdale, 14th batch.

Thunderbolt P-47D-26-RA, built at Evansville, 13th production batch.   (Photo: Republic Aviation Corp.)

East, the Thunderbolt was a familiar sight in England. They had been regularly escorting the Boeing Fortress and Convair Liberators of the 8th Air Force on daylight raids over Europe. Their first operations began in May 1943, and from March 1944 they carried auxiliary fuel tanks which extended their range, and enabled them to accompany the bombers as far as Berlin.

At about the same period they started operations with the 9th Air Force, escorting Marauders and Havocs, and engaging independently in train busting and ground attack sorties.

CAMOUFLAGE MARKINGS

All fighters and ground attack aircraft in Burma and the Far East, including Thunderbolts, had a consistent scheme, part of which was an aid to identification. A grey and green scheme on upper surfaces with sky undersurfaces was usual, with S.E.A.C. roundels of only eighteen inches in diameter in all positions, with a 24 inch by 27 inch light and dark blue fin flash. Eighteen-inch wide white bands were marked around the chord of mainplanes, just inboard of the ailerons, similar in style to those on Allied fighters, etc., taking part in the Normandy fighting.

The white band was repeated centrally around each tailplane. Finally, another eighteen-inch white band

P-47D-30-RE of the 18th and final batch built by Republic at Farmingdale. Operated with 353rd Fighter Squadron, 354th Fighter Group, 9th Air Force. (Photo: Imperial War Museum)

P-47D-27-RE of the 315th Fighter Squadron, 324th Fighter Group, 12th Air Force, Italy. (Photo: G. J. Letzer, via R. Ward)

was applied around the rudder, just above the fin flash. Unit code letters, eighteen-inches high, with individual letters, were applied fore and aft of the

Early production P-47D of the 8th Air Force in United Kingdom. Lacks wing guns.

Curtiss-built two-seat TP-47G trainer. Began life as a P-47G-15-CU of the 5th and final batch built at Buffalo. Converted to trainer configuration during 1942.
(Photo: Richard Ward)

roundel. Some squadrons, an example being No. 30, had their white bands completely encircling the wing, with no cut-out for control surfaces. No. 30 had a small, green, palm tree painted on the white band above the fin flash. This was the unit badge. Other squadrons had a white rim added to the engine cowling.

FOREIGN THUNDERBOLTS

A large number of other Air Forces operated the P-47D Thunderbolt and in alphabetical order they were:

Bolivia. As a signatory of the Rio Pact of Mutual Defence in 1947 Bolivia received a number of P-47Ds from the U.S.A., and as late as 1964 a few were still in service.

Brazil. It was in January 1944 that a band of pilots and ground staff reached America to undergo advanced and operational training before going on to Europe to serve with the U.S.A.A.F. After training they were equipped with P-47Ds and the squadron under the command of Lt.-Col. Nero Moura arrived in Italy on October 6th the same year. Attached to the U.S. 12th Air Force the squadron went into action for the first time on November 11th. Before the war ended the Brazilian Air Force received a total of 88 P-47Ds. An additional twenty-five were delivered during 1955 and they became standard equipment of two fighter-

P-47D-40-RA at Wright Field, 1945. Dayglow panel warns light aircraft to clear field during testing. (Photo: Richard Ward)

Below: *P-47D-28-RA of 405th Fighter Squadron, 371st Fighter Group, 70th Fighter Wing, 9th Air Force.* (R. Ward)

bomber groups, each group consisting of three squadrons of twelve aircraft. A small number of P-47Ds were still in service in late 1960s as fighter-bombers.

P-47D-40-RA, Republic-built (Evansville, 18th and final batch). Photographed during 1945. (Photo: Richard Ward)

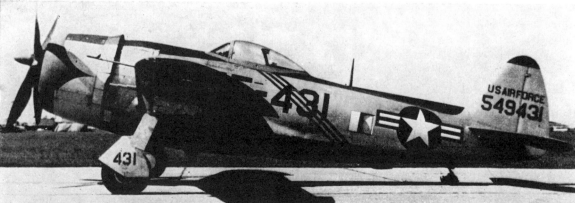

Chile. The first P-47Ds entered service with the Air Force during the late 1940s, and a further quantity was acquired in 1952. The Thunderbolts served with one combat group as front line aircraft as late as 1958.

China. The 11th Fighter Group of three squadrons was equipped with the P-47D in 1947, but after General Chiang Kai-shek's government was overthrown in 1949 only a small number was evacuated to the island of Formosa. *Nationalist China* took delivery of a number of P-47Ds during 1949 and they formed the equipment of two fighter-bomber wings. One of the wings exchanged their Thunderbolts for Sabres in 1954, and by 1958/59 only a small number remained in service.

Colombia. The Colombian Air Force acquired P-47Ds (or F-47Ds) in 1947, enough to equip one squadron. Eight were still flying as late as 1958.

Dominica. A number of F-47D Thunderbolts were acquired during 1948 and formed part of a mixed squadron of Vampires. They were being phased out of service in the late 1960s.

Ecuador. A number of surplus F-47Ds were delivered in 1947 and one squadron of this type was still in service in 1964.

France. A total of 446 P-47Ds was supplied to the Free French Forces during the war and by VE-Day they formed the equipment of two *Escadres de Chasse*. De Havilland Vampires began replacing the 47Ds during 1951 and the piston-engined fighters were transferred to Algeria, where they were used against the nationalist forces there. They were phased out of service in 1960.

Honduras. The first P-47Ds were delivered to the Honduran Military Air Arm in the early 1950s and a small number were still being flown as late as 1964.

Iran. In May, 1948, a group of Air Force officers went to the United States to undergo training, and on their return to their own country formed the basis of seven fighter/fighter bomber squadrons equipped with the F-47D Thunderbolt. These were being phased out in the late 1950s by modern jet fighters.

Early *P-47D-20RA showing three-tier 'bazooka-type' rocket tubes and folding fin rockets.* (Republic Aviation photo)

Mexico. Early in 1945 the 201st Fighter Squadron of the Mexican Air Force had completed its training, and was due to go overseas to serve with the American Forces in the South West Pacific. The squadron and their P-47Ds never went into action for Japan capitulated. Of the original twenty-five P-47Ds only a handful remain, and they are no longer operational.

Nicaragua. Enough P-47s were delivered to equip one fighter-bomber squadron in 1947, and they were still in service in 1960.

Peru. Twenty P-47Ds were supplied to Peru in 1947, but by 1955 they were relegated to second-line duties with the arrival of Sabre jet fighters. Two squadrons of F-47Ds were still operational in 1957, but these were being disbanded in 1964.

Turkey. In 1948 the U.S.A.F. began reconstruction of the Turkish Air Force under the military aid programme and among the first aircraft to equip the new squadrons were a number of F-47D Thunderbolts. By 1952 they were being phased out in favour of the first jet fighters.

Thunderbolts, P-47D-22 and 27-REs at Boxted, Colchester, U.K. "Miss Behave" (2nd from foreground) of 82nd Fighter Squadron, 78th Fighter Group, 8th Air Force.

P-47D-15-RE of the 353rd Fighter Group in D-Day markings, "Arkansas Traveller".　　　(Photo: Roger Freeman)

Venezuela. Republic F-47Ds arrived to equip the squadrons of the V.A.F. on the signing of the Rio Pact. They were replaced by the modern jet in 1957.

Yugoslavia. In 1951 Yugoslavia signed the Mutual Assistance Pact with the Western Powers, and among the first aircraft supplied were 150 F-47D Thunderbolts. By 1957 they had been relegated to the training rôle as the first jet fighters began to enter service.

Russia was allocated 203 P-47D-22-REs and 27-REs during the war under Lend-Lease agreements, but only 196 reached their destination.

THE P-47D DESCRIBED

Single-seat, long-range fighter/fighter-bomber. Low-wing cantilever monoplane with Republic S-3 section. Aspect ratio 5·61, incidence plus one degree. Dihedral (upper surface) 4 degrees. Wing was an all-metal structure built up around two main and one auxiliary spars and built in two main sections. Main spars of milled steel cap strips of "T" section with deep stiffening flanges and three webs. Lateral stringers were of "L" section to which was flush-riveted the light alloy stressed skin.

Fuselage was an all-metal, semi-monocoque stressed skin structure composed of eleven bulkheads and nine transverse frames of pressed channel section aluminium alloy with stringer cutouts, the latter supporting the light alloy skin. The two wing supporting bulkheads in the lower half of the forward fuselage were built into the main longerons.

Tail assembly was a full cantilever structure with all surfaces, including control, metal-covered. The complete assembly was bolted to the aft fuselage.

POWERPLANT

One Pratt & Whitney R-2800-21 or 59 Double Wasp, 18-cylinder, air-cooled, supercharged engine rated at 1,625 h.p. at 30,000 feet, with 2,300 h.p. available at take-off. Water injection boosted power to 2,535 h.p. in an emergency and air speed was increased to 437 at 30,000 feet. The water-alcohol tank held 15 gallons and was standardised from the D-5 onwards. From the D-5 to D-10 the pilot controlled water flow, but the procedure was automatic on the D-12 and subsequent models. Water injection in-

creased the maximum power rating by approximately 15 per cent and lasted for 15 minutes. A General Electric supercharger was located in the rear fuselage. The Double Wasp was fed from two self-sealing and armoured fuel tanks in the fuselage. Main tank (270

P-47D-20-RE of the 361st Fighter Squadron, 356 Fighter Group, 8th Air Force.　　　(Photo: Richard Ward)

Below: *P-47G-1-CU, built by Curtiss.* (Photo: Richard Ward)

P-47D-40-RA of the Maryland Air National Guard. Pilot, Major "Bob" Tyler, flew the aircraft with one prop blade white to get the stroboscope effect. To spectators it appeared that the blade remained static. (Photo: Major Robert Tyler, U.S.A.F.)

P-47D-30-RA, Republic, Evansville, 16th production batch.
(Photo: Richard Ward)

P-47D-28-RE of the 78th Fighter Group, Duxford, August, 1944.
(Photo: U.S.A.F.)

U.S. gallons) was located aft of fireproof bulkhead and the auxiliary tank (100 U.S. gallons) beneath the pilot's seat. The P-47 burned between 90 and 130 gallons per hour at normal cruising speeds and consumed about 25 gallons during warm-up and take-off. When full power was applied during combat consumption reached 275 gallons, while application of war emergency power raised this to 315 gallons. A fuel warning light went on in the cockpit when approximately 40 gallons remained.

ARMAMENT

Six or eight 0·5-in. calibre Browning machine guns,

three or four in each wing leading edge outboard of landing gear. Ammunition supply was 300 r.p.m., but this could be increased to 425 r.p.g. A combat cine camera was carried in port wing root. Maximum bomb load was two 1,000 lb. bombs under wings and one 500 lb. bomb under fuselage. Jettisonable rocket tubes in clusters of three under each wing, or ten 5-in. high-velocity rockets on stub fittings.

OTHER VARIANTS

Three "D" airframes were extensively modified by the installation of a 2,100 h.p. Pratt & Whitney R-2800-57 engine and dive brakes under the wing. As

P-47D-27-RE of the 15th Air Force, Italy.

(Photo: G. J. Letzer, via Richard Ward)

P-47D-30-RE, "Torrid Tessie", of the 15th Air Force, Italy. Black on natural metal.

(Photo: Imperial War Museum)

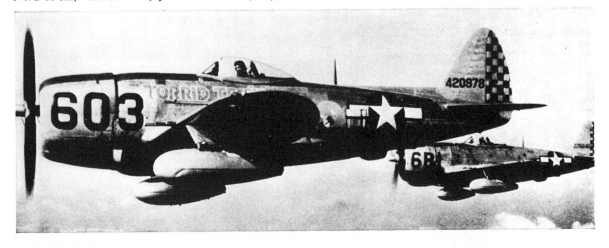

Probably the last Thunderbolt extant in the United States today is this P-47G-15-CU, built by Curtiss, at their Buffalo plant. Aircraft of the fifth and final batch. Sold to Republic during 1961 it carried the civil marks N5087V. (Air Force Museum photo)

such they carried the designation YP-47M and were among the fastest Thunderbolts ever built. During the latter half of 1944 they were shipped to Europe for use against the German V-1 flying bomb missile. 130 YP-47Ms were built.

Two of the Curtiss-built P-47Ds were converted into two-seat tandem trainers. One fuselage fuel tank was removed and an extra cockpit installed. Known as the TP-47G the type retained the eight-gun armament of the standard single seater.

PRODUCTION BATCHES

P-47D-RE, Republic, Farmingdale, New York.
47D-1-RE *42-7853 to 7957,* 47D-2-RE *42-7258 to 8402,* 47D-5-RE *42-8403 to 8701,* 47D-6-RE *42-74615 to 74964,* 47D-10-RE *42-74965 to 75214,* 47D-11-RE *42-75215 to 75614,* 47D-15-RE *42-75615 to 75864, 42-76119 to 76364,* 47D-16-RE *42-75865 to 76118,* 47D-20-RE *42-25274 to 25322, 42-76365 to 76613,* 47D-21-RE *42-25323 to 25466, 42-25467 to 25538,* 47D-22-RE *42-25539 to 26388,* 47D-25-RE *42-26389 to 26773,* 47D-27-RE *42-26774 to 27384* 47D-28-RE *44-19558 to 20307,* 47D-30-RE *44-20308 to 21107.*

P-47D-RA, Evansville, Indiana.
47D-RA *42-22250 to 22253, 42-22254 to 22363* 47D-2-RA *42-22364*

to 22563, 47D-3-RA *42-22564 to 22663,* 47D-4-RA *42-22664 to 22863,* 47D-11-RA *42-22864 to 23113,* 47D-15-RA *42-23143 to 23299,* 47D-16-RA *42-23114 to 23142,* 47D-20-RA *43-25254 to 25440,* 47D-21-RA *43-25441 to 25664,* 47D-23-RA *43-25665 to 25753, 43-27389 to 28188,* 47D-26-RA *42-28189 to 28438, 42-8439 to 29466,* 47D-30-RA *44-32668 to 33867, 44-89684 to 90483,* 47D-40-RA *44-90284 to 90483, 44-49090 to 49554.*

P-47G-CU Curtiss, Buffalo, New York.
47G-1-CU *42-24920 to 24939, 42-24940 to 24979, 42-24980 to 25039,* 47G-10-CU *42-25040 to 25119,* 47G-15-CU *42-25120 to 42-25273.*

Specification

RE-Republic Farmingdale	DIMENSIONS				PERFORMANCE					
RA-Republic Evansville					M.P.H. at			Climb Rate ft. min.		
	Span	Length	Height	Wing Area	5,000 ft.	20,000 ft.	30,000 ft.	5,000 ft.	20,000 ft.	Service Ceiling
P-47D-22-RE	40 ft. 9⅜ in.	36 ft. 1⅜ in.	14 ft. 7 in.	300 sq. ft.	353	406	433	2,751	2,140	40,000 ft.
P-47D-25-RE	40 ft. 9 in.	36 ft. 1 in.	14 ft. 2 in.	—	350	—	429	2,780	2,300	—
P-47D-35-RA	40 ft. 9⅜in.	36 ft. 1⅜ in.	14 ft. 7 in.	—	363	415	426	3,120	2,650	42,000 ft.

RE-Republic Farmingdale	WEIGHTS, lbs.			ENGINE		ARMAMENT
RA-Republic Evansville	Empty	Normal Loaded	Maximum Loaded	One Pratt & Whitney	Horse-power	P-47-22. Six or eight 0·5 in. Browning M/Gs with 267 or 425 r.p.g. plus one 500 lb. bomb.
P-47D-22-RE	9,900	13,500	15,000	2800-21	2,300	P-47-25. Six or eight 0·5 in. Browning M/Gs with 267 or 425 r.p.g. plus two 1,000 lb. bombs or ten 5 in. rockets.
P-47D-25-RE	10,700	14,600	17,500	2800-59	2,535	
P-47D-35-RA	10,000	14,000	—	—	—	P-47-35. As for 47-25.

The North American
P-51D Mustang

The North American P-51D Mustang

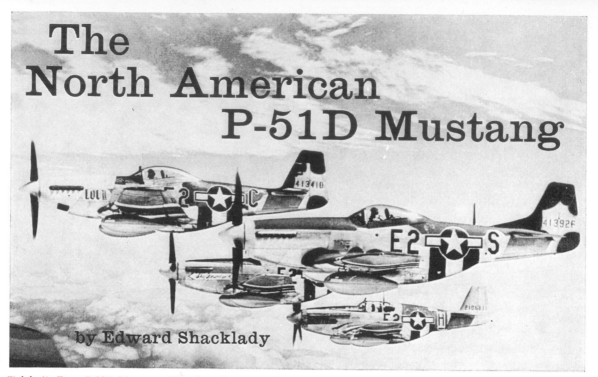

by Edward Shacklady

Eighth Air Force P-51D Mustangs. Note three distinct models—413410 (D-5) an early "D" without fin strake, 413926 (D-25) has strake while 2106811 is a 51B-15 with original canopy.
(Photo: Roger Freeman)

OF all the piston-engined fighters that took part in the great conflict that was World War II, perhaps the finest was the North American P-51 Mustang. Pilots swore by this sleek machine that looked right and whose performance outshone the majority of its contemporaries. That the basic design was fundamentally right can be seen in how the speed increased from the prototype's 382 m.p.h. to the final model's, the P-51H, 487 m.p.h. without too radical a change in outline or construction.

The story of how the Mustang was designed and constructed in one hundred days need not be told again in these columns, but it is not quite the whole truth, as the old story goes, that the Mustang was almost an inspiration of its designer James H. "Dutch" Kindelberger. The idea behind the Mustang design began, almost unintentionally, when Kindelberger went to Europe in 1938 for a tour of the aircraft industries of Great Britain and Germany. What he saw led him to sketch some plans of a fighter he thought would be able to better any other machine, should the United States become embroiled in the war that was imminent between Germany and the rest of Europe. He returned to his home state of California, but still maintained his oversea contacts.

The immortal P-51 Mustang was born two years later, and the most widely used variant was the P-51D. A grand total of 7,956 aircraft was constructed before the last machine rolled off the line.

The immediate predecessor of the 51D was the P-51C of which 1,750 examples were built. The "C" was an excellent aircraft but it lacked sufficient rearward view, and in spite of a number of them being fitted with the R.A.F.'s famed Malcolm cockpit canopy the U.S.A.A.F. decided that a new hood was required. At

about this period the first Hawker Typhoons were flying fitted with the "tear-drop" transparent canopy which afforded a 360-degree view. Two P-51B-10s were taken from the Inglewood production line and drastically modified in order to fit the Typhoon-type hoods. The North American type number for this hybrid fighter was NA-106, and in order to test the P-51D configuration complete with new hood both 51Bs were brought up to 51D standards, the modifications including a cut-down fuselage aft of the cockpit, the new "blown" canopy, provision for six wing-mounted 0·5-in. machine-guns and 1,800 rounds of ammunition.

The first fully equipped P-51D appeared in the latter half of 1944 with all the new innovations, which were introduced to the production line, and the first four aircraft, which had been built before the modifications were introduced, were retro-fitted at a later stage.

A total of 6,502 P-51D-5-NA to 25-NA were built at North America's Inglewood factory and 1,454 P-51D-5-NT to 20-NT at Dallas. Production models

The P-51D Mustang was a clean aeroplane, but it is seen here with everything down as it completes landing pattern.
(Photo: Richard Ward)

P-51D-5 of No. 55 Squadron, 67th Wing, 20th Group, U.S.A.F., taxiing out at Kingscliffe for an escort mission. Note girl motif on KI-S. (Photo: Richard Ward)

soon began to stream into U.S.A.A.F. squadrons in the Pacific, and it is interesting to record that the new 51D was the first American fighter to take part in strikes on the Japanese homeland. When the 51D reached Europe it was used primarily as a long-range interceptor, but as resistance of the Luftwaffe decreased they were used more and more in the ground-attack rôle.

As production increased the inevitable modification programme brought further changes to the basic airframe, one major modification being the introduction of a dorsal fin to compensate for loss of area of the cut-down rear fuselage. Tail warning radar was added at a later stage.

ROYAL AIR FORCE MUSTANGS

A large number of P-51D Mustangs was supplied to the R.A.F. under Lend Lease. An initial batch of 281 aircraft was delivered in 1944 and carried the designation Mustang Mark IV. They became standard equipment with the Nos. 19, 64, 65, 112, 118, 122, 154, 213, 249, 250, 303, 306, 442, and 611 Squadrons. The Mustang F.B.IV served with Nos. 26, 237 and 442 Squadrons. An additional 594 Mustang Mark IVs

served with the R.A.F., but they were P-51Ks not 51Ds.

During the invasion of Normandy the Mustang IVs were used in the fighter-bomber rôle with the 2nd Tactical Air Force, but by the end of 1944 they had rejoined Fighter Command's strength in England. Other Mustang IVs used for the interceptor rôle were kept busy during 1944 by the V-1 flying bombs, shooting down 232 of these missiles by September 5th. On April 16th 1945, Mustangs of No. 611 Squadron were the first R.A.F. aircraft to greet their Russian Allies over Berlin. A large number of Mustangs were sent to the Middle East to re-equip Hurricane and Kittyhawk squadrons in the Desert Air Force.

After the war a large number of Mustangs were returned to America, but a number continued to serve with the R.A.F. as late as May 1947.

Serial numbers of the Mustang Mark IVs supplied to the R.A.F. under Lend-Lease arrangements were. Mustang IV (P-51D) (one Packard-built Rolls-Royce V-1650-7 Merlin engine) *KH641* to *KH670*, 30 aircraft; *KM493* to *KM743*, 251 aircraft. Mustang IV (P-51K) (one V-1650-7 engine) *TK589*, this being an ex-U.S.A.A.F. aircraft (*44-13332*) and used for trials at A. & A.E.E.; *KN671* to *KN870*, 200 aircraft;

This is the P-51B-1-NA used to flight test the bubble canopy. (Photo: Richard Ward)

P-51D-5-NA Mustang of the 8th Air Force. Note shape of drop tank.

(Photo: Roger Freeman)

KM100 to *KM492*, 393 aircraft. The last two batches were fitted with the 4-bladed Aeroproducts propeller. An additional three P-51Ds were taken over in the Middle East from the 12th Army, U.S.A., and re-numbered *HK944* to *KH946*.

FOREIGN MUSTANGS

The P-51D was built in *Australia* under licence, but before the first licence-built aircraft appeared, enough machines to equip one squadron, No. 8, were supplied direct from America. It was during February, 1944, that the first erection jigs and tools were constructed, but the first of eighty aircraft assembled by the Commonwealth Aircraft Corporation did not fly until May 1945, too late to take part in the final assault on Japan. These eighty aircraft were constructed from components imported from America and as such were designated the CA-17 Mustang 20. Subsequent aircraft, 120 in all, built from Australian-made components, were designated C-18 Mustang 21. Fifteen Mark 21s (*A68-81* to *95*) were modified to the Mark 22 standard with the addition of F.24 cameras

and used for tactical reconnaissance duties. One hundred and seventy CA-18s were ordered but with the end of hostilities this was reduced to 120 aircraft.

The Australian contribution to the occupation of Japan consisted of three squadrons, No. 76, 77 and 82, of No. 81 Wing, equipped with P-51Ds, and they were shipped to Iwakuni and Bofu in the spring of 1946. They remained there until 1949 when Nos. 76 and 82 were withdrawn to Australia leaving No. 77. The latter was on the spot when the Korean conflict broke out in 1950 and it was immediately seconded to the U.S. Fifth Air Force for use as a fighter-bomber. In the first six months of operations in Korea No. 77 flew 2,600 sorties and they flew their Mustangs against tremendous odds until they took delivery of a number of Gloster Meteors in 1951.

It was inevitable that *Canada* would be interested in the P-51D and one hundred machines were supplied shortly after the war ended in 1945. These served with the Royal Canadian Air Force until the last went out of service in 1956.

The *Chinese Air Force* was re-equipped, with U.S. assistance, in 1946 and three squadrons of P-51Ds

"Little Lady" of the 55th Fighter Squadron, 20th Fighter Group, 8th Air Force, based on Kingscliffe, Northants. Compare with P-51Ds on pages 87, 94 and 96.

were supplied. With the overthrow of General Chiang Kai-shek's government in 1949, most of the Mustangs were evacuated to Formosa, but a number were left behind and they formed part of the Red Chinese Air Force. Some of these Mustangs were still in service when the Korean War broke out, but it is not known whether they were ever used against the United Nations forces.

Of the 160 aircraft that were evacuated to Formosa with the *Chinese Nationalist Air Force*, the majority were P-51Ds. By December 1954 two Mustang squadrons remained in service, one with F-51Ds and the other with RF-51D reconnaissance fighters.

Under the terms of the Rio Pact of 1947, *Cuba* was supplied with F-51D Mustangs, and these remained in front-line service until replaced by Russian equipment in the early 1960s.

Dominica introduced the P-51D to its Air Force when, in October, 1952, it purchased 32 surplus machines from Sweden, and they were still in service in 1962.

Guatemala bought a small number of F-51Ds in 1945, just after the war ended, but spares were a problem and as the Mustangs went out of service they were never replaced.

Six North American F-51Ds were purchased by *Haiti* just after the war, and some were still in service in 1961.

On signing the Rio Pact of 1947 *Honduras* received a number of Kingcobra and Lightning aircraft, but these were replaced a few years later by F-51Ds, a number of which were in service in the early 1960s.

During the war the Dutch forces in the Pacific were operating out of Australia with the P-51D, and on cessation of hostilities the Mustangs were used against the Indonesian Nationalists. Two squadrons, Nos. 121 and 122 fought the rebels, but to no avail for in June 1950, the Netherlands Indies Air Force was disbanded and its aircraft transferred to *Indonesia*. The Mustangs served for nine years with the I.A.F. until replaced by Russian equipment.

Mustang Mk. IV (P-51D) of No. 3 Squadron, R.A.A.F., 239 Fighter Bomber Wing, Desert Air Force, Lavarino, Italy.
(Photo: Richard Ward)

"Dallas Doll" P-51D-15-NA, subject of the five-view drawing on page 95. Flew with the 352nd Fighter Squadron.
(Photo: G. J. Letzer, via Richard Ward)

Despite restrictions imposed by the Western Powers *Israel* obtained 25 F-51D fighter-bombers from Sweden in 1952, these serving with the Israel Defence Force/Air Force until superseded by jet equipment in the late 1950s.

After the defeat of *Italy* the air force was supplied with American equipment, including P-51Ds. By October, 1948, 48 were in service and they remained as front-line equipment until replaced by Vampires and Sabres in 1953.

The *South Korean Air Force* first operated the F-51D in 1950, when they were used to stem the North Korean advance when the latter invaded South Korea. At first the Mustangs were used for defensive purposes, but as their numbers increased they went over to the ground-attack rôle. The Mustangs were

P-51D-5 "Ferocious Frankie" of the 8th Air Force.

(Photo: Roger Freeman)

89

P-51D-25 of the 457th Fighter Squadron, 506th Fighter Group, 20th Air Force based on Iwo Jima.

(Photo: G. J. Letzer, via Richard Ward)

phased out of service in 1960 with the arrival of the North American Sabre jet fighter.

Netherlands forces fighting in the Pacific in 1944/45 were equipped with the North American F-51D, and these same aircraft were used to try to crush the Indonesian Nationalists in the four years following VJ-Day. With the sovereignty of Indonesia recognised the Mustangs were transferred to the I.A.F.

Thirty P-51Ds were supplied to the *Royal New Zealand Air Force* in 1945, but they were not introduced into service for several years. The Mustangs were themselves replaced by Vampires in 1950.

In 1947 *Nicaragua* took delivery of a small batch of P-51Ds and a few were still in service in 1964.

The *Philippine Air Force* took delivery of a number of F-51Ds in 1946 and they formed the equipment of one fighter-bomber squadron until phased out of service in 1960.

The *South African Air Force* did not operate the F-51D until 1950 when, as part of the United Nations Forces in Korea they took delivery of a number of ex-U.S.A.F. machines at Johnson Air Force Base, Tokyo. On November 16th five Mustangs, plus personnel, were flown to K-9 airfield, Pusan, in South Korea, and three days later the S.A.A.F. flew its first sortie against the North Koreans. No. 2 Squadron, the one in question, was attached to the U.S. 18th Fighter-Bomber Wing, and with this Wing they moved to a number of airfields until settling down at K-10, near Chinhae, where they remained until re-equipped with Sabres in January, 1953.

During the early part of 1945 it appeared that *Sweden* would at last become involved in the war that was still raging in Europe, and in an effort to bolster air defences the government bought fifty P-51D Mustang fighters from America. Towards the end of the year the Swedish-built SAAB-21As, were coming off the production lines, but their introduction into

TP-51D trainer with dual seats under single bubble canopy.

Study in fuel tanks. Above: *the F-51D has bulky tanks and new style insignia.*   (Photo: Richard Ward)

This Air Training Command F-51D (note insignia on fin) has long, tapered tank.   (Photo: Richard Ward)

ETF-51D-25-NT of Air National Guard. Tall fin was introduced on the P-51H and several F-51Ds were retro-fitted during the early post-war period. Note "Bald Eagle" motif ahead of cockpit.   (Photo: R. F. Beseker, via Roger Freeman)

91

service was slow and a further 90 Mustangs were bought as an interim measure until the 21A became available in greater quantities. Eventually enough Swedish-built equipment became available and the Mustangs were either sold or phased out of service.

The *Swiss Air Force* just after the war consisted of mainly German aircraft, and with the advent of the jet fighter in the early post-war years the decision was taken to convert to this new form of propulsion. Whilst waiting for deliveries of the de Havilland Vampire the Air Force took delivery of 100 surplus F-51D Mustangs, these being phased out of service in 1956.

Uruguay took delivery of a limited number of P-51Ds just after the close of World War II, and these were still in service in the 1960s.

P-51 VARIANTS

A number of variations of the basic P-51D airframe were built and performed useful service. One major modification was the F-6D-20-NT to F-6D-25-NT tactical-reconnaissance aircraft built mainly at the Dallas plant. One hundred and thirty-six F-6Ds were built and they differed principally from the interceptor version in having oblique and vertical cameras installed in the rear fuselage. Other extra equipment included additional radio and D/F gear.

Another major modification was the TP-51D trainer, of which only a token batch of ten was constructed. An additional seat was installed behind the normal seat and was fitted with full dual control (the pupil sat in the front seat). The extra seat was accommodated under the normal bubble canopy, and the radio moved from its usual position to a place in the rear fuselage. One very special TP-51D was modified further for use as an observation aircraft and used by General Eisenhower, the Supreme Allied Commander in France, for inspection of the Normandy beach-head in June 1944.

Another "one-off" P-51D was *44-84900*, a war surplus machine that was used for testing the feasibility of using the Mustang as a ship-board fighter.

Above and below: *F-51Ds of the post-war period showing (top) old-style insignia and (below) contemporary-style insignia.*

The tail unit was modified by the addition of an extra-large fin strake, and the wings strengthened to absorb the landing loads of an arrester-hook deceleration. A series of deck-landing and take-off tests were initiated on the U.S.S. *Shangri-La*, the pilot, one Lt. R. M. Elder.

For the tests it bore the designation EFT-51D-25-NT, indicating that it had been constructed at Dallas. After the war it was allocated to the Pennsylvania National Air Guard, and for some curious reason re-designated TF-51D-NA (Inglewood), and as such served with the 148th Fighter Interceptor Squadron.

THE P-51D DESCRIBED

Structurally the Mustang was a low-wing cantilever monoplane with a N.A.A.—NACA laminar-flow wing section. The wing was built in two sections and bolted together on the fuselage centre-line, the upper surface forming the cockpit floor. It was a two-spar, all-metal structure with flush-riveted Alclad skin, the spars having single plate flanges and extruded top and bottom booms. The remaining structure was pressed ribs

F-51D of the South African Air Force is seen in Korea prior to take-off on raid. Note bulky tank, wing rockets and Cheetah motif under cockpit. Aircraft flew with the "Flying Cheetahs". (S.A.A.F. photo)

F-51D of the South Korean Air Force with rocket projectiles under wing.

with lightening holes and extruded spanwise stringers. Metal-covered ailerons were hinged to the rear spar, the port aileron having a controllable trim tab. Trailing-edge flaps were installed between the ailerons and fuselage.

The fuselage was an all-metal, semi-monocoque structure built in three sections—engine, main cockpit and tail section. The engine was mounted on two V-type cantilever bearers built up plate webs and top and bottom extruded members, each attached at two points to the front fireproof bulkhead of the main section. The latter was made up of two beams, each

Cockpit detail of P-51D Mustang.

comprising two longerons which formed the caps. The skin, reinforced with vertical frames, formed the webs. Aft of the cockpit the longerons extended into a semi-monocoque structure reinforced with vertical frames. The detachable tail section was similar in construction to the main section.

The tail plane was a cantilever monoplane built in one piece with detachable tips. Structurally it comprised two spars, pressed ribs and extruded stringers, the whole covered with a stressed Alclad skin. The fin was virtually similar. Rudder and elevators had aluminium-alloy frames with fabric covering. The control surfaces were dynamically balanced and had trim tabs. Two self-sealing fuel tanks were fitted as standard—one in each wing situated between the spars and each containing 92 gallons of fuel. An auxiliary tank containing 85 gallons was installed in the fuselage aft of the cockpit, and there was provision for two jettisonable tanks under the wings. These were of either 75- or 110-gallon capacity, and radii of action with various fuel loads were as follows: internal tanks only, 475 miles; with two 75-gallon tanks, 650 miles; with two 110-gallon tanks, 850 miles.

ARMAMENT

Main armament of the P-51D was six 0·5-inch Browning machine-guns installed three per wing, with a maximum ammunition capacity of 400 rounds per gun for each of the inboard and 270 rounds for the centre and outboard guns, providing a total of 1,880 rounds. The centre guns could be removed, reducing armament to four guns and the same amount of ammunition, but the Mustang could then carry either two 1,000-lb. bombs; ten 5-inch, high-velocity rockets or six bazooka-type rocket launching tubes installed in banks of three under each wing. As the potency of the unguided rocket became known they were fitted to the P-51D and for the record the final 1,100 P-51D-25-NAs constructed had two zero-length launching stubs for the 5-inch rockets installed under each wing, thus obviating the need for the weighty rocket tubes. The machine-guns were adjusted to

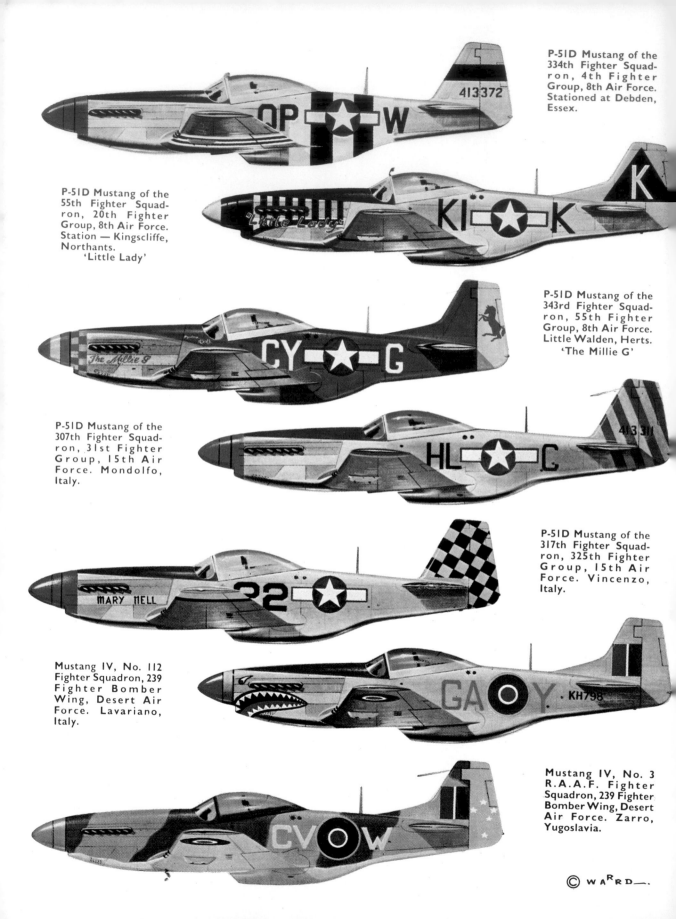

P-5ID Mustang of the
334th Fighter Squad-
ron, 4th Fighter
Group, 8th Air Force.
Stationed at Debden,
Essex.

413372

P-5ID Mustang of the
55th Fighter Squad-
ron, 20th Fighter
Group, 8th Air Force.
Station — Kingscliffe,
Northants.
'Little Lady'

'Little Lady'

KI K

P-5ID Mustang of the
343rd Fighter Squad-
ron, 55th Fighter
Group, 8th Air Force.
Little Walden, Herts.
'The Millie G'

The Millie G

CY G

P-5ID Mustang of the
307th Fighter Squad-
ron, 31st Fighter
Group, 15th Air
Force. Mondolfo,
Italy.

HL C

413311

P-5ID Mustang of the
317th Fighter Squad-
ron, 325th Fighter
Group, 15th Air
Force. Vincenzo,
Italy.

MARY NELL

32

Mustang IV, No. 112
Fighter Squadron, 239
Fighter Bomber
Wing, Desert Air
Force. Lavariano,
Italy.

GA Y. KH798

Mustang IV, No. 3
R.A.A.F. Fighter
Squadron, 239 Fighter
Bomber Wing, Desert
Air Force. Zarro,
Yugoslavia.

CV W

© WARD.

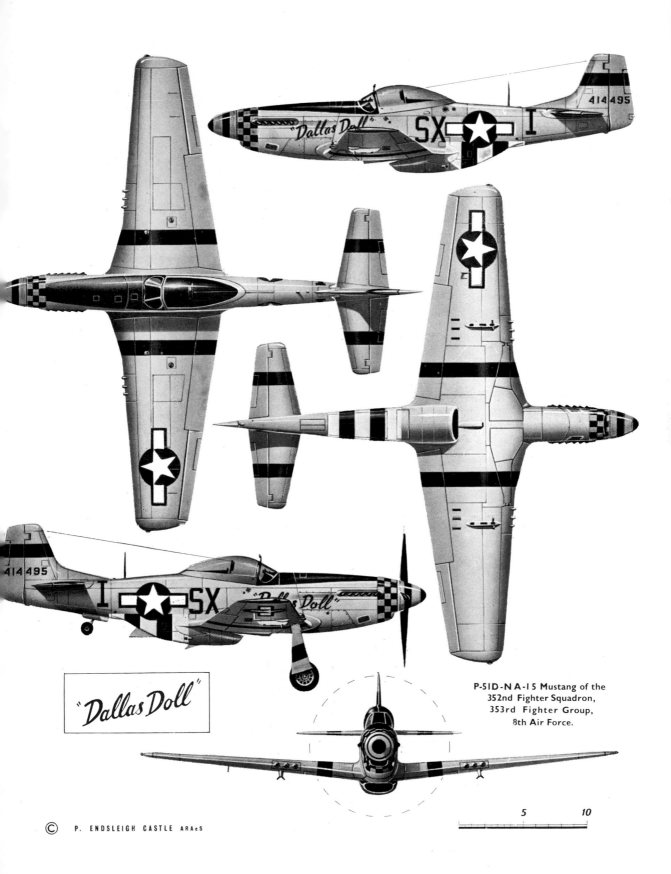

414 495

"Dallas Doll"

SX I

I SX "Dallas Doll"

414 495

P-5ID-NA-15 Mustang of the
352nd Fighter Squadron,
353rd Fighter Group,
8th Air Force.

5 10

© P. ENDSLEIGH CASTLE ARAeS

converge at 300 yards range, but some pilots preferred to narrow the range to as little as 250 yards and adjusted their guns to suit.

THE MUSTANG ENGINE

Standard engine for the P-51D was the liquid-cooled, 12-cylinder, Packard-built, Rolls-Royce Merlin V-1650-3 or -7 developing 1,400 h.p. at take-off. The original Mustangs were fitted with the low-altitude rated Allison engine, but as the possibilities of the Mustang as a high-altitude fighter became realised it was decided to fit a Merlin engine. For this purpose four Mustang Mark Is were sent to Rolls-Royce for use as development aircraft—*AL963, AL975, AM203* and *AM208*. They had Merlin 61 series engines installed with a frontal radiator in addition to the normal ventral scoop. The Mustang/Rolls-Royce combination was an instant success and it was adopted as standard for all the Mustang variants. To increase

"Sad Sack", P-51D of the 55th Fighter Squadron, 20th Fighter Wing, 8th Air Force. Based on Kingscliffe, Northants. Compare with colour side views, page 94 and "Little Lady" also pages 94 and 95. (Photo: Richard Ward)

the flow of engines the Packard Car Company of America built the Merlin under licence.

The Merlin was fitted with an injection-type carburettor and a two-stage supercharger. With the supercharger working, the -3 engine cut-in at 19,000 feet and on the -7 between 14,500 and 19,000 feet. The supercharger was automatic but could be manually overridden. In order to give the engine an extra burst of power during an emergency, the throttle could be pushed past the gate stop, breaking the safety wire. If used longer than five minutes there was a risk of severe engine damage.

Mustang pilots were left in no doubt when the supercharger cut-in to the high-blower position for the aircraft shuddered violently. They had to learn to anticipate the cut-in and reduce throttle. When descending the change to low-blower took place at about 14,500 feet, and the only indication of the event was a drop in manifold pressure.

The Packard Merlin drove either a four-blade Hamilton-Standard Hydromatic or Aeroproducts automatic, constant-speed airscrew. Coolant (30/70 ethylene-glycol/water) and oil radiators were installed in the pronounced belly scoop radiator fairing under the fuselage.

One weakness of the Merlin was that it could be put out of action by a single bullet or piece of shrapnel, but this applied to all liquid-cooled, in-line engines and did not detract from the Mustang's all-round capabilities, and the aircraft was a welcome sight to the Fortress crews as they plunged deep into German skies during the daylight offensive against the Nazi armament industries.

Price of the P-51D Mustang with the Packard-Merlin engine was 50,985 dollars, a remarkably low figure for such an efficient and graceful aeroplane.

Study in shark's smile, the latter pioneered by No. 112 Squadron, Desert Air Force. (Photos: Richard Ward)

Specification

Dimensions: Wing span 37 ft. 7/16 in.; length 32 ft. 3¼ in.; height 13 ft. 8 in.; wing area 233·19 sq. ft.

Weights: Empty 7,125 lb.; gross weight 10,100 lb.; maximum weight (with 489 gallons of fuel) 11,600 lb.

Performance: Maximum speed at 25,000 ft.—437 m.p.h., at 15,000 ft. —413 m.p.h., at 5,000 ft.—395 m.p.h.; cruising speed 362 m.p.h.; landing speed 100 m.p.h.; service ceiling 41,900 ft.; climb rate 3,475 ft. per min.; range 950 miles with minimum 269 gallons, 2,300 miles with maximum 489 gallons.

The Albatros D V

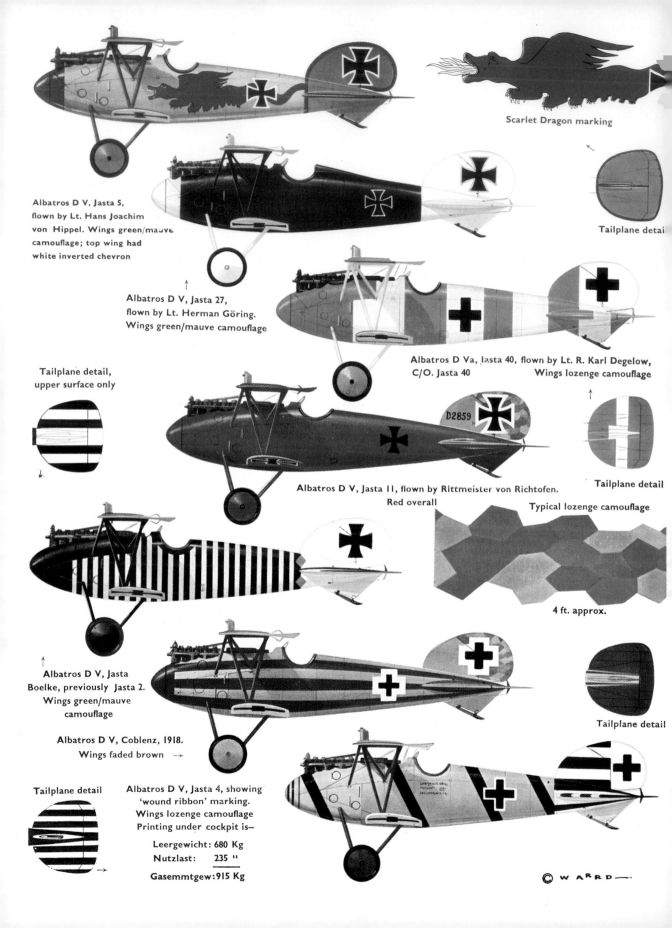

Scarlet Dragon marking

Albatros D V, Jasta 5, flown by Lt. Hans Joachim von Hippel. Wings green/mauve camouflage; top wing had white inverted chevron

Tailplane detail

Albatros D V, Jasta 27, flown by Lt. Herman Göring. Wings green/mauve camouflage

Albatros D Va, Jasta 40, flown by Lt. R. Karl Degelow, C/O. Jasta 40   Wings lozenge camouflage

Tailplane detail, upper surface only

Albatros D V, Jasta 11, flown by Rittmeister von Richtofen. Red overall

Tailplane detail

Typical lozenge camouflage

4 ft. approx.

Albatros D V, Jasta Boelke, previously Jasta 2. Wings green/mauve camouflage

Tailplane detail

Albatros D V, Coblenz, 1918. Wings faded brown →

Tailplane detail

Albatros D V, Jasta 4, showing 'wound ribbon' marking. Wings lozenge camouflage Printing under cockpit is—

Leergewicht: 680 Kg
Nutzlast: 235 "
Gasemmtgew: 915 Kg

© WARD

ALBATROS DV (1917) flown by Hpt. Eduard
Ritter von Schleich, C.O. of Jasta 21.

0   5′

The Albatros D.V.

by Peter Gray

Fuselage and fin of this Albatros D V appear to be over-painted: rudder, tailplane, and wings are covered with lozenge-patterned fabric. The skull motif is almost identical to that on the Fokker D VII in which Wüsthoff was shot down, but it is not confirmed that the Albatros was Wüsthoff's.
(Photo: Peter M. Grosz)

HIGH above the French sector of the Western Front in the summer of 1917 a shark-like shape, resplendent in red and white candy-striped decor and gleaming jewel-like in the early morning sun, sliced through a tuft of cumulus and pounced upon the unsuspecting Breguet reconnaissance machine pursuing its lawful occasions below. Its twin Spandau machine guns spoke briefly and the luckless observer slumped to the floor of his cockpit. Climbing away the striped machine poised for another attack from out of the eye of the sun; another stammer of bullets was unleashed into the Frenchman—the Bruguet now began to burn, fell off on one wing and with increasing steepness plunged torch-like to the ground trailing a funeral pyre of black smoke.

This streamlined destroyer was the Albatros D V, fast becoming the mainstay of the German fighter units (the *Jagdstaffeln*) which had been organised towards the end of the previous summer. It was not exactly a new aeroplane, but more a logical development and refinement of an existing design which had begun with the Albatros D I in 1916. The brain behind this streamlined series was Dipl. Ing. Robert Thelen, then chief designer to the *Albatros-Werke* at Johannisthal; with assistance of two other aeronautical engineers, Dipl. Ing. Schubert and Ing. Gnaedig.

Progress had been made through the initial D I and D II types with the equal chord wings, to the D III with its much narrower lower wing inspired by the French Nieuport chaser machines. The Albatros D IV which followed, featured a return to the equal chord wing format of the D I–D II series; power unit was an experimental geared 160 h.p. Mercedes which enabled it to be completely enclosed in the nose. However, teething troubles with this engine plagued the design and it was not proceeded with.

Retaining the fuselage of the D IV, which was more oval and of better aerodynamic shape than the D III, the D V was evolved with a return to the sesquiplane wing structure of the D III. Initially the Albatros D I had been designed to regain the supremacy which the

notorious Fokker monoplanes had lost to the British D.H.2 and French Nieuport scouts, which it did with admirable effect. Progression to the D V was a continued attempt to retain the balance of fighter supremacy in Germany's favour, in the face of the Camels, Spads and S.E.5s of the Allies. Although vast numbers of Albatros D V and D Va's were built by the parent company at Johannisthal, and by the subsidiary, *Ostdeutsche Albatros Werke* at Schneidemühl, no really decisive ascendancy over the Allied types was achieved.

THE D V DESCRIBED

Certainly the Albatros D V (and its D Va development) was a fine looking machine. In endeavouring to improve performance over that of the D III the airframe was carefully made lighter and the fuselage contours considerably improved. Initially the same 160 h.p. Mercedes engine was used, but later the compression ratio was raised and eventually oversize cylinders and pistons were fitted, which up-rated the power to 170–185 h.p. at varying altitudes. The fuselage itself was a semi-monocoque structure consisting basically of lightened ply formers and eight spruce longerons, to which was pinned and screwed the outer covering of carefully shaped plywood panels. This method of construction was of considerable

The Albatros D IV, sleek forebear of the D V, was fitted with a closely-cowled, geared engine.

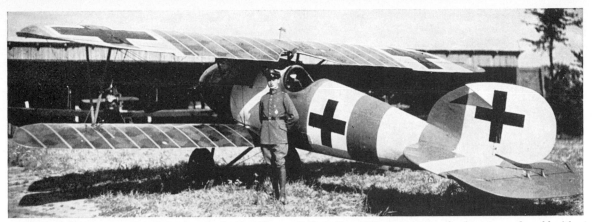

Lt. Helmuth Dilthey, Jasta *40, with his green and white Albatros D Va in June 1918. Authenticity of colours is confirmed by* (then) *Lt. Degelow, C.O.* Jasta *40.*
(Photo: Egon Krueger)

strength and called for no internal bracing at all. In section it varied from completely circular at the nose and developed through truly elliptical formers to a horizontal knife-edge aft. The engine was neatly installed but with much of the cylinder block exposed to facilitate servicing. A large bulbous spinner was fitted to the laminated (ash, walnut, mahogany) airscrew, of slightly less diameter than the fuselage immediately aft, in order to admit cooling air to the crankcase. Removable metal panels were adjacent to the cylinder block and around the first section, otherwise the fuselage and lower wing root stubs were completely ply skinned. A neat headrest fairing was fitted, but as this tended to restrict vision to the rear it was often removed on active service.

Tail surfaces were similar to the D III, in fact the tailplane and elevator were interchangeable with that aircraft. The fin was built integral with the fuselage and ply skinned in like manner to the fuselage, as was also the triangular under-fin which formed the support for the stout ash tailskid. The tailplane was wooden framed and fabric covered. A D III-type rudder with straight trailing edge was used on the prototype D V but thereafter the more familiar rounded rudder was fitted. This surface, like that of the one-piece elevator, was constructed from light-gauge steel tube and fabric covered. Large removable inspection panels were situated between the tailplane and fin to facilitate access; these were square and positioned at 45 degrees to the vertical.

In the main, the wing structure followed the usual all-wood tried and trusted Albatros practice, certainly

the upper wing did with its two box-spars located well forward and the front spar connected to the leading-edge with a plywood capping strip. A wire trailing-edge member imparted the distinctive scalloped effect. Ribs were of ply considerably fretted with lightening holes and were narrowly flanged with spruce. Ailerons were of inverse taper and of steel tube framing and in their operation departed from former practice. The cables now ran up through the fuselage decking, into the centre-section, and along the inside of the wing and were attached to pulleys mounted on the aileron leading-edge—small shrouds housed the cables where they emerged through the wing surface. A Teeves and Braun radiator was mounted in the starboard side of the centre-section; a shutter beneath it was manually operated by the pilot to partially blanket off the surface giving the required degree of cooling. Centre-section struts were of "N" pattern, with a bracing member across the upper extremities, and were of streamlined steel tube from which medium the interplane Vee struts were also fabricated.

The lower wing followed the same general method of construction as the upper but due to its considerably reduced chord it was based on a single spar, as on the French Nieuports, from which type the idea was adapted. It was in this single spar wing that the inherent weakness of the "Vee Strutters" (as they were

Green tailed D V of Oblt. Flashar, Jasta *5, displays "mailed gauntlet" motif on fuselage and chevron on lozenge fabric-covered wings. Note early type "Balkankreuz" with white outline.*
(Photo: Egon Krueger)

This Albatros D Va—D6553/17, (O.A.W.), thought to be Jasta *4, was a Schneidemühl-built machine. Note auxiliary strut from interplane strut to leading-edge.* (Photo: Egon Krueger)

101

Another view of "Blitz" showing arrow motif more clearly.

(Photo: Egon Krueger)

dubbed by the Royal Flying Corps) lay, i.e. the unfortunate tendency to break up in a prolonged dive. At the time the reason was not fully understood, as the structural strength of the wings proved to be more than adequate under static load tests. It was eventually discovered that the single spar was located too far aft, this causing vibrations which, in a prolonged dive, increased proportionately eventually resulting in structural failure. A degree of safety was achieved by the fitting of a short auxiliary strut from the leading-edge to the Vee interplane strut; but this was no more than partially effective and pilots were cautioned not to over-dive their Albatroses. All flight surfaces were fabric covered, the fabric being sewn and tacked to the ribs on both surfaces with rib tapes.

An orthodox streamline steel tube undercarriage chassis was fitted: a single spreader bar behind the axle joined the apices of the vees and this assembly was covered by a streamlined fairing. The wheels were sprung with elastic shock cord which bound the axle to the vees. Tyres fitted were of 700 mm. diameter and 100 mm. section and the wheel discs were generally of fabric or metal, although on one captured machine (D 5253/17) they were of three ply.

Armament consisted of twin fixed Spandau machine guns mounted on the decking immediately in front of the pilot and synchronised to fire through the airscrew disc by a direct flexible drive interrupter gear. They were fired from twin triggers on the control column actuated through a Bowden type cable and could be operated independently.

The Albatros D Va which soon succeeded the D V on the production lines differed very little—the airframe was strengthened which resulted in an increase in the all-up weight of some 80 kg. (132 lb. approx.). Aileron operation reverted to the earlier system used on the D III where the cables were led through the lower wing and then ran vertically up adjacent to the interplane strut station to connect to the aileron crank lever. D Va and D III upper wings were in fact completely interchangeable, the only difference being that the aileron crank was somewhat shorter in the D Va. It was *only* in the method of aileron operation that positive visual identification between D V and D Va was possible.

INTO SERVICE

Summer 1917 saw the introduction of the Albatros D V to the *Jagdstaffeln*, to be joined by the D Va in the late autumn of that year. It is not known exactly how many D V and D Va's were built (the factory did not differentiate between the types) but prodigious orders —for those days—must have been placed judging by the numbers that eventually came to be in service. In September 1917 some 424 D Vs were at the Front which figure peaked to 526 in November 1917, thereafter numbers gradually decreased: correspondingly D Va figures increased until March 1918 when 928 Albatross D Va's were with Front Line units compared with 131 D Vs. It may be safely assumed that all 80 *Jastas* (as the *Jadgstaffeln* were abbreviatedly known) that were formed in time for the big German offensive

"Blitz", Albatros D Va of Lt. von Hippel Jasta 5 showing areas of mauve and olive green camouflage on upper wing surface. Arrow device on fuselage was red and white.

(Photo: W. Puglisi)

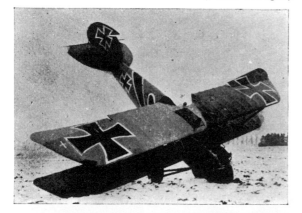

Hermann Göring (2nd from left) and his D V of Jasta 27, after 8th victory over Lt. Slee, R.F.C. Black fuselage with white nose and tail.

(Photo: Egon Krueger)

Albatros D V prototype. Note D III-type rudder with straight trailing edge, and that fuselage and fin have been painted in same style as lozenge fabric on flight surfaces.

Oblt. Benz of Jasta 78 with D Va D6924/17 (O.A.W.) showing ultimate style of "Balkankreuz". (Photo: Egon Krueger)

of March 1918 at one time or another had D V and D Va's upon their establishment. Strangely enough D III manufacture was not immediately discontinued, they continued to come off the production line alongside the later machines until early 1918. Consequently *Jastas* often had a mixed bag of Albatros D III, D V and D Va's on strength; it was possible that some may have had Pfalz D III, D IIIa and Fokker Dr.I.

Certainly the Albatroses were the most widely used German fighters and continued in service until the Armistice although from mid-1918 onward the Fokker D VII came increasingly into use. The disadvantage of the Albatros D V and D Va series was that it was introduced into service when already more-or-less obsolescent and then had to operate with a restriction on its diving performance. Its main asset was the usual numerical superiority it obtained over the smaller Allied patrols.

COLOUR SCHEMES

Many and varied were the colour schemes adopted by Albatros pilots with all sorts of colourful, and even bizarre, unit and individual devices. Most often though these were confined to the fuselage and tail surfaces but inevitably there were exceptions to the rule and machines with over-all colour schemes were reported by Allied pilots. Evidence of this is confirmed by Eduard von Schleich, C.O. of *Jasta* 21 from May 1917, who, after the death of his friend Lt. Limpert, painted over the whole of his Albatros D V with black paint. It is of interest to mention that earlier von Schleich had intended to use the blue and white background of his Bavarian Lion insignia as a scoreboard, marking the date and place of his victories on the lozenges. It has often been reported that Manfred von Richthofen flew all-red aircraft but this does not seem to be supported by modern research in this field, and it is now generally supposed that the red was confined to the complete fuselage, all struts and possibly tail unit, only.

As these Albatros fighters were often such colourful aircraft digression on to the basic "ex works" finish seems worthwhile. Albatros D V and D Va came from the two factories at Johannisthal (Berlin) and Schneidemühl in two types of camouflage finish applied to the fabric covered surfaces. From 12th April 1917 a shadow shading style of camouflage was applied to the upper wing and tail surfaces: the wing being divided into no more than two (roughly half and half), or at the most three, large irregular patches of darkish olive green and a drab mauvish purple. Underneath surfaces were finished in a light blue shade approximated to sky blue. Serial numbers were painted in black, in an ornate style, along the base of its fin followed by an oblique stroke with the last two digits (in a smaller size) of the year in which the production order was placed e.g. *D 5787/17*.

A major development in German aircraft camouflage was the introduction of fabric which was pre-printed in a pattern of irregular polygons, which has become more widely known—for simplicity of designation—as "lozenge" fabric. It has now been established with reasonable certainty that only two basic patterns existed, one consisting of a five-colour combination and the other a four-colour combination. Each pattern was printed in two sets of colours, that to be used for the upper and side surfaces was in darker shades than that to be applied to the under surfaces. In respect of the five-colour fabric the shades of the upper surface

Albatros D Va of Lt. Schlömer, Jasta 5, fuselage motif black with white border. (Photo: Egon Krueger)

Black tailed D Vs of Jasta *12. Rear aircraft is A.E.G. C IV, squadron "hack", also with black tail.* (Photo: Egon Krueger)

were approximately: indigo blue, blue-grey, deep mauve, sage green and yellow ochre. The under surface shades were: pale pink (tinged with blue), cream (tinged with crimson), bright reddish pink, leaf green (tinged with grey) and pale cerulean blue (tinged with grey). Upper surface shades of the four-colour fabric were: violet, dark blue-green, beige, light sage green. Under surface shades were: pale cobalt (tinged grey), pale leaf green (tinged grey), pale terra cotta, reddish pink (tinged grey). It will be seen that the under surface shades were much less saturated than the top surface, more of pastel colour tinged with grey. Not all fabrics were absolutely identical however, and varied slightly with differing dye batches. Another point is that although it was laid down that two types of fabric should be applied to aircraft, they were not always so covered and if one or other fabric was in short supply an airframe would be covered in a single type of fabric.

The fuselage was left in its natural wood (birch ply) finish with a coating of protective varnish which gave a warm yellow appearance. All steel struts and metal panels were given a coat of grey or olive green protective paint. Exhaust manifolds and induction pipes were of copper and water line piping from the radiator was of brass or copper. Near full chord Patee crosses

with narrow white outlines were positioned on top of the upper wing tips and underneath the lower wing tips, also on the fuselage sides and on fin/rudder. This type of cross remained in force until 15th April 1918 when the form was changed to the straight sided *Balkankreuz*, at first surrounded by a white outline 150 mm. wide. On 25th June 1918 the white outline was revised and confined only to the sides of the cross and to be only a quarter of the width of the bars of the cross.

OPERATIONAL EXPERIENCE

When issued to the *Jastas* in the summer months of 1917 the Albatros D V was received with varying degrees of enthusiasm, the older pilots having hoped for a machine with a considerably improved performance over that of its Albatros D III forebear—a hope that was doomed to disappointment. The psychological effect of a suspect wing strength when diving for any appreciable length of time was considerable and the fighter gained an unenviable reputation. A tendency to failure of the cantilever ends of the upper wings, due to vibration and flexing, was largely cured by the addition of a bracing cable running from the apex of the interplane Vee struts to the centre of the

Albatros D V flown by Lt. Billick of Jasta *12. Has black fuselage emblazoned with swastika and wings of green/mauve camouflage.*
(Photo: W. Puglisi)

Sleek lines of the D Va are displayed in this head-on view. Note absence of auxiliary strut.

Black and white striped Albatros D V, thought to be of Jasta 2 (Boelcke).

Captured Albatros D Va stripped of engine and fabric covering for display in London during 1918.

rear spar on the overhanging outer portion. However, repeated crashes occurred due to continued lower wing failure which was eventually partially remedied as mentioned earlier in the text.

Lt. von Hippel, a member of *Jasta* 5, experienced an uncanny escape when, following a prolonged dive of some 3,000 feet during combat in the vicinity of Le Catelet on 18th February 1918, the lower port wing of his D V failed; not then having been fitted with the auxiliary strut to the leading-edge. It eventually broke completely away from the rest of the fuselage and the fact that it did so—and did not continue to assume a distorted shape setting up uncontrollable forces— doubtless facilitated von Hippel's eventual escape as he managed to nurse the damaged airframe down the remaining 13,000 feet but unfortunately overturned on landing. The lower wing which broke away was eventually located more than twelve miles distant.

In the hands of a skilled pilot however the Albatros was able to give a lively account of itself and during the winter months of 1917–1918 Major J. B. "Jimmy" McCudden V.C. in his autobiography "Flying Fury" refers several times to the agility and elusiveness of opposing Albatros fighters. In particular to a green tailed Albatros with whom his flight tangled several times, but whom he was unable to line up in his sights. On 6th December 1917 whilst patrolling at 12,000 feet over Gouzancourt McCudden writes:

I led my patrol north and then turned west behind the six V-strutters, who still flew on looking to the

Left-hand side of D Va cockpit (British A.S.I. fitted); Right-hand side of D Va cockpit. 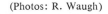 (Photos: R. Waugh)

Line-up of Jasta *5 Albatros D IIIs and D Vs at Boistrancourt, 1917.* (Photo: Egon Krueger)

The Dragon-inscribed D V in which von Hippel had such a remarkable experience. (Photo: Egon Krueger)

west. We closed on them and I gave everyone of my men time to pick a Hun before I fired and drew their attention. It seemed to me very funny that six of us should be able to surprise six Huns so completely as to get within range before being seen. I closed on the Hun I had selected and fired a short burst at him after which he went down vertically with a stream of petrol following him. I noticed he had a tail painted light blue.

By now I was in the middle of these Albatroses and saw that they were a patrol of good Huns whom we had fought before, they all had red noses and yellow fuselages but each had a different coloured tail. There was a red, light blue (whom I sent to the sports), black, yellow, black and white striped, and our dear old "green tail". By Jove! They were a tough lot. We continued scrapping

with them for half an hour and they would not go down although we were above them most of the time.

A few days later on the 9th December he reports:

We now flew up towards Bourlon Wood, where we encountered "green tail" and a brown Pfalz. We scrapped these two for half an hour and with no result, for these two co-operated wonderfully and put up a magnificent show, for we could not attack either of them without having the other after us. There were now only three of us and we did our very best to get one of them but to no avail. After a time they both went down, apparently for some more petrol or ammunition and we flew home.

McCudden was eventually to destroy the "green tail" Albatros D V. On 18th February 1918 he remarks:

D Va displays what appears to be a carrot-type insignia. Pilot thought to be Lt. Mohr. (Photo: Peter M. Grosz)

Eduard von Schleich with his Bavarian Lion D V. Note large, rear-view mirror on cockpit. See also 5-view drawing on page 99. (Photo: Egon Krueger)

Captured Albatros D V, D2129/17, with spiral ribbon marking. Note British A.S.I. pitot head on port interplane struts.

Very soon we sighted a patrol of Albatroses below us—I signalled to attack and down we went with the sun behind us.

I singled out the leader and fired a good burst from both guns and I must have riddled the pilot, for he still flew on straight until the machine burst into flames, and then it fell over sideways. I got a plain view as it fell a flaming wreck. It was "green tail". The pilot had fallen from the machine and was hurtling to destruction faster than his aircraft. This Albatros was the identical one that had shot down Maybery (Capt. R. A. Maybery, M.C.) in December. It had the green tail, the letter K and the white inverted V across the top of the wing. I was very lucky to get him.

Capt. F. Adams, a Bristol Fighter gunner with 11

Lt. Meierdirks of Jasta *12 in D V with simple geometric insignia across encircling ribbon. Tail and nose black, spinner white, lozenge fabric wings.* (Photo: Egon Krueger)

Another "Blitz", D Va, slightly pranged. Lozenge fabric highlights the blue rib tapes. (Photo: Egon Krueger)

Sqdn., R.F.C., was able to testify as to the viciousness with which Albatroses were able, on occasion, to press home an attack. During the second week of July 1917 he writes:

Before reaching Flampoux (near Arras), we saw the two German artillery buses streaking for home and after waiting for some time for them to reappear, started on patrol down the lines. Near Cambrai we ran into a formation of seven Albatros scouts led by a machine painted red with black stripes and obviously the same *staffel* we had fought previously. There was now no doubt that we were absolutely "for it". West (piloting the Bristol) and I attacked the leader while Pern and Day attacked one of the others. West's bullets appeared to be going right through the Hun's fuselage, but quick as lightning the Boche turned and, coming at us nose on, soon had a bullet through the petrol tank and another through me. Spinning down to 500 feet we straightened out but the red machine was still on our tail, so I kept the Lewis firing at him as best I could, although I could now hardly see the gun sights through the loss of blood. Eventually we crashed in the grounds of a Casualty Clearing Station near Boyelles; how we managed to get so far I never knew as West was killed three weeks later and I was sent home unfit for further active service.

Albatros-Werke entered four D Va's in the first of the competitions the German authorities organised at Adlershof (Berlin) airfield during January and Feb-

Specification

Manufacturer: Albatros-Werke G.m.b.H. Johannisthal. Ostdeutsche Albatros-Werke, Schneidemühl.
Power Plant: 160 h.p. Mercedes D III Albatros D V. 170/185 h.p. Mercedes D IIIa Albatros D Va (Basically standard DIII engine with higher compression ratio, later oversize cylinders and pistons were fitted).
Dimensions: Span 9·05 m (29 ft. 8¼ in.). Length 7·33 m (24 ft. 0⅜ in.). Height 2·7 m (8 ft. 10¼ in.). Wing area 21·2 sq. m (229 sq. ft.). Chord Upper 1·5 m (4 ft. 11½ in.). Chord lower 1·1 m (3 ft. 7⅜ in.). Gap 1·5 m (4 ft. 11⅛ in.). Dihedral 2° lower wing only.
Weights: Albatros D V.—Empty 620 kg (1,367 lb.). Loaded 852 kg (1,874 lb.).
Albatros D Va.—Empty 687 kg (1,511 lb.) including 30 kg (66 lb.) cooling water. Loaded 937 kg (2,061 lb.).
Fuel: Petrol: Main tank 17 gallons approx. Reserve tank 5 gallons approx. Oil: 2 gallons approx.
Maximum speed: 165 km.hr. (103 m.p.h. approx.).
Climb: to 3,280 feet (1,000 m) in 4·0 minutes—to 6,560 feet (2,000 m) in 8·8 minutes—to 9,840 feet (3,000 m) in 14·8 minutes—to 13,120 feet (4,000 m) in 22·8 minutes—to 16,400 feet (5,000 m) in 35·0 minutes.

Albatros D Va brought down by an R.E.8 of No. 5 Squadron, Australian Flying Corps., now in the War Memorial Museum at Canberra.

(Photo: Kevin McKay)

Early production Albatros D V. 2004/17 "Ex works".

N.B.:—Albatros D Va D7117/17 fitted with 185 h.p. B.M.W. IIIa engine achieved a ceiling of 10,500 m (34,440 feet)—uncorrected barograph record—on 6th February 1918 at Adlershof D Types Competition. Piloted by Diemer at a loaded weight of 872·8 kg (1,920 lb.) and fitted with Axial airscrew of 2·9 m (9 ft. 6½ in.) diameter and 1·9 m (6 ft. 2⅞ in.) pitch two climbs were made to 6,000 m (19, 680 feet) in 24·5 and 25·5 minutes.

sion of a clamping device on the control column by which the elevators could be locked, this enabled pilots to use both hands to clear machine gun jams. A tendency to spin easily was a characteristic of the type—which trait had caused quite a few accidents—but there was no difficulty about recovery. McCudden tried his hand on a captured D Va example and expressed surprise that their pilots managed to wring from them the agility that they did.

ruary 1918. These competitions were instituted in an endeavour to ensure their fighting squadrons received the best equipment, and manufacturers were invited to submit D type (i.e. single seat fighter) machines for evaluation by Front Line pilots in addition to their own test pilots in competitive speed and climb tests. Of the four Albatros D Va machines entered, two: D 7089/17 and D 7090/17 were fitted with standard Daimler Mercedes D III engines, 4563 (Factory No. —military serial not recorded, if allocated) was fitted with a Mercedes D IIIaü (überkompressen = high compression ratio) engine and D 7117/17 was powered by a B.M.W. IIIa engine developing some 185 h.p. However, no startling performances were recorded and the eventual winner of the first competition was adjudged to be the Fokker V 11, which, after slight modification went into production as the D VII. Front Line pilots who were invited to assess the machines were: Manfred von Richthofen, von Tutschek, von Jastrow, von Der Osten, Bruno Lörzer, Klein and Busse.

Most of the Albatros production fighters had agreeable flying qualities and were by no means difficult machines. A useful feature of the type was the inclu-

Production

Production figures for Albatros D V and D Va are not available but the following table of the numbers of aircraft that were with the Front Line units gives some indication of the numbers that were produced:—

		D V	D Va
July	1917	216	—
September	1917	424	—
November	1917	526	53
January	1918	513	186
March	1918	250	475
May	1918	131	986
July	1918	91	604
September	1918	20	307

Known serial numbers of Albatros D V and D Va machines:
D 1021 D 1024 (von Tutschek Jasta 12) D 1027 (Hermann Göring Jasta 27) D 1033 (Manfred von Richthofen Jasta 11) D 1040 (No. 1 Marine Feld Jagdstaffel) D 1172 (No. 1 M.F. Jasta) D 1177 (Manfred von Richthofen Jasta 11) D 1179 D 1189 D 1199 D 2016 (Karl Thom Jasta 21) D 2024 D 2055 (von Tutschek Jasta 12) D 2059 D 2042 D 2065 (Jasta 5) D 2068 (Jasta 5) D 2076 D 2078 D 2093 D 2108 (von Griem Jasta 34) D 2130 D 2144 D 2161 (Linsingen Jasta 11) D 2164 (Karl Thom Jasta 21) D 2172 (von Schleich Jasta 21) D 2190 (Jasta 5) D 2194 (von Tutschek Jasta 12) D 2240 D 2284 (Waldhausen Jasta 37) D 2299 (Bruno Loerzer Jasta 26) D 2311 D 2312 (No. 1 M.F. Jasta) D 2343 (Jentsch Jasta 61) D 2349 D 2361 D 4023 D 4409 (Paul Baumer Jasta 5) D 4430 (Baumer Jasta 5) D 4509 4515 4519 4545 (Captured) D 4550 D 4552 D 4562 (Jasta 5) D 4563 D 4565 (Vzfw Barth Jasta 10) D 4566 (von Der Osten Jasta 4) D 4596 D 4628 (Gussmann Jasta 11) D 4629 (Jasta 5) D 4640 D 4680 D 4688 (No. 1 M.F. Jasta) D 4693 (Manfred von Richthofen Jasta 11) D 5222 (Hans Adam Jasta 6) D 5253 (Captured) D 5313 (von Schweidnitz Jasta 11) D 5358 D 5360 D 5361 D 5363 D 5372 D 5375 D 5384 (Italian Front) D 5388 D 5390 D 5401 (Helmann Jasta 10) D 5405 (Max Muller Jasta Boelcke) D 5410 (Baumer Jasta 5) D 5416 D 5496 D 5601 D 5602 D 5612 D 5621 D 5624 D 5635 D 5639 D 5677 D 5787 D 5808 D 5815 D 6530 (Jasta 5) D 6550 D 6560 D 7089 (D Type Tests) D 7090 (D Type Tests) D 7098 D 7117 (D Type Tests) D 7132 D 7145 D 7167 D 7174 (No. 1 M.F. Jasta) D 7179 D 7202 D 7212 D 7234 D 7236 D 7310 D 7330 D 7332 D 7337 D 7516.

All above Serials were 1917 allocations and were accordingly suffixed /17.

The Gloster Gauntlet

The Gloster Gauntlet

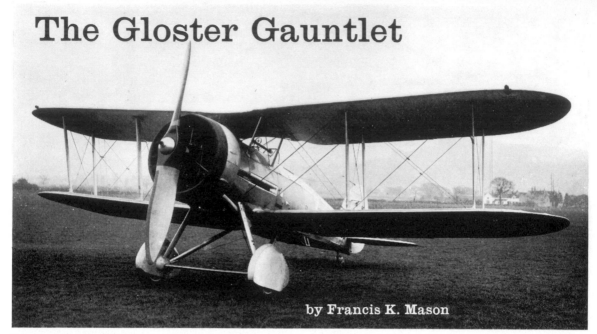

by Francis K. Mason

First production Gauntlet I fitted with wheel spats. Serialled K4081, it flew for the first time during December 1934.

(Air Ministry photo)

THE Gloster Gauntlet is perhaps often overshadowed by its more illustrious successor, the Gladiator, yet apart from its greater popularity as a "pilot's aeroplane" in its own right, it should be remembered that had war been declared at the time of the Munich Crisis, Britain's first-line fighter strength at that time depended more upon the Gauntlet than any other type of aircraft.

Developed from a long line of fighter biplanes (which, designed by H. P. Folland, had included the well-known Grebe and Gamecock of the mid-'twenties), the Gauntlet's true origin lay in the Gloster S.S.18. Specification F.9/26, initially issued in 1926, was intended to produce a successor to the Gamecock, in service with the Royal Air Force, to be constructed primarily in steel or duralumin. While this Specification undoubtedly spurred British aircraft designers to great efforts and spawned numerous advanced designs, it did not in fact bring forth a service fighter directly. Instead, experience gained from examination of the prototypes submitted (which included the Gloster Goldfinch and Bristol Bulldog*) was formulated into a new Specification, F.20/27, issued in 1927. Again numerous prototypes were submitted, including the revised Bulldog, Hawker Hawfinch, Boulton Paul Partridge and Armstrong Whitworth A.W.XVI. Folland's entry was the Gloster S.S.18 (*J9125*) and, although it was beaten during competitive trials by the Bulldog and Hawfinch (the former being judged the winner), the small margin by which it was beaten encouraged Gloster to persevere with its design.

Originally powered by the recalcitrant Bristol Mercury IIA, the S.S.18 was first flown by Howard Saint in 1928 and achieved 183 m.p.h. at 10,000 feet—no mean speed with two-bay wings and uncowled radial engine. The success of the *Bulldog, however,

prompted Folland to adopt the well-tried Bristol Jupiter, and, with the Jupiter VIIF installed, *J9125* became the S.S.18A in 1929. The following year further power demands led to the adoption of the Armstrong-Siddeley Panther III (and later the IIIA) the designation changing to S.S.18B. These engines (together with their Townend ring "cowlings") however, severely penalised the design owing to their much-increased weight and once again Folland reverted to the Jupiter.

By 1931 the arrival of the in-line Rolls-Royce Kestrel in British fighters and light bombers was, by bestowing much increased speeds, bringing about new thoughts on interceptor armament; already Specification F.7/30 had foreshadowed the end of the traditional twin synchronised Vickers guns which had been retained since World War I. Unfortunately the old Vickers gun, prone as it was to frequent stoppages, had to be placed in the fuselage so that the pilot could reach the breeches to clear jams. Folland, realising that short lethal bursts from large batteries of guns could achieve much the same results as fewer, faster-firing guns, decided to mount drum-fed Lewis guns on the wings of his old *J9125* prototype, placing them clear of the airscrew arc—thus allowing them to fire without interruption.

Thus in 1931 *J9125* re-emerged at the Gloster works at Brockworth with Townend ring over a Jupiter VIIFP, two synchronised Vickers guns on the sides of the fuselage. and no fewer than four Lewis guns, two under the upper and two under the lower wings. Such was the load now carried that *J9125* (now termed S.S.19) grossed 3,900 lb., compared with 3,200 lb. in its early form, but with the fully-rated Jupiter the speed had also risen—to 188 m.p.h.

By now Glosters had reached the basis of a first-rate interceptor, but the Air Staff remained sceptical of the

110   * *See pages 62-67 for the complete Bulldog story.*

The Gloster S.S.19, J9125, fitted with the six-gun armament of four Lewis guns on wings and two Vickers guns in fuselage.

very heavy armament and recommended replacement of the Lewis guns by night flying equipment. With wheel spats added as refinements, increased fin area to improve lateral control and night flying equipment added, the S.S.19A embarked on full Service evaluation trials at Martlesham Heath in November 1931. In this form, *J9125* achieved 204 m.p.h. at 10,000 ft.— a full 30 m.p.h. margin over the Bulldog, and almost exactly the same as the in-line engined Hawker Fury.

THE ARRIVAL OF THE MERCURY

This undoubtedly represented the limit of *J9125*'s performance with the old Jupiter engine. It had for

more than four years been realised that if the reliability of the Bristol Mercury could be improved this engine would allow substantial performance improvement. The Mercury IIA had been discarded long since, but in 1932 the first flight example of the Mercury VIS, giving 536 b.h.p. for take-off, was delivered and fitted in *J9125*.

This version, the S.S.19B, can be said to have been the Gauntlet prototype and, when test-flown by Martlesham pilots during the spring of 1933, returned a maximum speed of 212 m.p.h. at 14,500 feet, and attained 20,000 feet in 12 minutes 15 seconds. *J9125* still retained the large wheel fairings as well as a "spatted" tailwheel, but it soon became evident that

The Gloster S.S.19B (J9125) under test as the Gauntlet prototype.

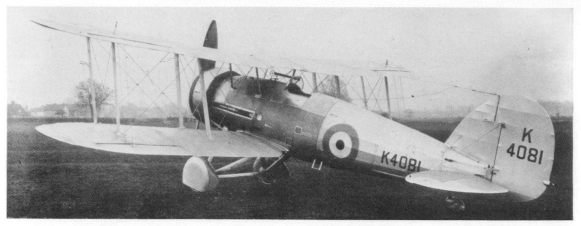

Two further views of the first production Gauntlet I. Note Vickers gun troughs in fuselage and sight ahead of windscreen.
(Air Ministry photos)

these were more trouble than they were worth, especially when operating from soft ground. Service recommendations (made in June 1933) for their removal were agreed by Glosters, but it is an unexplained fact that the first production machines were produced many months later equipped with wheel fairings.

As experience with the Mercury continued, a new version, the Mercury VIS2 of 570 b.h.p., was fitted in *J9125* with a Boulton Paul Townend ring and, with full military load on board, the old prototype was officially tested at 215·5 m.p.h. at 16,500 feet.

This 40 m.p.h. margin that existed over the Bulldog now prompted the draft issue of Specification 24/33 to Gloster in September 1933. This called for the production of twenty-four aircraft by March 1935, based upon the S.S.19B. By the time the final Specification and Contract were issued in February 1934 a narrow-chord N.A.C.A. cowling, R.A.E. Mark IIA air starter (in place of the Hucks starter claw), Vickers Mark V guns and production 640 h.p. Mercury VIS2 were specified.

The first production Gauntlet I, *K4081*, was flown in December 1934 by P. E. G. ("Gerry") Sayer, who had come to Glosters from Brooklands when Hawker Aircraft Limited took over the Brockworth company that year. Once more the performance had increased, the increased power available from the Mercury VIS2 raising the speed to 230 m.p.h. at 15,800 feet. The climb to 20,000 feet from unstick now occupied only 9 minutes 28 seconds.

By the end of April 1935, twenty Gauntlet Is had been completed and on 25th May the first true deliveries were made to No. 19 (Fighter) Squadron, commanded by Squadron Leader J. R. Cassidy. (One aircraft, *K4086*, had in fact been taken on charge by the Squadron for trials on 18th February.) This Squadron was to fly Gauntlets until after the Munich Crisis, and throughout the three-and-a-half year period gained an outstanding reputation through the brilliance of its pilots. One of its Flight Commanders, Flight Lieutenant (later Air Chief Marshal Sir) Harry Broadhurst won the Fighter Air Firing Challenge Trophy at Sutton Bridge in 1935 and 1936. No. 19 Squadron, first to receive Gauntlets in 1935, were also

The first five production Gauntlet Is (K4081–K4085). Note differences in undercarriage wheel fairings.   (Gloster Aircraft photo)

No. 19 Squadron was the first to fly Gauntlets. The first nine aircraft are seen here at Duxford.

the first to fly the Spitfire in August 1938, although the last of the biplanes were not disposed of until January 1939.

THE GAUNTLET II

Following Gloster's take-over by Hawker Aircraft in 1934, studies were conducted to integrate production techniques, and it was decided that Glosters should adopt the Hawker system of construction. As the national military expansion programme slowly got under way in 1935, the Air Ministry placed a second production order for 104 Gauntlets in April that year, and a further contract for 100 the following September.

Designated Gauntlet IIs, these follow-on aircraft employed the Hawker structure in the rear fuselage which consisted basically of two Warren trusses built-up with lengths of steel and aluminium tube swaged to square section and bolted together with fish plates. Ball-ended tubes, butting into cupped bolts passing through the fish plates, separated the trusses and the whole structure was braced by crosswires with turnbuckles. Also included in the

After serving with No. 111 (Fighter) Squadron, this Gauntlet II was seconded to the R.A.E. for experiments as a radar "target".

Gauntlet II were Hawker wing spars which employed pairs of steel strip rolled to form flanged octagonal tubes and connected together with a steel strip web.

May 1936 saw the first Gauntlet II deliveries, twenty-four aircraft being delivered to Northolt for equal distribution between Nos. 56 and 111 (Fighter) Squadrons, in both cases replacing Bulldogs. For some months these two units remained below established strength owing to a number of accidents resulting from engine failures and fires. The faults were traced to a breakdown of the valve gear lubrication, a weakness that was to recur several times both on the Gauntlet and Gladiator during the period 1936–40. (It should be explained here that during the latter half of the nineteen-thirties Fighter Command squadron strength was officially fourteen aircraft at first-line state, these usually being ex-factory deliveries. In reserve were a further five aircraft, these probably possessing the highest number of flying hours, having been "rotated" from another unit.)

The two Northolt Gauntlet squadrons participated in a review fly-past over the unveiling ceremony at the Vimy Ridge memorial performed by King Edward VIII on 26th July 1936.

It was during July that the next Gauntlet squadron was formed, this time No. 66 (Fighter) Squadron coming into being at Duxford from a nucleus provided by "C" Flight of No. 19 Squadron, commanded by Sqdn. Ldr. Victor Croome. Working up on this unit continued smoothly throughout the remainder of 1936, but the following year was marred by a number of accidents, no fewer than five of the Squadron's aircraft being destroyed in mid-air collisions.

No. 151 Squadron was another unit re-formed—on 4th August 1936—with a nucleus from an established squadron, this time from No. 56. Provisionally classified as a reserve squadron, No. 151 flew an odd assortment of replacement Gauntlets and seldom possessed a strength of more than half a dozen, and

Gauntlet IIs of No. 151 (Fighter) Squadron. Note upper wing markings. A number of aircraft have the older Watts wooden propeller, whilst others have the three-blade Fairey metal type.
(Air Ministry photo)

Gauntlet Is of No. 111 (Fighter) Squadron at Northolt in 1936.

did not receive its full quota until March 1938.

The famous zig-zag markings of No. 17 Squadron at Kenley, so familiar on Woodcocks and Bulldogs since the mid-1920s, now appeared in August 1936 on Gauntlets, as sixteen new aircraft, *K5343–K5350* and *K5356–K5363*, were delivered. These aircraft were to become unique in the newly-constituted

No. 46 (Fighter) Squadron based at Kenley carried these distinctive markings on fuselage and upper wing. Upper fin portion of the Flight Commanders' aircraft carried Flight colours. See page 119 for full colour scheme.

Another view of a Gauntlet of No. 56 Squadron showing the markings on upper wing surfaces. (The Aeroplane photo)

Fighter Command in being painted with Flight colours extending over the entire upper decking of the fuselage, as well as on wheel discs. Within a month another famous squadron was to reform with Gauntlets from No. 17; this was No. 46 Squadron, formed from "B" Flight under Flt. Lt. M. F. Calder.

Nos. 32 and 54 Squadrons also received Gauntlets in 1936 and, of these, No. 32 must lay claim to the greater place in history. It was in November 1936 that, participating in trials accorded the utmost secrecy at the time, a Section of the Squadron's Gauntlets *K7797, K7799, K7800* was directed by the experimental radar at Bawdsey Manor to intercept an inbound airliner—the first successful radar-controlled fighter interception.

Neither No. 54 at Hornchurch nor No. 80 at Kenley (the latter formed early in 1937) retained their Gauntlets for more than a few months, their place being taken by Gladiators. No. 213 (Fighter) Squadron, re-formed on 8th March 1937 under Flt. Lt. J. R. MacLachlan at Northolt, moved almost immediately to Church Fenton in Yorkshire as part of the new No. 12 Group in the re-organised Fighter Command, and went on to win the Air Firing Challenge Trophy from No. 19 in the 1937 competition.

Engine failures in Service Gauntlets during 1937 again caused numerous accidents, one of the hardest-hit units being the newly-formed No. 79 (Fighter) Squadron at Biggin Hill—formed from "B" Flight, No. 32 Squadron. The cause of the engine failures was found to be the exhaust valve stems seizing—remedied by reaming out all Mercury exhaust valve guides.

Last R.A.F. squadron to receive Gauntlets during 1937 was No. 74, "Tiger" Squadron. Always tending towards the flamboyant, 74's Gauntlets were conspicuous in contravening current Air Staff instructions by extending their famous black and yellow "tiger's

Gauntlet I, K4101, was fitted with low pressure tyres for service in the Middle East. (Air Ministry photo)

teeth" markings to the tailplane leading edge, thereby excluding the fuselage serial number. Based at Hornchurch, 74 received its Gauntlets *after* having discarded Gladiators in June 1937; this anomaly has never been explained authoritatively, but it is thought that owing to the previous equipment with two-seat Demon fighters and the subsequent replacement by specialist single-seat pilots from a Gauntlet squadron (No. 80), a preference for the Gauntlet was universally expressed—a preference officially acknowledged in order to avoid the necessity to re-convert on the Gladiator. (It should be remarked here that Gladiator conversion occupied, on average, almost twice the flying time of that required for the Gauntlet. The essence was *speed* in the R.A.F.'s expansion during 1937.)

No. 74 Squadron justified its flamboyance with the Gauntlet, many of its pilots during those last years of peace achieving undying fame in Spitfires and Hurricanes in 1940. Among its pilots who won the Air Firing Challenge Trophy in Gauntlets in 1938 was a certain Fg. Off. A. G. ("Sailor") Malan.

The Gauntlet reached the climax of its first-line R.A.F. career in May 1937, fourteen squadrons being thus equipped. By the end of the year, Gladiators were beginning to replace the older aircraft, while the first monoplane fighters—Hurricanes—started to arrive on No. 111 Squadron at Northolt before Christmas 1937.

During 1938 almost all the old Gauntlet Is disappeared from front-line squadrons at home, and three-blade metal Fairey propellers were introduced on most Mark IIs (necessitating modifications to the gun interrupter gear and slowing the rate of fire). Just how unprepared for war Britain was at the time of Munich is shown by the fact that not one Gauntlet or Gladiator squadron was available at combat readiness, all R.A.F. Gauntlet squadrons being on leave. Within four days all had been recalled, some moving to war stations and most of the aircraft being hurriedly and inconsistently daubed with various camouflage "schemes". While some aircraft were painted the dark brown and green, others (in particular, one Flight of No. 79 Squadron's Gauntlets) were doped black overall for their rôle as night fighters.

Not only did the R.A.F. Gauntlets assume the anonymity of drab camouflage in the autumn of 1938, but the gaudily painted aircraft of the Auxiliary Air Force. No. 615 (County of Surrey) Squadron, for some

K7804, a Gauntlet II, of the Met. Flight, Duxford. Upper photo was taken during 1936; the same aircraft (below) photographed during 1938, showing modifications. (Air Ministry photos)

months an auxiliary army co-operation squadron flying Audaxes and Hectors, received its first Gauntlets just before Munich and, with its change of rôle to interception, became, at Kenley, merged into the London defences. Another auxiliary army co-operation squadron to receive Gauntlets was No. 601 (County of London) at Hendon on 31st October 1938, though Blenheims replaced the biplanes early in 1939.

No. 616 (South Yorkshire) squadron received Gauntlets at Doncaster on 30th January 1938, and, under the command of the Earl of Lincoln, were the only home-based squadron to retain the biplanes until after the outbreak of war in September.

No. 17 Squadron's Gauntlets at Kenley during the Munich crisis of 1938. Camouflage was crudely applied.

GAUNTLETS OVERSEAS

No. 616 Squadron's Gauntlets never fired their guns in anger, and though they were not listed in the first-line Order of Battle on 4th September 1939, there were others that were.

Gladiators had been shipped to the Middle East early in 1938, Nos. 33 and 80 Squadrons being thus equipped in the defence of the Suez Canal zone. Later in the year a number of Gauntlets were despatched to No. 102 Maintenance Unit at Abu Sueir as back-up equipment and for training purposes.

Another squadron, based in Palestine since the mid-1930s, was No. 6, equipped with Hawker Hardys, and on 23rd August 1939 the first of several Gauntlets was delivered to the Squadron whose "A" Flight was then based at Ramleh. The Squadron was engaged in co-operation with the Army and the Palestine Police in their efforts to curb the activities of renegade nomadic Arab gangs in their illicit trading, slaving and looting in remote Palestine villages. Having forced a gang of suspected Arabs to take refuge in a particular village, the ground forces and police would conduct a thorough search while patrolling aircraft kept watch for any would-be "cordon breakers", and, if necessary, use guns and light bombs to discourage such sorties. Within three days of delivery, the first Gauntlets of No. 6 Squadron were in action at Yatta, one of the pilots being Plt. Off. Sir R. A. MacRobert—one of three brothers all of whom served with the R.A.F. and later lost their lives in action.

By the beginning of 1940, No. 6 Squadron, commanded by Sqdn. Ldr. N. C. Singer, D.S.O., possessed nine Gauntlets (K4085, K4101, K5292, K5331, K7792, K7863, K7870, K7871 and K7881) and, together with two Lysanders and eighteen Hardys, launched a determined "Airpin" operation in conjunction with the Army to put an end to these diverting troubles. Eventually the Squadron took on a full strength of Lysanders, the last Gauntlet, K5292, being flown to Helwan on 7th June 1940 and handed over to No. 112 Squadron.

Nos. 33 and 112 Squadrons took over most of the available Gauntlets during 1940 as useful means to pursue training techniques while conserving Gladiator flying hours. No. 33 took on charge six Gauntlets (K5273, K5286, K5299, K5316, K7793 and K7884) at Mersa Matruh during February 1940, and these

Gauntlet IIs being refuelled in pairs. (*Flight* photo)

machines were still listed at reserve strength when Italy declared war on 10th/11th June that year. No. 112 also possessed five Gauntlets at Helwan on this date.

The last known instance of Gauntlets on active strength in the Royal Air Force was in 1943 when, due to a temporary shortage of replacement Gladiators in East Africa, four Gauntlets were delivered for training purposes to No. 1414 Met. Flight at Eastleigh on 1st May that year. There is no record of the aircraft

Gauntlets in Service

Representative aircraft with R.A.F. units:
No. 3 (F) Squadron, Kenley: (Mk.IIs only), *K3315, K7845.*

No. 6 (F) Squadron, Ramleh, Palestine: (Mk.I), *K4104;* (Mk.II), *K5290, K7792.*

No. 17 (F) Squadron, Kenley: (Mk.IIs only), *K5267, K7798.*

No. 19 (F) Squadron, Duxford: (Mk.I), *K4087* (crashed 26/1/37); (M.II), *K5270, K7808.*

No. 32 (F) Squadron: (Mk.II), *K5273, K7797.*

No. 33 (F) Squadron, Mersa Matruh, 1940: (Mk.II), *K5286.*

No. 46 (F) Squadron, Kenley: (Mk.II), *K5315, K7795* (crashed 14/12/36).

No. 54 (F) Squadron, Hornchurch: (Mk.II), *K5301, K7815.*

No. 56 (F) Squadron, North Weald: (Mk.II), *K5298* (caught fire and crashed 7/7/36; Sgt. Davis safe), *K7812.*

No. 65 (F) Squadron, Hornchurch: (Mk.II), *K5331, K7857.*

No. 66 (F) Squadron, Duxford: (Mk.II), *K5300, K7809.*

No. 74 (F) Squadron, Hornchurch: (Mk.II), *K5308, K7875.*

No. 79 (F) Squadron, Biggin Hill: (Mk.II), *K5310, K7799.*

No. 80 (F) Squadron, Kenley: (Mk.II), *K5339, K7863.*

No. 111 (F) Squadron, Northolt: (M.II), *K5264* (crashed 3/9/36), *K7811.*

No. 112 (F) Squadron, Helwan, Egypt, 1940: (Mk.II), *K5292.*

No. 151 (F) Squadron, North Weald: (Mk.II), *K5288, K7873.*

No. 213 (F) Squadron, Northolt and Church Fenton: (Mk.II), *K5301, K7857.*

No. 601 (County of London) Squadron, Northolt: (Mk. II), *K5336, K7881.*

No. 602 (City of Glasgow) Squadron: (Mk.II), *K5319, K7858.*

No. 605 (County of Warwick) Squadron, Castle Bromwich: (Mk.II), *K5269.*

No. 615 (County of Surrey) Squadron, Kenley: (Mk.II), *K5294, K7826.*

No. 616 (South Yorkshire) Squadron, Doncaster: (Mk. II), *K5357, K5364.*

Other R.A.F. units—No. 8 F.T.S. *K5281;* No. 9 F.T.S. *K4090;* No. 10 F.T.S. *K5278;* No. 1 Anti-Aircraft School *K4098;* Aldergrove Met. Flight *K5282;* No. 3 Bombing & Gunnery School *K5283;* No. 24 (Communications) Sqdn. *K5357;* Eastchurch Station Flight *K5291;* No. 325 Sqdn., 1940 *K5301;* Aldergrove Met. Flight *K5280, K5282, K5283.*

Representative Gauntlets sold abroad:
Sold to Rhodesia, 1936: *K5277;* 1939: *K7825.*
Sold to Finland, 1940: *K5352, K7813.*
Sold to South Africa, July 1940: *K5276, K7833.*
Aircraft also sold to Denmark, identities unknown.

Close-up of engine of Gauntlet I. (*Flight* photo)

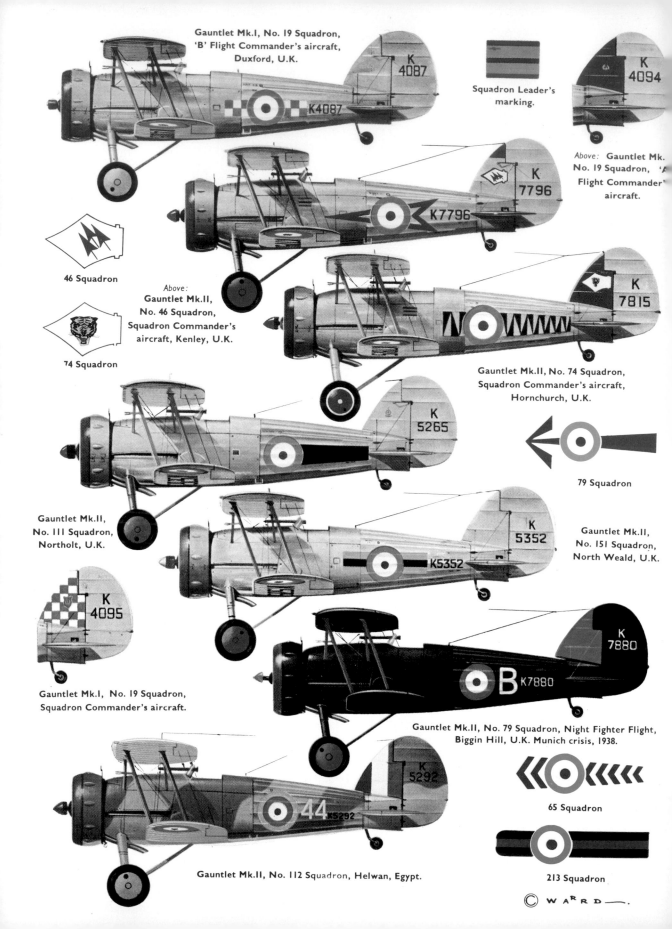

Gauntlet Mk.I, No. 19 Squadron, 'B' Flight Commander's aircraft, Duxford, U.K.

K4087

Squadron Leader's marking.

K 4094

Above: Gauntlet Mk. No. 19 Squadron, 'A' Flight Commander's aircraft.

46 Squadron

Above:
Gauntlet Mk.II, No. 46 Squadron, Squadron Commander's aircraft, Kenley, U.K.

74 Squadron

K 7796

Gauntlet Mk.II, No. 74 Squadron, Squadron Commander's aircraft, Hornchurch, U.K.

K 7815

K 5265

79 Squadron

Gauntlet Mk.II, No. 111 Squadron, Northolt, U.K.

K 5352

Gauntlet Mk.II, No. 151 Squadron, North Weald, U.K.

K 4095

Gauntlet Mk.I, No. 19 Squadron, Squadron Commander's aircraft.

K 7880

K7880

Gauntlet Mk.II, No. 79 Squadron, Night Fighter Flight, Biggin Hill, U.K. Munich crisis, 1938.

65 Squadron

K 5292

44 K5292

213 Squadron

Gauntlet Mk.II, No. 112 Squadron, Helwan, Egypt.

© WARD

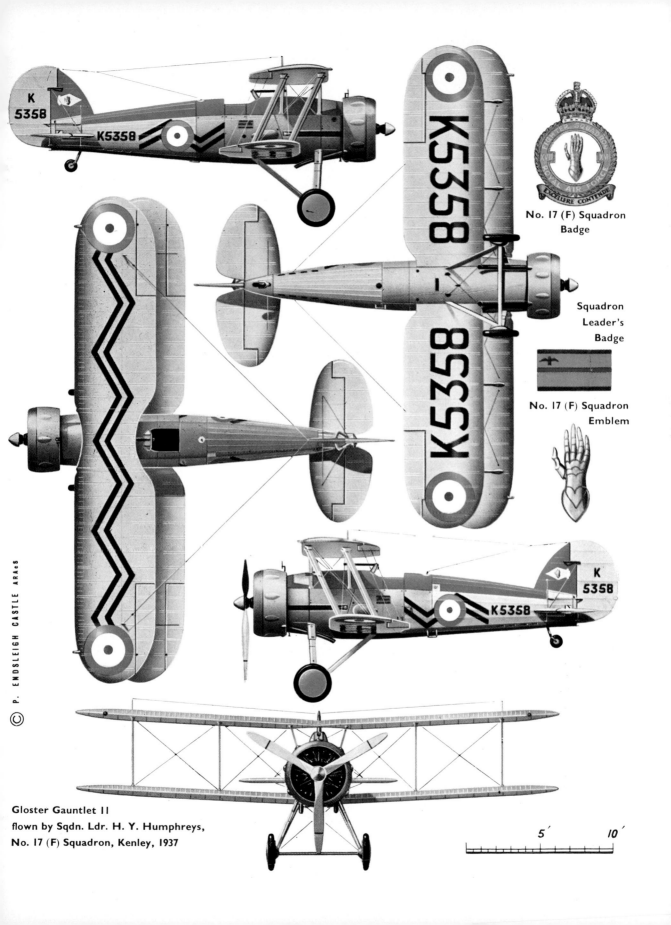

No. 17 (F) Squadron
Badge

Squadron
Leader's
Badge

No. 17 (F) Squadron
Emblem

© P. ENDSLEIGH CASTLE AR&aS

Gloster Gauntlet II
flown by Sqdn. Ldr. H. Y. Humphreys,
No. 17 (F) Squadron, Kenley, 1937

5′   10′

involved, yet it seems quite possible that they may have served on one of the operational squadrons in Palestine and the Western Desert three years previously, and in Fighter Command before that!

FLYING THE GAUNTLET

It has been said that the Gauntlet was the last truly aerobatic biplane fighter in the R.A.F., the Gladiator displaying distinctly "tricky" tendencies, especially at low airspeeds. The closed cockpit and landing flaps of the later aircraft undoubtedly contributed to the sense of flying a "monoplane with a top wing".

Grossing more than 1,200 lb. heavier than the Gauntlet, the Gladiator never acquired the popularity of the earlier aeroplane. The Gauntlet would become airborne in under 100 yards at full load with a light (5 knot) headwind, climbing to 20,000 feet in under ten minutes. In the dive prior to a loop, there was always the tendency to overspeed the engine but the airspeed quickly built up and only light pressure on the stick brought the aeroplane round and "over the top" without tendency to stall. Slow rolls were relatively difficult to perform without losing height, and were forbidden below 3,000 feet. Approaching to land, the airspeed was maintained at about 55 m.p.h. up to the boundary hedge, easing back to touch down at slightly over 50. Using wheelbrakes the ground run

was about 150 yards. Visibility in the air was good, but it was necessary to weave on the ground to see ahead.

Production

All aircraft built by the Gloster Aircraft Co. Ltd., Brockworth, Gloucester.

One prototype, *J9125*, progressively developed from Specification F.9/26, through S.S.18 to S.S.19B.

Gauntlet I. One production batch, *K4081–K4101*, 24 aircraft.

Gauntlet II. First production batch, *K5264–K5367*, 104 aircraft; second production batch, *K7792–K7891*, 100 aircraft.

Specification

Powerplant: Mk.I and II. One 640 h.p. Bristol Mercury VIS2 nine-cylinder air-cooled radial engine, driving 2-blade wooden Watts (on early aircraft) or 3-blade Fairey metal propeller (on late production aircraft).

Dimensions: Span 32 ft. 9½ in., length (Mk.I) 26 ft. 2 in., (Mk.II) 26 ft. 5 in., height (with Fairey prop.) 10 ft. 3 in., wing area 315 sq. ft.

Weights: (Mk.II)—empty 2,775 lb., loaded 3,970 lb.

Performance: (Mk.I and II similar)—maximum speed 230 m.p.h. at 15,800 feet. Initial climb 2,300 ft./min. Time 9 minutes to 20,000 feet. Range 455 miles. Service ceiling 33,500 feet.

Armament: Two Vickers Mk.V synchronised machine-guns with 600 rounds per gun.

Gauntlet Is of No. 19 (Fighter) Squadron in formation. Note variations of fin markings. (*Flight* photo)

The Handley Page Halifax III, VI, VII

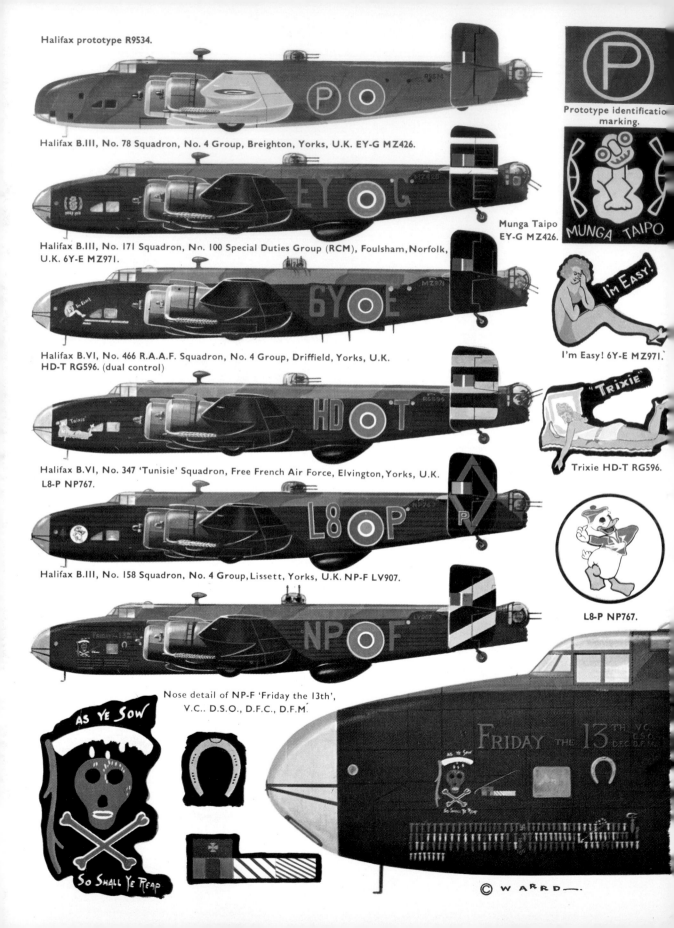

Halifax prototype R9534.

Halifax B.III, No. 78 Squadron, No. 4 Group, Breighton, Yorks, U.K. EY-G MZ426.

Halifax B.III, No. 171 Squadron, No. 100 Special Duties Group (RCM), Foulsham, Norfolk, U.K. 6Y-E MZ971.

Halifax B.VI, No. 466 R.A.A.F. Squadron, No. 4 Group, Driffield, Yorks, U.K. HD-T RG596. (dual control)

Halifax B.VI, No. 347 'Tunisie' Squadron, Free French Air Force, Elvington, Yorks, U.K. L8-P NP767.

Halifax B.III, No. 158 Squadron, No. 4 Group, Lissett, Yorks, U.K. NP-F LV907.

Prototype identification marking.

Munga Taipo EY-G MZ426.

I'm Easy! 6Y-E MZ971.

Trixie HD-T RG596.

L8-P NP767.

Nose detail of NP-F 'Friday the 13th', V.C.. D.S.O., D.F.C., D.F.M.

AS YE SOW

SO SHALL YE REAP

© W ARRD

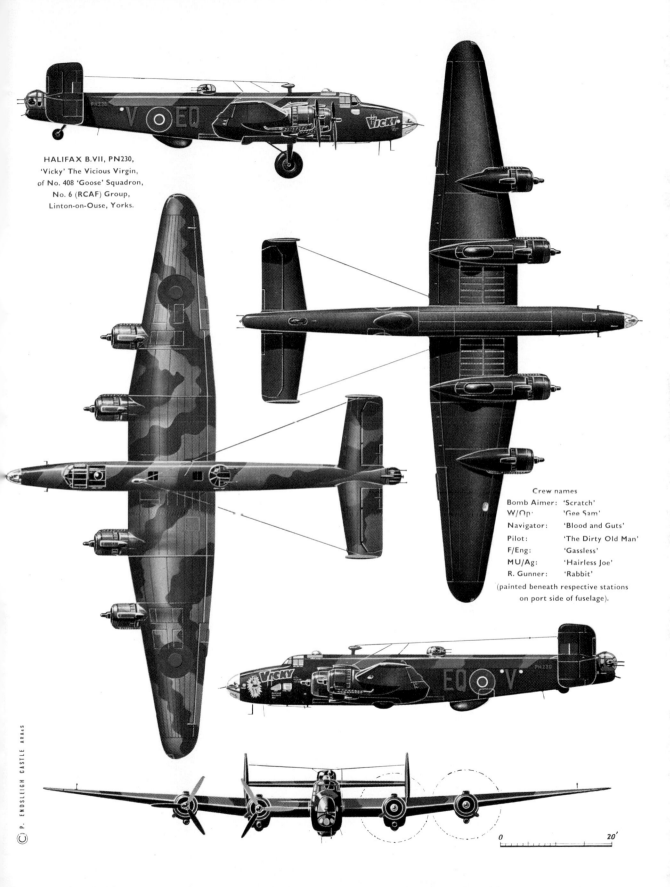

HALIFAX B.VII, PN230,
'Vicky' The Vicious Virgin,
of No. 408 'Goose' Squadron,
No. 6 (RCAF) Group,
Linton-on-Ouse, Yorks.

Crew names
Bomb Aimer: 'Scratch'
W/Op: 'Gee Sam'
Navigator: 'Blood and Guts'
Pilot: 'The Dirty Old Man'
F/Eng: 'Gassless'
MU/Ag: 'Hairless Joe'
R. Gunner: 'Rabbit'
(painted beneath respective stations
on port side of fuselage).

0   20'

The Handley Page Halifax B.III, VI, VII

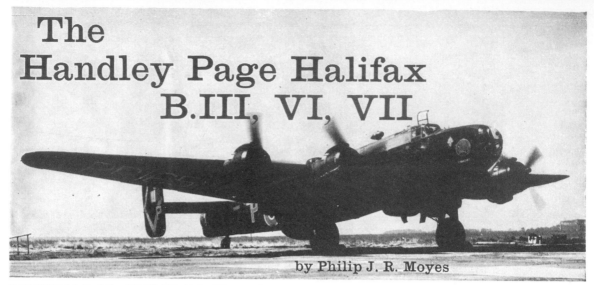

by Philip J. R. Moyes

B.VI PP165 L8–P of No. 347 (F.A.F.) Sqdn. (Groupe 1/25 "Tunisie") seen after V.E. Day. Groupe 1/25's "moonlit bison" badge appears on nose, also name "C. Brachet".
(Photo: French Air Force)

ONE of the truly famous aircraft of World War II, the Handley Page Halifax had its real beginning in Air Ministry Specification P.13/36 which called for an all-metal, mid-wing cantilever monoplane "heavy-medium" bomber powered by two Rolls-Royce Vulture liquid-cooled engines, then still under development. Two prototypes of the H.P.56, as the Vulture-powered aircraft was called, were ordered in April 1937, but the following August, when the doubtful prospects of the Vulture had become apparent, the Air Ministry induced Handley Page to re-design the bomber (apparently "much against the company's wishes"*) to take four Rolls-Royce Merlins instead. The prototype of the new aircraft, which was designated the H.P.57, first flew on 25th October 1939, piloted by Major J. L. Cordes. It had now grown considerably in size and weight compared with the original design. Its wing span was nearly 100 ft. and its all-up weight was around 55,000 lb. by the time it was ready for service.

The H.P.57 was ordered into production before the first prototype flew, the first "pilot" order—for 100—

* *The Design and Development of Weapons, H.M.S.O., 1964*

being placed in January 1939. A second prototype, which first flew in August 1940, was quickly followed by the "first off" less than two months later.

Lord Halifax foreshadowed his namesake's lethal powers at the official christening ceremony (featuring a late production Mk.I and with Lady Halifax officiating) at Radlett in September 1941. Quoting an old Yorkshire prayer, "from Hull, Hell and Halifax, good Lord deliver us", he said that the Germans might well use the same plea during the months and years to come.

There was nothing very unorthodox about the design of the Halifax. Briefly it was a mid-wing monoplane of moderate aspect ratio with four engines and twin fins and rudders. It was of all-metal construction with smooth, stressed-skin covering except for the control surfaces which were fabric-covered. The fuselage was "slab-sided" and contained a 22 ft.-long bomb bay, further cells being provided in the wing centre-section. The cockpit was flush with the top of the fuselage. Fat nacelles of Handley Page design and not the slim, Rolls-Royce designed standard "power-eggs" were used. These had a higher

First prototype B.III (Hercules VI engines), formerly Handley Page's "hack" B.II. Serialled R9534, this aircraft is the subject of a side-view colour drawing.

drag, but they later proved valuable since they were readily adaptable to the larger Bristol Hercules radial engines.

Four 1,145 h.p. Merlin X engines driving Rotol constant-speed compressed-wood airscrews gave the Halifax B.I a maximum speed of 265 m.p.h. at 17,500 ft. Normal range with 2,242 Imp. gal. of fuel and a 5,800 lb. bomb load was 1,860 miles. Maximum bomb load was 13,000 lb. Wing span was 98 ft. 10 in., length 70 ft. 1 in., and wing area 1,250 sq. ft. Defensive armament consisted of nose and tail Boulton Paul power-operated turrets, mounting two and four 0·303 in. Browning guns respectively. At first these were supplemented by beam guns poking out from the sides of the fuselage.

PRODUCTION PROGRAMME

To undertake the large production programme, an organisation known as the Halifax Group was formed. Besides the parent company, it comprised four main members, the first of which was English Electric, renowned for its production methods while building Hampdens. Its first Halifax—a B. Mk.II—flew in August 1941. Other companies brought into Halifax production were: the London Aircraft Production Group (Chrysler Motors, Duple Bodies and Motors, Express Motor and Body Works, Park Royal Coachworks and the London Passenger Transport Board), Rootes Securities and Fairey Aviation.

During its period of peak production, the Halifax Group comprised 41 factories and dispersed units (7½ million square feet), 600 sub-contractors and 51,000 employees. One complete Halifax was produced by it each working hour.

Two techniques which Handley Page helped to pioneer, photo-lofting and split construction and assembly, were the main factors behind the high rate of production. Out of 10,018 British heavy bombers built between 1940 and mid-1944, 4,046 were Halifaxes—more than 40 per cent. In all, 6,176 Halifaxes

were produced, the last one, an A (for Airborne Forces) Mark IX, being delivered to the R.A.F. at the end of 1946.

OPERATIONAL DEBUT

The Halifax made its operational debut on the night of 11th/12th March 1941, when No. 35 Squadron of No. 4 Group, R.A.F. Bomber Command, attacked the docks and shipping at Le Havre. Not until the following July, however, was the existence of the Halifax disclosed officially to the British public. The announcement following a daring daylight attack made by Halifaxes on the notorious *Scharnhorst* at La Pallice. The German battle-cruiser had slipped out of Brest but five direct hits and a hot time in general compelled her to return. She remained in Brest until an escape with the *Gneisenau* enabled them both to regain their home ports in a very battered condition.

The Halifax was withdrawn from daylight bombing operations after a final raid on the two battle-cruisers at Brest at the end of 1941 because increasing fighter opposition threatened to make the casualty rate in such raids prohibitive.

The Halifax B.II rapidly followed the B.I into service. It had various combinations of turrets and guns and sacrificed speed for fire-power or vice-versa.

By the end of 1943 a complete bomber Group (No. 4) based in Yorkshire was equipped entirely with Halifaxes. It operated with them throughout the remainder of the European war. The R.C.A.F. Bomber Group (No. 6) which formed in Yorkshire in late 1942 also adopted the Halifax. Although this was not its only aircraft, each of its ultimate total of 14 squadrons was for a time solely equipped with them.

Bomber Command reportedly had no less than 76 Halifax squadrons and other units at the time of its peak strength.

In the autumn of 1942, the original Halifax squadron, No. 35, was one of the five units chosen to form

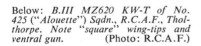

Right: *Thirteenth production B.III, HX-238, bearing "prototype" marking and allotted to Boulton Paul, R.A.F. Llandwrog (for air-firing trials), H.P., A and A.E.E., 48 M.U., and H.P. Rawcliffe in turn.*

Below: *B.III MZ620 KW-T of No. 425 ("Alouette") Sqdn., R.C.A.F., Tholthorpe. Note "square" wing-tips and ventral gun.* (Photo: R.C.A.F.)

B.III LL599 Z5-E of No. 462 (R.A.A.F.) Sqdn. Note "square" wing-tips. Ventral gun position was removed from photograph by wartime censor.
(Photo: R.A.A.F.)

the nucleus of the famous Pathfinder Force, later given Group status (No. 8 Group). In 1943 the first Canadian Halifax squadron, No. 405, joined it.

When the Pathfinder Force began to operate, a vast improvement was effected in the technique of night bombing. The Halifaxes lent their weight to the mounting round-the-clock offensive which Air Chief Marshal Arthur Harris (later M.R.A.F. Sir Arthur) had promised would "scourge the Third Reich from end to end".

By now the Halifax B.II Srs. IA was entering service. It retained the standard 4-gun Boulton Paul rear turret but in the mid-upper position was a compact Boulton Paul "Defiant"-type turret, mounting four guns instead of the earlier "Hudson"-type turret's two. It also had a neat moulded Perspex nose mounting a single hand-operated 0·303-in. Vickers "K" gun. Powered by Merlin XXs or XXIIs, this cleaned-up model had an edge of about 20 m.p.h. in cruising speed over the earlier versions. An interim version of the Halifax Mk.II known as the Mk.II Srs. I (Special) was produced and eventually this also had a "Defiant"-type dorsal turret. To overcome a shortage of Messier

undercarriages, the Halifax Mk.V which used a Dowty undercarriage was introduced and the two main versions of this—the Mk.V Srs. I (Special) and Srs. IA—corresponded to the above-mentioned Mk.II variants. It is hoped to describe in detail the development of these and also the earlier Merlin-powered Halifaxes in a later publication in this series.

HALIFAX B.III

Although the Merlin-engined Halifax did valuable work with Bomber Command, its all-round performance was always unsatisfactory because it was underpowered. Labouring along at only moderate heights it was easy prey for enemy fighters and by 1943 losses had become serious. The type continued to be unsatisfactory throughout 1943 and, to quote the Official History, "it was not until about February 1944, when the Mark III [Bristol Hercules air-cooled radial engines] became available in quantity, that the Halifax began to hold its own against the formidable fighter defences of the Third Reich".

The decision to produce the Halifax III (company

Left: *B.III LL573 "L8–B" of No. 347 (F.A.F.) Sqdn. seen at Rawcliffe, York, Xmas, 1945. Note ventral gun position.*

Below: *B.IIIs LL596 "KW–U" and MZ454 "KW–S" of No. 425 ("Alouette") Sqdn., R.C.A.F., Tholthorpe. Note wingtips and "mid-under" installations.*
(Photo: R.C.A.F.)

designation H.P.61) was taken after tests, begun in 1942, with Handley Page's "hack" Mk.II *R9534* re-engined with 1,615 h.p. Bristol Hercules VIs. The first production aircraft, *HX226*, made its first flight in July 1943.

The extra power afforded by the Hercules power plants boosted the Halifax's performance, and permitted a maximum all-up weight of 65,000 lb. Hercules XVIs driving de Havilland hydromatic airscrews were fitted and during production the wing span was increased from 98 ft. 10 in. to 104 ft. 2 in. The increase in wing area improved the operational ceiling and extended, curved wing-tips became standard on all subsequent marks. No. 2 fuel tank was transferred from the intermediate-section to the centre-section of the wings and provision made for additional (optional) fuel tanks in the outboard bomb cells in the centre-section. Other features of the Mk.III included a retractable tailwheel and an *H2S* scanner or a ventral gun position (one 0·50-in. Browning) as standard.

The Halifax III began to enter service with Bomber Command in November 1943 (the first squadrons to receive the type being Nos. 433 and 466 which received their first aircraft on 3rd November) and by the end of the year several squadrons of Nos. 4 (R.A.F.) and 6 (R.C.A.F.) Bomber Groups were so equipped.

Transformation of the war situation came in 1944 with the invasion of Europe. Attacks were made on French marshalling yards. Halifaxes returned to their early rôle of daylight bombers as a semi-tactical force. Gun emplacements on the French coast, strong points and troop concentrations were attacked with uncanny accuracy.

During an attack on Vaires marshalling yards at Paris on the evening of 18th July 1944, crews were given a convincing demonstration of the sound construction and airworthiness of the Halifax when B. Mk.III *MZ313*, captained by F./Lt. P. H. Finley of No. 466 (R.A.A.F.) Squadron, was severely damaged by a shell exploding in the fuselage. The rudders were u/s, the elevators would not respond and it seemed highly probable that the Halifax would break in two. Finley ordered his crew to bale out and his mid-upper gunner, while floating earthwards, considered that the aircraft's back was broken as the tail unit was swinging from side to side. Nevertheless, Finley and his bomb-aimer attempted to fly the aircraft back to base, and by great physical exertion managed to coax it back across the sea to the Dungeness area, where it became unmanageable; they baled out shortly before it disintegrated in the air. It appeared incredible but very praiseworthy that such a large part of the return flight had been made in such a condition, and general confidence in the rugged qualities of the Halifax was increased.

The only V.C. awarded to a Halifax pilot (or to any Halifax crew-member) went to P./O. Cyril J. Barton who displayed great gallantry in bringing his crippled Halifax of No. 578 Squadron back from a raid on Nuremberg on 30th/31st March 1944. Barton crash-landed in England and lost his life but his remaining crew (some had baled out earlier) survived. His aircraft was Halifax III *LK797* LK-E named *Excalibur* and bearing on its nose an emblem depicting a hand emerging from the base of a cloud and grasping the legendary sword of King Arthur.

In addition to disorganising enemy communications, Halifaxes waged a vigorous offensive against flying-bomb sites. The high water mark was reached in August 1944 when No. 4 Group alone flew 3,629 sorties. By this time the *Luftwaffe* was too enfeebled to offer very serious resistance although as recently as June this Halifax Group created a Bomber Command record by destroying 33 fighters.

This Group also undertook emergency transport work and in little more than one week ferried nearly half a million gallons of petrol to an airfield near Brussels to meet the urgent needs of the British Second Army during the heroic struggle at Arnhem.

The massive weight of Bomber Command was next hurled into the renewed offensive against oil targets.

Right: B.VI RG607—one of several presented to France after the war—of Groupe "Tunisie", F.A.F. seen at Mauripur, India, 12th Oct. 1947. Note freight pannier. (Photo: G. A. Cull)

Below: B.III NR169 "G-AGXA"—formerly "HD-T" of No. 466 (R.A.A.F.) Sqdn.—which Mr. G. N. Wickner purchased and flew to Australia in 1946.

Modified B.VI RG815 "Mercury" of the Empire Radio School, Debden. In 1946–47 this aircraft made a 25,000-mile radio and radar demonstration flight.

B.VI PN369, operating in S.E.A.C., seen on a mission against the Japanese. Note streamlined fairing beneath rear fuselage.
(Photo: Imp. War Mus.)

Of special significance was an attack on the oil plant at Homberg in the Ruhr on 27th August. A force of 216 Halifax IIIs from No. 4 Group and 27 Mosquitoes and Lancasters from No. 8 (Pathfinder) Group were despatched and were accompanied by an almost equal number of Spitfires of Fighter Command. Only one German fighter—a Bf. 110—was sighted by the Bomber Command crews and it was driven off by the Spitfires before it could do any damage. Heavy A.A. fire was encountered in the target area but none of the bombers was brought down and all the aircraft subsequently returned safely home. This was the first major daylight operation by Bomber Command against a German target in 1944 and the first also in which Bomber Command had ever penetrated beyond the Rhine with fighter cover. The target was partly obscured by cloud and although the damage done to it was somewhat scattered it was, in places, quite severe.

Some indication of the size of the Halifax's contribution to the war effort during 1944 can be gained from the activities of No. 4 Group alone. It flew 25,464 sorties (on all types of operation including bombing, sea-mining and emergency transport) at a cost of 402 aircraft.

Smashing attacks on Hanover, Magdeburg and Stuttgart came at the beginning of 1945. Cologne, Münster, Osnabruck and many other "old favourites" of Bomber Command—mostly homes of synthetic oil plants—also returned to the target list. Halifaxes bombed them by day and by night until the time came to pound the great railway centres preparatory to the climax of the war on the ground, the crossing of the Rhine.

In March, No. 4 Group dropped its record weight of bombs on Germany in a series of outstandingly successful raids. The loss rate for this month was the lowest in the Command.

B. MKS. VI AND VII

Two new marks of Halifax were in service alongside the B.III in the closing months of the European war—the Mks.VI and VII. Both had a pressure-transfer fuel system, with "grouped tanks" (one group per engine), additional tankage, special carburettor filters over the carburettor intakes and an *H2S* scanner permanently fitted. More and more attention was being paid to preparations for a final campaign in the

B.III NA497 "IP(?)–C", "Pubwash", No. 434 ("Bluenose") Sqdn., R.C.A.F.

Unidentified Halifax of No. 6 (R.C.A.F.) Group.

B.VI NP763 H7–N of No. 346 (F.A.F.) Sqdn. (Groupe 2/23 "Guyenne") in storage at No. 29 M.U., High Ercall, Feb. 1946. Close-up of Brer Rabbit insignia (white and blue on orange disc with red outer circle) appears on following page.

B.VI PP206 DY–P of No. 102 (Ceylon) Sqdn. photographed at No. 29 M.U. High Ercall, Feb. 1946.

Above: *B.VI RG867 L8–H of Groupe 1/25 "Tunisie", F.A.F. after the war. Note Boulton Paul "D"-type rear turret.*

Below: *B.VII NP808 of No. 426 ("Thunderbird") Sqdn. R.C.A.F. Named "I'm Easy" it is seen here shortly after transfer from No. 424 ("Tiger") Sqdn., R.C.A.F., and when its new codes "OW" had only been chalked on.*

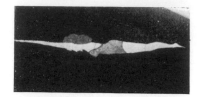

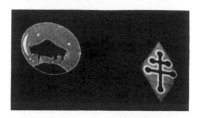

NOSE INSIGNIA. Top to bottom: *B.III NA499 "SE–W", No. 431 ("Iroquois") Sqdn. R.C.A.F.; B.III "IP(?)–Q", No. 434 ("Bluenose") Sqdn. R.C.A.F.; B.III MZ913, No. 462 Sqdn. R.A.A.F.; B.III "DT–B" "Babe", No. 192 Sqdn.*

Top to bottom: *B.III NP957 "KW–Q", No. 425 ("Alouette") Sqdn. R.C.A.F. (Photo: R.C.A.F.); B.VII NP756 "EQ–P", No. 408 ("Goose") Sqdn. R.C.A.F.; B.VI RG607 "X" (ex "H7–X") of Group "Guyenne", F.A.F. carrying insignia of Groupe "Tunisie". (Photo: G. A. Cull); B.VI NP763 "H7–N", No. 346 (F.A.F.) Sqdn.*

Top to bottom: *B.III MZ587 "PT–C", No. 420 ("Snowy Owl") Sqdn. R.C.A.F.; B.III NP995 "EY–Z", No. 78 Sqdn.; B.III MZ857 "BM–N", No. 433 ("Porcupine") Sqdn. R.C.A.F.; A B.III of No. 434 ("Bluenose") Sqdn. R.C.A.F. (Photo: R.C.A.F.)*

Far East, and "tropicalisation" was the order of the day for new types. The B.VI had four 1,675 h.p. Hercules 100 engines which gave it a maximum speed of 312 m.p.h. at 22,000 ft. and improved its all-round performance. It had an all-up weight of 68,000 lb. and the first B.VI, *NP715*, first flew on 10th October 1944. The B.VII had Hercules XVI engines—the power-plant of the B.III. This mark came into being because airframe production exceeded supply of Hercules 100 engines. It was used primarily by the squadrons of No. 62 (Beaver) Base and its sub-stations in No. 6 (R.C.A.F.) Group, i.e. Nos. 408, 426, 432 and (to a small extent) 415 Squadrons. The B.VI served in

Nos. 76, 77, 78, 102, 158, 346 and 640 Squadrons of No. 4 Group but was only just becoming estab-lished when hostilities in Europe ended.

FINAL OPERATIONS AND WAR RECORD

The last time that Halifaxes of Bomber Command operated in force against the enemy was on 25th April 1945, when a heavy daylight attack was made on coastal gun batteries on Wangerooge Island in the East Frisians. On 2nd/3rd May 1945, Halifaxes of No. 100 (Bomber Support) Group flew diversionary

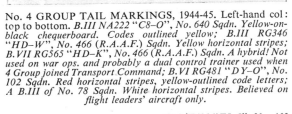

No. 4 GROUP TAIL MARKINGS, 1944-45. Left-hand col:
top to bottom. *B.III NA222 "C8–O", No. 640 Sqdn. Yellow-on-
black chequerboard. Codes outlined yellow; B.III RG346
"HD–W", No. 466 (R.A.A.F.) Sqdn. Yellow horizontal stripes;
B.VII RG565 "HD–K", No. 466 (R.A.A.F.) Sqdn. A hybrid! Not
used on war ops. and probably a dual control trainer used when
4 Group joined Transport Command; B.VI RG481 "DY–O", No.
102 Sqdn. Red horizontal stripes, yellow-outlined code letters;
A B.III of No. 78 Sqdn. White horizontal stripes. Believed on
flight leaders' aircraft only.*

Right-hand col: top to bottom. *B.III MZ431 "Z5–J", No. 462
(R.A.A.F.) Sqdn. Yellow vertical stripes; B.VI NP763 "H7–N",
No. 346 (F.A.F.) Sqdn. Red "trellis-work", yellow-outlined codes,
French fuselage roundels; B.III NA233 "NP–T", No. 158 Sqdn.
Yellow diagonal stripes; Z.VI RG669 "L8–G", No. 347 (F.A.F.)
Sqdn. Red "hollow-diamond", yellow-outlined codes, French
fuselage roundels.*

R.C.M. (sometimes with bomb-dropping) sorties
against Flensburg, Schleswig-Holstein and elsewhere,
in support of a Main Force attack on Kiel—Bomber
Command's last raid of the war.

Halifaxes of Bomber Command flew more than
82,000 operational sorties during the war, and dropped
nearly a quarter of a million tons of bombs. One
thousand eight hundred and thirty-three Halifaxes
were reported missing.

With No. 100 Group of Bomber Command Halifaxes waged a fantastic war of their own—a war of the
ether, jamming and confusing the enemy's radio and
utterly confounding his fighter controllers. Other
Halifaxes, operating with "Special Duties" squadrons
of Bomber Command, dropped secret agents in
enemy-held territory and countless loads of arms and
supplies to resistance movements.

At the end of the European war, Bomber Command's Halifax squadrons were either disbanded,
transferred to Transport Command and soon re-
equipped with Dakotas, Yorks or Liberators, or else—

in the case of some units of No. 6 Group—re-armed with Lancasters before returning to Canada. Nearly all the Halifaxes of Nos. 4 and 6 Groups found their way to Rawcliffe (York) or 29 M.U., High Ercall (Salop) and by 1947 most of them had been scrapped.

After V.E. Day, Halifaxes were sent to the Far East to harass the Japanese but the advent of the atom bomb almost made their journey unnecessary. Some of these bombers, fitted with extra fuel tanks in their bomb bays and carrying radar-detection equipment, did get an opportunity to pin-point enemy radar stations which were afterwards bombed.

One of the finest tributes to the Halifax was paid by F./Lt. N. G. Gordon (R.C.A.F.) of No. 158 Squadron, R.A.F., based at Lissett, near Bridlington. He was captain of the fourth crew to complete a tour of operations on *Friday the Thirteenth*. This renowned Halifax, despite its name and the skull and crossbones, scythe, inverted horseshoe and other unlucky signs painted on it, completed 128 operational sorties by V.E. Day. On his return from Gelsenkirchen, *Friday's* 100th op. on 22nd/23rd January 1945, F./Lt. Gordon said: "We always feel absolutely confident in her. She flies right and she always gets there . . ." *Friday* had by then undergone two major inspections and had 550 flying hours to its credit. It had never been left behind when due for an operation—a record which it maintained throughout the rest of its career.

Three more Halifaxes—all B.IIIs—passed the century mark on operations and details of these are as follows:

Serial	Sqdn.	Code and Ident. Letters	Date taken on charge	Op. Sorties
LV937	578	LK-X & 'R	March 1944	At least 100
	51	MH-J, 'M & 'E	April 1944	
LW587	578	LK-V & 'A	Feb. 1944	At least 104
MZ527	578	LK-W & 'D	March 1944	At least 105

The last two of these aircraft did their 100th ops. together—to Kamen on 3rd/4th March 1945. Another Halifax III, *LV917* NP-T, 'H and 'C of No. 158 Squadron is known to have flown 99 operations and seems to have had an extra op. "chalked up" on its nose for luck.

Halifax B.III Specification

Powerplants: Four Bristol Hercules XVI radial engines rated at 1,615 h.p. at 2,900 r.p.m. for take-off, 1,675 (5-min. limit) at 4,500 ft., and 1,455 h.p. at 12,000 ft.
Dimensions: Span 99 ft. (later a/c 104 ft. 2 in.); length 71 ft. 7 in.; height 20 ft. 9 in.; wing area 1,250 sq. ft. (later a/c 1,275 sq. ft.).
Weights: Tare, 38,240 lb., max. t/o 65,000 lb., max. landing 55,000 lb. Max. fuel capacity 2,688 Imp. gal.
Performance: (At normal loaded wt.) 278 m.p.h. at 6,000 ft., 282 m.p.h. at 13,500 ft.; most economical cruising speed 215 m.p.h. at 20,000 ft.; range (with 1,150 Imp. gal. and 13,000-lb. bomb load) 1,030 mls., (with 1,986 Imp. gal. and 7,000-lb. bomb load) 1,985 mls.; Service ceiling (normal loaded) 24,000 ft., (max loaded) 20,000 ft.; initial rate of climb 960 ft./min., time to 20,000 ft., 37·5 min. (max. wt.) 50 min.
Armament: One flexible 0·303 Vickers "K" gas-operated gun with 300 rounds in nose and four 0·303 in. Browning guns with 1,160 r.p.g. in each of Boulton Paul dorsal and tail turrets. Some early a/c had one flexible 0·5 in. Browning gun in a ventral "blister". Max. bomb load 13,000 lb.
Alternative fuselage bomb loads, six 1,000-lb. plus two 2,000-lb., one 8,000-lb., two 4,000-lb., four 2,000-lb., eight 1,000-lb., two 1,500-lb. (mines) plus six 500 lb., or nine 500-lb. bombs, plus six 500-lb. bombs in wing cells.

Production

101 B.III (H.P.) *HX226–247, HX265–296, HX311–357.*
104 B.III (Fairey) *LK747–766, LK779–812, LK826–850, LK863–887.*
60 B.III (Rootes) *LL543–559, LL573–615.*
225 B.III and 15 B.VII (H.P.) *LV771–799, LV813–842, LV857–883,*

LV898–923, LV935–973, LV985–999, LW–113143, LW157–179, LW191–195, B.III; *LW196–210,* B.VII (most of these B.VIIs went to No. 426 (R.C.A.F.) Sqdn.).
260 B.III (English Electric) *LW346–348, LW361–397, LW412–446, LW459–481, LW495–522, LW537–559, LW572–598, LW613–658, LW671–696, LW713–724.*
180 B.III (London Acft. Prodn. Gp.) *MZ282–321, MZ334–378, MZ390–435, MZ447–495.*
360 B.III (English Electric) *MZ500–544, MZ556–604, MZ617–660, MZ672–717, MZ730–775, MZ787–831, MZ844–883, MZ895–939.*
219 B.III (Rootes) *MZ945–989, NA102–150, NA162–205, NA218–263 NA275–309.*
180 B.III (Fairey) *NA492–531, NA543–587, NA599–644, NA656–704.*
105 B.VII and 95 B.VI (H.P.) *NP681–723, NP736–781, NP793–820,* B.VII except for *NP715, 748, 752, 753, 758, 760, 762–767; NP821–836, NP849–895, NP908–927* B.VI.
200 B.III (English Electric) *NP930–976, NP988–999, NR113–156, NR169–211, NR225–258, NR271–290.*
42 B.III and 20 (or 21?) B.VII (Fairey) *PN167–208,* B.III; *PN223–242 (and PN343 ?)* B.VII.
80 B.III (London Acft. Prodn. Gp.) *PN365–406, PN423–460.*
37 B.VI (H.P.) *PP165–187, PP203–216.*
80 B.III, 20 B.VII and 400 B.VI (English Electric) *RG345–390, RG413–446,* B.III; *RG447–458, RG472–479,* B.VII; *RG480–513, RG527–568, RG583–625, RG639–679, RG693–736, RG749–790, RG813–853, RG867–879,* B.VI.
25 B.VI and/or G.R.VI (H.P.) *ST794–818* (16 of these converted to G.R.VI and 3 others supplied to French Air Force).
23 B.VII (and A.VII?) (H.P.) *TW774–796* (originally allotted serials *PP142–164* but re-numbered as these compromised Short Sunderland serials).

Halifax B.IIIs, 'VIs and 'VIIs in Service

Examples of aircraft used by operational squadrons.‡
No. 4 Group:
No. 10 Sqdn., Melbourne: *MZ902* 'ZA-R' (B.III†, H2S).
No. 51 Sqdn., Snaith: *LL548* 'MH-D' (B.III*, v.g.), *LK843* 'C6-F' (B.III*, no H2S or v.g., 'C' Flt.).
No. 76 Sqdn., Holme-on-Spalding Moor; *NA571* 'MP-M' 'Die Fledermaus' (B.III), *TW794* 'MP-A' (B.VI).
No. 77 Sqdn., Full Sutton: *MZ769* 'KN-R' (B.III, H2S), *RG531* 'KN-R' (B.VI).
No. 78 Sqdn., Breighton: *NP995* 'EY-Z' 'Zooloo Mk.II' (B.III), *RG662* (B.VI).
No. 102 Sqdn., Pocklington: *LW159* 'DY-P' 'Popeye' (B.III), *RG485* 'DY-J' 'Joanie' (B.VI).
No. 158 Sqdn., Lissett: *MZ373* 'NP-O' 'Otophelia, Bert's Bag' (B.III†, H2S), *RG644* 'NP-R' (B.III), *RG495* 'H7-A' (B.VI).
No. 347 (F.A.F.) Sqdn., Elvington: *LL573* 'L8-B' (B.III*, v.g.), *RG669* 'LG-G' (B.III).
No. 462 (R.A.A.F.) Sqdn., Driffield: *NP989* 'Z5-F' (B.III).
No. 466 (R.A.A.F.) Sqdn., Driffield: *NR127* 'HD-M' (B.III).
No. 578 Sqdn., Snaith and Burn: *LW473* 'LK-P' (B.III).
No. 640 Sqdn., Leconfield: *MZ856* 'C8-S' (B.III), *RG588* 'C8-S' (B.VI).
No. 6 (R.C.A.F.) Group:
No. 408 (Goose) Sqdn., Linton-on-Ouse: *MZ904* 'EQ-G' (B.III), *NP742* 'EQ-U' 'Embraceable "U"' B.VII.
No. 415 (Swordfish) Sqdn., East Moor: *LK766* '6U-Q' (B.III*, v.g.), *PN240* '6U-W' (B.VII).
No. 420 (Snowy Owl) Sqdn., Tholthorpe: *LW380* 'PT-B' 'The Bird of Prey—Achtung Gallopin' Buzzard' (B.III†).
No. 424 (Tiger) Sqdn., Skipton-on-Swale: *HX346* 'QB-U' (B.III).
No. 425 (Alouette) Sqdn., Tholthorpe: *MZ425* 'KW-U' 'Little Lulu' (B.III, H2S).
No. 426 (Thunderbird) Sqdn., Linton-on-Ouse: *LK880* 'OW-C' (B.III) *NP740* 'OW-C' 'Cowan's Cowards' (B.VII).
No. 427 (Lion) Sqdn., Leeming: *MZ823* 'AL-E' 'Tondelayo' (B.III).
No. 431 (Iroquois) Sqdn., Croft: *MZ881* 'SE-A' (B.III).
No. 432 (Leaside) Sqdn., East Moor: *LK754* 'QO-Z' (B.III), *NP774* 'QO-Z' 'Overseas Zombie' (B.VII).
No. 433 (Porcupine) Sqdn., Skipton-on-Swale: *MZ883* 'BM-S' (B.III).
No. 434 (Bluenose) Sqdn., Croft: *NA522* 'IP(?)-U'.
No. 8 (P.F.F.) Group:
No. 35 Sqdn., Gravely: *HX321* 'TL-K' (B.III).

No. 100 (Bomber Support) Group:
No. 171 Sqdn., North Creake: *NA694* '6Y-H' (B.III).
No. 192 Sqdn., Foulsham: *MZ817* 'DT-Q' (B.III).
No. 199 Sqdn., North Creake: *PN374* 'EX-N' (B.III).
No. 462 (R.A.A.F.) Sqdn., Foulsham: *MZ306* 'Z5-X' (B.III).

*98 ft. 10 in. span.
†104 ft. 2 in. span.
v.g. = ventral gun.

‡In addition to the squadrons, many Halifaxes served at Heavy Conversion Units, the Bomber Command Instructors' School and other training units.

The Gloster Meteor F.8

The Gloster Meteor F.8

by C. F. Andrews

Meteor F.Mk.8s of No. 63 Squadron, circa 1953. Note squadron marks on fuselage and wing tips.

THE 5th of March 1943 was a day of great significance for the Royal Air Force, for it was then that Britain's first jet-propelled fighter, the Gloster Meteor, took off from Cranwell's runway on its maiden flight.

The supremacy of the piston-engined aeroplane was about to be challenged by a new method of propulsion, and although the early Meteor marks were only marginally faster than the contemporary Tempest, Mustang, etc., the potential was obvious.

Only a few, short years were to pass before jet-engined fighters superseded those equipped with the reciprocating powerplant, but it had been a long, hard struggle against tremendous odds to put the first Meteor into the air on that March day.

Meteor Mk.1s. were produced in sufficient numbers to enable them to take part in the last few weeks of the war against Germany, and from this basic design was evolved the Meteor Mk.3 and 4, which served with the regular and auxiliary squadrons of the Royal Air Force.

By the end of 1947 the Meteor had been in continuous production for just over four years, and the airframe differed very little from that as originally developed for the prototype F.9/40s. But so rapid was the progress made in improving performance of jet propelled aircraft, largely through great increases in the thrust of new types of turbo-jet engines, that by the end of the year the Meteor in its Mark F.4 version was beginning to fall behind other jet fighters.

Consequently the Gloster design office undertook a major design at that time to improve the performance of the Meteor and to provide for new equipment demanded by changing operational requirements. For production facility as many F.4 components were retained as possible as well as suitable constructional and tooling jigs.

The new Mark of Meteor was designated F.8 as the intervening numbers had been taken up by the F.R.5, intended for photographic reconnaissance, and the projected F.6, which was similar in drawing board outline to the subsequent F.8, and the two-seat Meteor trainer T.7, which was produced in quantity for the R.A.F. and for the Navy.

The Meteor F.8 was to be Britain's number one fighter for five years, and with this mark it reached its peak of efficiency and performance, and it formed the

The prototype Meteor F.8, originally an F.4, with the Gloster E1/44. Fin and rudder of the latter was successfully adopted for the F.8.

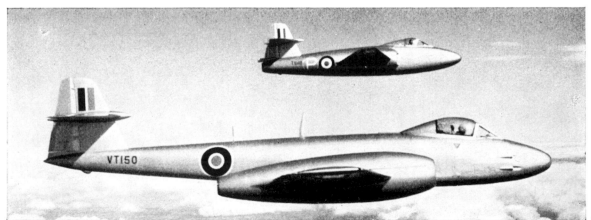

WA982 was used to flight test the Rolls-Royce Soar engine, weighing a mere 275 lb. Only one Soar was installed, the port fixture being a dummy.   (Photo: Rolls-Royce)

bulk of Fighter Command of the Royal Air Force from 1950 to 1955. The F.8 was the only British jet fighter to take part in major air actions since the end of World War II, and it served with many other nations well into the early 1960s. It was a classic example of re-engineering a basic design to squeeze the utmost development out of an already successful and, indeed, historic aeroplane.

Progressive strengthening of the Meteor airframe, increases in engine weight and additional equipment stowage in the rear fuselage necessitated the introduction of more and more ballast in the nose to maintain a reasonable c.g. position. In the F.4 no less than 1,000 lb. of ballast was required. This consisted of lead weights attached to the mounting structure of the nose undercarriage and heavy alloy rings comprising the engine intake leading edges to the nacelles.

All this dead weight had to be lost and the most promising project was for a lengthening of the nose itself to correct the c.g. position, the additional space provided being used to house an extra fuel tank and so give increased range.

A Meteor F.4, *RA382*, was modified to take a 30 in. additional section between the existing centre section and the front fuselage. This involved a forward shift of the armament bay and its 800 lb. of ammunition. As the latter was gradually expended by the firing of the guns so the nose became progressively lighter leading to the pitch instability of the aeroplane. Control with the existing Meteor tail became difficult but by one of those strange fates that sometimes occur in aeronautical development, it was found in the R.A.E. wind tunnel that the tail of the Gloster single engine E.1/44 fighter, a project that never entered production, suited the case admirably.

Accordingly, a substitute installation of this tail was made on *RA382* and the handling trials were instantly successful, the new tail giving the necessary control. Although contracts had been placed for the old tail assembly a decision was made to equip all F.8s with the E.1/44 type, so much better was the aircraft in this form. Only minor modifications were needed, one being the replacement of the wooden upper component of the E.1/44 fin (to take a suppressed radio aerial) by a metal assembly.

A true prototype, *VT150*, was constructed to continue trials. This featured a new, one-piece blown canopy which provided much improved rearward vision, and with this modification *VT150* made its first flight on 12th October 1948. Flight trials con-

Meteor VZ460 of the Central Fighter Establishment was used for tests with rocket projectiles and bombs. (Photo: Gloster Aircraft)

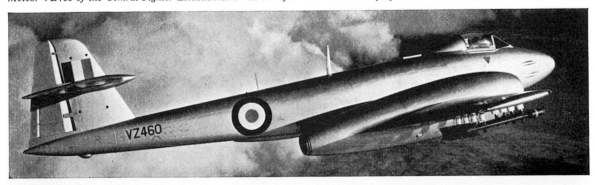

The most powerful Meteor 8 flown was WA820, fitted with two Armstrong-Siddeley Sapphire engines providing 15,200 lb.s.t.
(Photo: Hawker Aircraft)

tinued with this F. Mark 8 prototype and confirmed the promise that the new version of the Meteor was a great improvement on all previous variants, general handling being easy and delightful at all speeds. On test quite high Mach numbers were obtained, but these were not considered sufficiently free from control difficulties to be permitted to the average Service pilot in the course of normal flying.

Various components in the airframe were strengthened to meet increased stress requirements consequent upon the higher performance and loadings of the Mark F.8. The power units were Rolls-Royce Derwent 8s each developing 3,500 lb. thrust. These were mounted between the spars as in the earlier marks. The Meteor airframe was in fact quite a conventional structure and one of the points often overlooked when considering Meteor development was that the design generally was based on piston engine practice. The only feature which characterised the Meteor as a jet-propelled fighter was its short undercarriage rendered possible by the absence of need for propeller clearance.

The Meteor F. Mark 8, powered by two Royce Derwent turbo-jet engines, attained a maximum speed of 529 m.p.h. (Mach 0·78) at sea level, 550 m.p.h. (Mach 0·81) at 30,000 ft. and 530 m.p.h. (Mach 0·8) at 40,000 ft. The first F.8 was delivered to the Royal Air Force, No. 43 (F) Squadron, on 2nd August 1949 and was serialled *VZ440*. The first production F.8 of an initial batch of 128 on order for the R.A.F. was *VZ438* and it went to No. 1 (F) Squadron on 10th December 1949.

The Meteor F.8 was the standard equipment of the following regular R.A.F. Squadrons—Nos. 1, 2, 13, 19, 25, 29, 33, 34, 41, 43, 54, 56, 63, 64, 65, 66, 72, 91, 92, 111, 153, 208, 209, 211 A.F.S., 222, 226 O.C.U., 245, 247, 257, 263 and the Auxiliary Squadrons Nos. 500 "County of Kent", 504 "City of Nottingham", 600 "City of London", 601 "County of London", 604 "County of Middlesex", 609 "West Riding", 610 "County of Chester", 611 "West Lancashire", 614 "City of Glamorgan", 615 "County of Surrey", and 616 "South Yorkshire". It started regular service in the R.A.F. with No. 245 Squadron at Horsham St. Faith on 29th June 1950 and continued in that service until 1955 when it was largely replaced in the Squadrons by Hawker Hunters. The last R.A.F. Meteor F.8 actually went from No. 245, in April 1957.

Interesting F.8 conversion was WK935. Second cockpit accommodated pilot in prone position.

THE METEOR IN KOREA

No Meteor F.8 went overseas in Squadron service or went into action with the R.A.F. but it fought with distinction against superior enemy fighters in the Korean War in the hands of the Royal Australian Air Force.

These Meteors served with No. 77 Squadron, R.A.A.F., which at the outbreak of the Korean War

The Armstrong-Siddeley Screamer rocket motor was tested in VZ517.

High-altitude tests were carried out with VZ439, fitted with strengthened hood.

was stationed at Iwakuni, Japan, equipped with North American F-51 Mustang piston-engined fighters. Its first action was in July 1950, and after nearly two years of hard flying and fighting with the Mustangs, No. 77 heard that it was to be re-equipped with jet fighters with which to meet the formidable MiG 15s, in service with the Chinese Air Force, after the intervention of the People's Republic into the struggle between North and South Korea.

Hopes that the Squadron would get the F-86 Sabre were soon dashed and it was learned that it would be re-equipped with the Meteor F.8 as the most modern jet fighter available to the Australian Government, short of the Hunter, which was in fact making slow development progress at that time. No. 77 therefore

returned to its home base at Iwakuni to receive the Meteors at the end of February 1951.

Some uncertainty became evident as to the best use of the F.8. It was inferior to the Mig 15 which was capable of a speed of Mach 1 at least and was very efficient at high altitude, while the Meteor was much slower and lacked manoeuvrability at height. American assessments emphasised these shortcomings as well as the restricted rear view (later a fully transparent hood was fitted to R.A.F. F.8s). Further difficulties arose over the lack of radio compass but this was ironed out by providing one for each flight of aircraft and flying to a minimum 1,000 ft. cloud base.

No. 77 flew its first mission with Meteors on 29th July in a fighter sweep with Sabres but not until

Meteor F.8 (VZ461) of No. 43 Squadron.

Squadron Leader's aircraft, No. 610 Squadron.

WK921 of No. 29 Squadron.

WK655 bore Nos. 85 and 141 Squadron markings.

WH359 of No. 611 Squadron.   (Photo: M. Bowyer)

WK810 of No. 615 Squadron. Green/grey camouflage. Note fin flash.

Meteor F.Mk.8s of No. 41 Squadron. Note squadron leader's badge under cockpit of aircraft in foreground. (Photo: Gloster Aircraft)

29th August did the Meteors go into action when, in a sweep over Chongju in the notorious "MiG Alley", eight F.8s had the worst of a brush with about 30 MiGs, one pilot being lost as a prisoner-of-war after baling out. A further engagement a week later was similarly indecisive, one Meteor returning to base in a damaged condition but it was clear that the MiG 15 was in fact undoubtedly superior. Accordingly the rôle of the F.8 was modified in agreement with the U.S. Air Force Commanders, and it was allocated the task of escorting B-29 bombers. On one of these missions 16 Meteors in four sections ran into a battle between Sabres and MiGs but were unable to fire for fear of hitting the American aircraft.

After the Americans had abandoned daylight precision bombing because of the losses suffered against the armada of Chinese MiGs operating from safe airfields in Manchuria, the Australian Meteors continued to patrol regularly in a defined area south of the Chongchon. On 1st December 1951 No. 77 was in action against a large formation of MiGs. Three aircraft were lost and one or possibly two MiGs were destroyed in return.

A spell of airfield defence followed for No. 77 in which the superior climbing powers of the Meteor over the Sabre were utilised. At the end of 1951 a new commander arrived in the Squadron, Wg./Cmdr. Ronald Susans, and he eventually obtained sanction for the Meteor to be used for ground attack, a rôle for which the aircraft was specially suited because of its rugged construction and low altitude performance. A successful sortie of this nature, with cannon fire and rocket strike, on a water tower, proved the point that the Meteor was a good platform for this brand of air warfare.

During January 1952 the Australian Squadron flew 769 sorties in ground attack and in February over one thousand, and in the course of these four pilots and

Although a Gloster private venture aircraft G–7–1 was basically a Mark 8, it could carry 24 rockets or four 1,000 lb. bombs, plus tip tanks. It was named the Reaper.
(Photos: Gloster Aircraft)

Another Gloster P.V. was G–AMCJ, also based on the Mark 8. It could carry a variety of stores and was stressed for R.A.T.O.G.
(Photo: M. Bowyer)

aircraft were lost. In May No. 77 reverted to fighter sweeps and on the 8th of that month flew no fewer than 70 sorties. The last encounter of Meteor and MiG was in March 1953 when Sgt. John Hale managed to record a victory.

When the Korean War ended in July 1953, the tally for No. 77 Squadron, R.A.A.F., was 18,872 individual sorties, pilots lost 42, 32 of them in Meteors. To their credit, they had three confirmed victories over the redoubtable MiG 15s, as well as other successes and had wrought enormous damage to enemy ground installations. Although the Meteor was by then ten years old, No. 77 had proved that it still had plenty of life left in it during the hectic days of Korea.

THE EXPERIMENTAL F.8s

More Meteor F.8s were produced than any other mark and many were used in consequence for experimental purposes. Some of the more important of these special variants of the basic F.8 are set out below.

VT150. Prototype F.8 later used for testing spin parachute installations for the Javelin and also for investigation into influence of gun blast on nose structures.

VZ438. First production F.8 later used at Farnborough for experiments leading to the Meteor F.R.9 before final conversion to the target towing rôle T.T.8. A number of F.8s were converted to T.T.8 standard after the F.8 had left first-line service and the last Meteor in the Far East Air Force was T.T.8 *WH398*, which retired from Seletar air base at the end of 1961.

VZ460. Acceptance trials with bomb pylon carriers and R.P. tests. Also flown with spring tab ailerons.

VZ468. Captured the London–Copenhagen record.

VZ500. Used to investigate the effect on an auto-stabiliser on yaw.

VZ517. After serving at Rolls-Royce Hucknall for investigation into engine surge in the Derwent 8 engine, was used to conduct flight tests with the Armstrong-Siddeley Screamer rocket engine.

VZ657. Used for finding a solution to the problem of preventing damage to the ventral fuel tank of the F.8 by spent cartridge cases.

VZ442. A series of trials on this aircraft provided a satisfactory remedy for faulty canopy fastenings.

With the addition of a target-towing lug to the belly tank, the F.8 became the T.T.8. It had yellow undersides with black bands.

Large numbers of F.8s were converted to unmanned target drones. WH344 was a typical example of the U.Mk.16 aircraft.
(Photo: Flight Refuelling)

WA775. Experiments with nose radar for Firestreak missile for Hunter fighters.

WA820. Test bed for Armstrong-Siddeley Sapphire engines each of 7,600 lb. thrust. Needed extensive modifications and strengthening of airframe.

WA823, WA828 to *830, WA832, WA834, WA836, WA837, WA936, WA938, WA941, WA946* and *WA952*. All these aircraft were used in "probe and drogue" flight refuelling trials notably with No. 245 Squadron stationed at Horsham St. Faith.

WA982. Modified to flight test the Rolls-Royce Soar lightweight jet engines. These were mounted at the wing tips so this Meteor was in fact the only four-engined example of the Meteor to fly.

WE855. Used in 1957 for experiments with over-run "catch" barriers on airfields.

WH301. Many F.8s were converted to advanced trainers and redesignated the T.8. This aircraft was one of the first to be converted.

WH483. Tests with spring tab ailerons to improve rate of roll and reduction of lateral stick forces at higher speeds.

WK935. Converted for most interesting series of experiments into prone pilot position for Bristol Type 185 rocket interceptor project.

THE FOREIGN F.8s

When the war ended in August 1945, the demand for the Meteor was almost insatiable and Glosters were swamped with orders from the Air Ministry. But, other countries were beginning to re-equip their air forces, and it was inevitable that their first thoughts would be for the new jet fighter.

Large numbers of the Mark 3 and 4 were exported, as were the F.8s. In alphabetical order there follows a list of countries which took delivery of the Gloster fighter.

After cessation of hostilities in Korea No. 77 Squadron of the *Royal Australian Air Force* returned home taking with them their F.8s. In 1955 these were exchanged for the Australian-built Commonwealth CA-27 Sabre Mk.30s and the F.8s were relegated mainly to training duties, while a few were issued to the Citizen Air Force. With this force the Meteors operated with No. 22 and No. 23 Squadrons. A small number were converted to the U.Mk.16, 21 and 21A configuration for use as pilotless drones, and a number were utilised for target towing. The final front-line unit to operate the F.8 was No. 75 Squadron, which was also the first to form a three-unit aerobatic team known as "The Meteorites".

The F.8 could be converted to the F.R.9 by the attachment of a camera nose. VW360 was an F.R.9, but here it lacks a camera nose and is carrying eight HVAR rockets.

Above: *Meteor 8, 1st Squadron, 1st Fighter Group, Brazilian Air Force. Blue trim on nose and fin.* Below: *Danish F.Mk.8.*

Belgium operated large numbers of Meteors, exchanging the obsolete F.4s for F.8s in late 1949. Twenty-three ex-R.A.F. machines were delivered, serials running from *EG-201* to *EG-223*, but the second batch of 150 (serials *EG-1* to *EG-150*) aircraft were built under licence by Avions Fairey of Holland, who had been building the aircraft under licence since April 1949. Two further batches of 30 and 37 aircraft were acquired, these being assembled by Fairey from components supplied by Fokker Aircraft. The F.8 remained in service with the B.A.F. until 1956, when it was replaced by the Hawker Hunter.

Sixty Meteor F.8s were sold to *Brazil*, these replacing most of the ageing Thunderbolts and remaining in service for over ten years. Serial numbers ran from *4400* to *4459* and were in black on an overall silver finish.

The *Danish* Government placed an order with the Gloster Aircraft Company for 20 F.Mk.8 Meteors in April 1950, and the first was delivered in January 1951. Serials ran from *481* to *500* and the aircraft were finished in a grey and green camouflage. The F.8s served with No. 742 Squadron until replaced by Hunters in 1956. A number of Meteors remained in use as target tugs until as late as March 1962.

Modernisation of the *Egyptian Air Force* was started in 1949, and in the October of that year an order was placed with Glosters for 19 Meteor F.8s. An additional five were ordered in the December, but work on both contracts was suspended a year later when an arms embargo covering the Middle East was put into effect. In December 1952 seven F.8s were delivered, followed by 15 more three years later. Serial numbers of the original seven aircraft (ex-R.A.F. machines) were *WK877, 878, 885* to *889*, and the other 15 were *WL183, 186* to *189, 191, WH371, 1415, 1419* to *1421, 1423* to *1426*. Two Meteors were destroyed during the fighting in the Suez campaign in 1956, and some were still serving in 1958.

Biggest employer of the Meteor outside the United Kingdom was *The Netherlands*, who purchased a grand total of 226 of the F.4, F.8 and T.7 versions. The F.4s served from June 1947 until January 1951, when they were replaced by the F.8. The majority of Netherlands Meteors were licence-built by Fokker but the first eight delivered in July 1951 were ex-R.A.F. machines, serials (*WF697* to *699*) *I-90* to *I-94*. Fokker delivered 155 Mk.8s in the following batches: *101* to *199, 201* to *204, 206* to *208, 210* to *212, 214* to *220, 223, 225, 226, 228* to *231, 233* to *248, 250* to *255*. Squadrons operating the F.8 were No. 322, 323, 324, 325, 326, 327 and 328. The Meteor remained in service from 1951 until 1956.

Production

	Gloster-built Aircraft		Armstrong Whitworth-built	Aircraft
Contract 6/ACFT/2430/CB7 (b) 4th September 1949.				
VZ438 to VZ485	..	48	VZ518 to VZ532 ..	15
VZ493 to VZ517	..	25	VZ540 to VZ569 ..	30
		73		45
Contract 6/ACFT/2983/CB7 (b) 25th November 1948.				
WA813 to WA857	..	45	WA755 to WA994 ..	40
WA867 to WA909	..	43	WA965 to WA969 ..	5
WA920 to WA964	..	45	WA981 to WA999 ..	19
			WB105 to WB112 ..	8
		133		72
Contract 6/ACFT/4040/CB7 (b) 29th September 1949.				
WE903 to WE939	..	37	WE852 to WE891 ..	40
WE942 to WE976	..	35	WE895 to WE902 ..	8
		72		48
Contract 6/ACFT/5043/CB7 (b) 4th May 1950.				
WF689 to WF716	..	28	WF693 to WF662 ..	24
WF736 to WF760	..	25	WF667 to WF688 ..	12
		53		36
Contract 6/ACFT/5621/CB7 (b) 8th August 1950.				
			WH249 to WH263 ..	15
			WH272 to WH320 ..	49
			WH342 to WH386 ..	45
			WH395 to WH426 ..	32
			WH442 to WH444 ..	3
			WH445 to WH484 ..	40
			WH498 to WH513 ..	16
				200
Contract 6/ACFT/6066/CB7 (b) 15th January 1951.				
WK647 to WK696	..	50	WK707 to WK756 ..	50
WK783 to WK827	..	45	WK906 to WK934 ..	29
WK849 to WK893	..	45		
WK935 to WK955	..	21		
WK966 to WK944	..	29		
WL104 to WL143	..	40		
WL158 to WL191	..	34		
		264		79
Total	..	595	Total	500

Total number of F.Mk.8s built 1095.

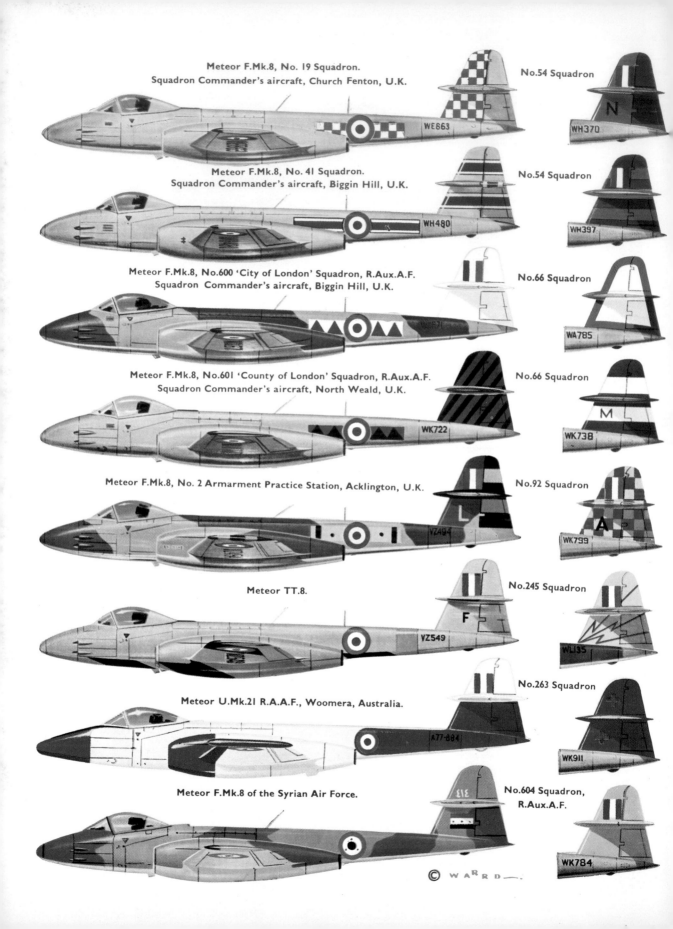

Meteor F.Mk.8, No. 19 Squadron.
Squadron Commander's aircraft, Church Fenton, U.K.

No.54 Squadron

WE863

WH370

Meteor F.Mk.8, No. 41 Squadron.
Squadron Commander's aircraft, Biggin Hill, U.K.

No.54 Squadron

WH480

WH397

Meteor F.Mk.8, No.600 'City of London' Squadron, R.Aux.A.F.
Squadron Commander's aircraft, Biggin Hill, U.K.

No.66 Squadron

WA785

Meteor F.Mk.8, No.601 'County of London' Squadron, R.Aux.A.F.
Squadron Commander's aircraft, North Weald, U.K.

No.66 Squadron

WK722

WK738

Meteor F.Mk.8, No. 2 Armament Practice Station, Acklington, U.K.

No.92 Squadron

VZ494

WK799

Meteor TT.8.

No.245 Squadron

VZ549

WL135

Meteor U.Mk.21 R.A.A.F., Woomera, Australia.

No.263 Squadron

A77-884

WK911

Meteor F.Mk.8 of the Syrian Air Force.

No.604 Squadron,
R.Aux.A.F.

WK784

© WARD

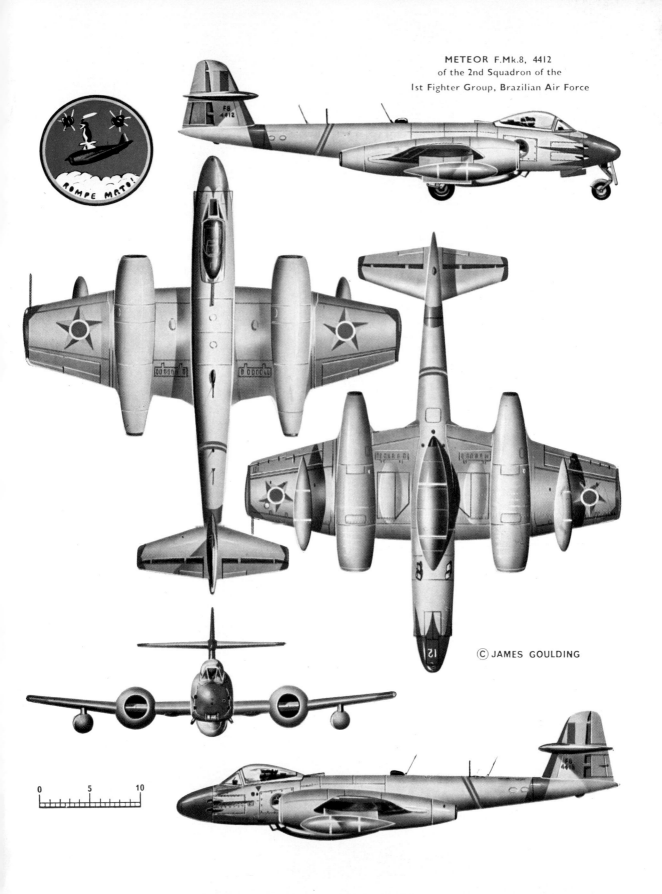

METEOR F.Mk.8, 4412
of the 2nd Squadron of the
1st Fighter Group, Brazilian Air Force

ROMPE MATO!

© JAMES GOULDING

0   5   10

A number of F.8s were supplied to the Syrian Air Force.

(Photo: Gloster Aircraft)

Twelve Meteor F.8s were ordered by *Syria* in 1950, and the specification called for a camouflage system of light earth and green on upper surfaces with sky-blue undersurfaces, serials *101* to *112* were in white. The Meteors *WK814* to *WK817, 824* to *827* and *862* to *865* were earmarked for delivery, but with the application of the Middle East arms embargo in 1951 they were diverted to the R.A.F. The dozen aircraft eventually reached Syria in 1952, followed by a batch of seven in 1956. The latter were ex-R.A.F. machines serialled *WA785, WL174, WK868* and *984, WH503, WE965, WH260.* Syrian serials were *101* to *112, 480* and *481*—four were not numbered. They served with the S.A.F. as ground attack aircraft.

Israel ordered eleven Mk.8s in February 1953, and these were modified to undertake duties as target tugs in addition to the fighter rôle. The cannon armament was supplied by Israel, and the aircraft modified to allow installation of American HVAR rocket projectiles. Serials were *2166* to *2169* and *2172* to *2178,* and they were delivered in a silver overall finish, this being replaced by the Israel authorities with a camouflaged pattern. They remained in service until replaced by the Dassault Mystère.

THE METEOR STRUCTURE

Construction of the Meteor 8 was virtually identical to that of the earlier variants and followed accepted aircraft practice and the emphasis was on sub-assembly units which could be readily dismantled for transportation.

Wing was a cantilever structure, the centre section of which formed an integral part of the fuselage and included the two jet engine nacelles and landing-gear units. It was built up of two parallel spars, heavy ribs and transverse diaphragms covered with a heavy-gauge, stressed duralumin skin. Upper and lower air-brakes and flaps were also carried on the centre section. Outer panels were built up of two spars and pressed ribs covered with a metal skin.

Fuselage aft of the centre section was an all-metal, stressed-skin structure with closely-spaced light-alloy "Z" section frames and four longerons. The tail unit, built as a separate section, incorporated the lower fin and tailplane, and was attached to the rear fuselage by four pick-up points.

Specification

The Gloster G41K METEOR F. MARK 8

Dimensions: Span 37 ft. 2 in.; length 44 ft. 7 in., height 13 ft.
Powerplant: Two Rolls-Royce Derwent Series 8 turbojets of 3,500 lb. static thrust at sea level.
Aerodynamic Data: Aerofoil section EC1240 merging to EC1040 at wing tip. Aspect ratio 3·9. Gross wing area 350 sq. ft. Incidence, one degree. Outerplane sweepback 4:8. Outerplane dihedral 6 degrees.
Weights: Structure 10,684 lb. Gross weight in normal operational trim 15,700 lb.
Loadings: Wing loading at normal take-off weight as above: 45 lb/sq. ft. Power loading 2·24 lb. per lb. static-thrust.
Performance: Max. level speed at sea level 592 m.p.h. (Mach ·78); at 30,000 ft. 550 m.p.h. (Mach ·81); at 40,000 ft. 530 m.p.h. (Mach ·80). Max. rate of climb (clean) at sea level 7,000 ft. per min.; at 30,000 ft. 2,700 f.p.m.; at 40,000 ft. 1,200 f.p.m. Time to 30,000 ft. (clean) 6·5 min.; to 40,000 ft. 11·6 min. Take-off run 480 yards, landing run 510 yards; range including climb at 40,000 ft. with normal tankage (420 galls.) 690 stat. miles; comparative endurance 1·6 hr.

An F.8 of the Belgian Air Force, constructed by Avions Fairey from components supplied by Fokker Aircraft.